VISIONS OF PRACTICE

Sonia Nieto, *Series Editor*

Families With Power:
Centering Students by Engaging With Families and Community

Mary Cowhey

D1569492

Families With Power

Centering Students by Engaging With Families and Community

Mary Cowhey

Foreword by Sonia Nieto

TEACHERS COLLEGE PRESS

TEACHERS COLLEGE | COLUMBIA UNIVERSITY
NEW YORK AND LONDON

*For my husband, Bill Blatner, and my children, Robeson Cowhey
and Mairead Blatner, who keep me grounded and growing.
And for my sister, Amy Cowhey-Brown*

Published by Teachers College Press,® 1234 Amsterdam Avenue, New York, NY 10027

Copyright © 2022 by Mary Cowhey

Cover and interior photographs by Mary Cowhey, unless otherwise credited.

Library of Congress Cataloging-in-Publication Data

Names: Cowhey, Mary, 1960– author.
Title: Families with power : centering students by engaging with families
   and community / Mary Cowhey ; foreword by Sonia Nieto.
Description: New York : Teachers College Press, [2022] | Series: Visions of
   Practice series | Includes bibliographical references and index.
Identifiers: LCCN 2021060376 (print) | LCCN 2021060377 (ebook) |
   ISBN 9780807766385 (Paperback : acid-free paper) | ISBN 9780807766392
   (Hardcover : acid-free paper) | ISBN 9780807780749 (eBook)
Subjects: LCSH: Families with Power (Organization) | Students with social
   disabilities—Education—United States. | Poor children—Education—
   Social aspects—United States. | Educational equalization—United States. |
   Popular education—Philosophy.
Classification: LCC LC4065 .C69 2022 (print) | LCC LC4065 (ebook) |
   DDC 379.2/60973—dc23/eng/20220218
LC record available at https://lccn.loc.gov/2021060376
LC ebook record available at https://lccn.loc.gov/2021060377

ISBN 978-0-8077-6638-5 (paper)
ISBN 978-0-8077-6639-2 (hardcover)
ISBN 978-0-8077-8074-9 (ebook)

Printed on acid-free paper
Manufactured in the United States of America

Contents

Foreword

Mary Cowhey is a born storyteller. What is especially remarkable about her stories is that they are all true, authentic, and based on her experiences as a teacher and community organizer. Having known Mary as her teacher, mentor, and friend for over 20 years, I am well acquainted with her considerable talents as an activist for social justice in schools and communities, many of which are evident in this beautiful book.

In these pages you will not find any cookie-cutter recipes for parent involvement. Instead, Mary takes readers through a series of stories and events that describe in vivid detail the evolution of Families with Power (FWP), a transformative model of family engagement that she created with families at Jackson Street School in Northampton, Massachusetts. It is a model that works particularly well with families of marginalized communities who are often unheard and unseen in school matters, but the underlying message of respect will work well with any community. Regardless of the issue about which she writes, her tremendous sensitivity and integrity shine through. Part memoir, part family engagement text, and part grassroots organizing manual, *Families With Power: Centering Students by Engaging With Families and Community* is the most inspired and significant book on family involvement in education that I've encountered in my long career.

This book explores a host of topics that often go unaddressed in typical family outreach efforts, the most significant among which is, I believe, what it means to work with humility and grace with families of diverse ethnic, racial, social class, and linguistic backgrounds. At the same time, teachers and educators are treated with the same kindness and empathy as the families in FWP. For instance, Mary Cowhey writes perceptively of the fears and uncertainties new teachers face when reaching out to their students' families. Learning to become catalysts for change in one's school and community, something that few books tackle, is another matter that she addresses. Even matters of nutrition, physical and mental health, and immigration, among others, that to some readers at first glance may seem tangential to teaching, are given full attention in this text. *Families With Power* encourages readers not simply to learn how to work effectively with families but, more importantly, to listen deeply and learn through their interactions with them.

There are countless examples of bravery in this book, ranging from the very vision that led to the creation of FWP, to the courage needed by teachers who want to initiate contact with families they do not know and whose languages and experiences they may not understand. A particularly powerful example is the extraordinary valor shown by parents speaking before a school committee meeting, something they had never before done. In these instances, and many others, Mary Cowhey shines a light not on herself but on the families and children that are the subject of this book. The lessons she describes can serve as a model for other educators interested in working authentically with families of diverse backgrounds.

I still recall how, as a new teacher some 50 years ago, I felt completely unprepared to work with my students' families. We certainly had never addressed this topic in my teacher education courses. Being Puerto Rican and having been raised among communities of people of color, I thought I was prepared to work with families. I was wrong. Never having had the opportunity to experience how teachers can develop respectful relationships with families, I had no model to follow. As immigrants with a limited education, my parents were not taken as seriously as middle-class, highly educated, English-speaking families. I only wish I had had a Mary Cowhey to consult with then; I relied instead on my instincts and some vague notions of parent involvement. It was rough going at first, yet this aspect of my job became one of the most important and fulfilling of my professional career, first as a teacher and, later, as a teacher educator and researcher. Having a book such as this would have been a lifesaver, not because it would have told me exactly what to do and how, but because it presents such a humane model of interacting with families. Instead of claiming that she has the answer to all the challenges of family engagement, Mary Cowhey asks provocative questions that make you think; this alone will make you a better teacher and advocate for your students. Most importantly, her writing will move you to ask your own questions.

A major goal of the Visions of Practice series is to address the fact that so few practitioners, especially teachers and others who work closely with students and their families, are visible in discussions of school improvement, leadership, and change. This series places experienced classroom teachers and other practitioners at the center of the conversation. It is my hope that this and forthcoming titles in the series will result in richer and more inclusive conversations, policies, and practices focused on educating our nation's children.

—Sonia Nieto

Acknowledgments

I want to start by thanking Luz Eneida García (Eneida) and Maribel Abrego,* the two parents who helped found Families with Power/Familias con Poder, along with Kim Gerould, my colleague and coconspirator for more than 2 decades. I also want to thank the other "pillars" who represented their neighborhoods: Irma Lucena in Florence Heights, Nydia Canales* in Meadowbrook, Janet Namono in Hampshire Heights, as well as the many leaders who emerged later, including Elba Heredia Cartagena, Josefina Rodriguez, Santa Garcia, Edwin Gomez,* Jennifer Brinson, Pallavi Bandalli, Rania Al-Qudsi,* Carmelo Vega-Hernandez, Lilly Pastor, Roque Sanchez, Doña Lucas García, Lourdes Santiago-Campos, Andrea Raphael and Sue Brow. Thank you for sharing your stories and for reviewing the manuscript, to help tell the story of Families with Power as accurately as possible.

I want to thank the children of Families with Power for their leadership and active participation in annual retreats, dinners, and so many of our programs, for speaking up and making their voices heard. These include Freddy Ramírez, Juan Montañez, Jorge Montañez, Samuel and Jazmari Abrego,* Mike and Alex Vega-Lucena, Mateo Canales,* Anjelica Gomez,* Mwalye David Martin, A.J., Eliaz, and Angela Robles, Reneury and Joseury Rodriguez, Desiree Moore-Brinson, Alexus Brinson, Karen Plaza, Anaisha Feiciano, Rasha Al-Qudsi,* Blanca Diaz, Amélie Acevedo-Velez, Jennifer Buri-Yunga, Melissa Lisboa-Soler, Camila Guerrero-Soler, Aaliyah and Mya Grant, Raymond Heredia, Lanaiya Rodriguez, and Jordan Lopez-Brow.

Speaking of families, thanks to my incredibly supportive husband, Bill Blatner, who cooked dinner, did bedtime, and kept the home fires burning countless times while I was out in the community or writing. Thanks to our children, Robeson Cowhey and Mairead Blatner, who participated in many of the FWP activities described in this book and shared their mom with our community. I am proud of the fine adults they've become. Thanks to my siblings, for their support, encouragement, memories, and good humor, and to our parents, Mary Rose and Bob Cowhey, who both passed away in 2018. They were storytellers and teachers in their own unique ways.

---

* Names marked with asterisks are pseudonyms to protect participants' privacy.

Thank you to the Jackson Street School community, especially my colleagues and fellow union members, including Linda Barca, Mary Bates, Barbara Black, Joan Cameron, Tom Chang, Sadie Cora, Talia Cossin, Sue Ebitz, Vivian Flores, Maria García, Holly Ghazey, Deirdre Johnson, Alfred Kimani, Kathy Malynoski, Linda Mondschien, Joan Morvidelli, Lily Pastor, Marilyn Rivera, Karen Schipellite, Maria Vega, and Janice Totty. Thanks to my principal, Gwen Agna, for her educational leadership, friendship, and countless cups of tea. Thanks to all the caregivers, grandparents, and community members who volunteered at Morning Math Club and to those who joined the dozens of standouts for equitable school funding, immigration rights, and a fair contract.

Thanks to the Western Mass Writing Project for supporting Teachers as Writers, which was my teacher-writer home while writing *Black Ants and Buddhists*. Thanks to Bruce Penniman, for agreeing to help me rebuild that home for this book in early 2020, especially for the encouragement to organize a remote teachers-as-writers summer retreat when the pandemic threatened to shut down our revived program. I would not have become a writer, a teacher, or an activist, if not for the love and guidance of two middle school English teachers, Rita and Terry Rowan. Thanks to Janice Sorenson and the Raspberry Shed at her Magpie Farm for giving me a quiet and COVID-19–safe place to write in nature when everything else closed.

I want to remember those who have gone to join the ancestors. We appreciate the gifts of their wisdom, dedication, and compassion. Doña Lucas García (1940–2013) was a great-grandmother and founding member of Families with Power. She had a beautiful voice and was generous in sharing her songs. She especially loved Family Reading Parties, the Family Writing Project and annual retreats. Andrea Raphael (1964–2012) was a loving parent, a skilled teacher, and an energetic organizer. I met Andrea when she worked in my classroom as a paraprofessional; she went on to become a special education teacher. Andrea was very active in Families with Power, especially the development of How Schools Work. She often brought her children, Christopher and Maeve Reily, to Family Reading Parties and the Family Writing Project. Andrea took many of the photographs that appear in this book. Giada Rodriguez (2007–2021) was my student in kindergarten and 1st grade and promptly became an active member of Morning Math Club, like her older siblings, Devin and Celinette. She especially loved the school garden and hatching chicks. She had hoped to study animal science at Smith Vocational High School.

I would not have written this book or *Black Ants and Buddhists* without the mentorship and encouragement of my teacher, friend, and now editor, Dr. Sonia Nieto, whose persistent invitations and countless cups of coffee transformed me from a teacher who wrote journal reflections to a published author. I appreciate her leadership in creating the Visions of Practice series at Teachers College Press to lift the voices of practitioners. Thanks also to Brian Ellerbeck, Lori Tate, Nancy Mandel and the rest of the Teachers College

Press team for their advice, guidance and patience in bringing this book to fruition.

Here's a shoutout to all the community organizations, farmers, public health workers, and leaders who have collaborated with FWP, including Casa Latina, Center for New Americans, Pioneer Valley Workers Center, Grow Food Northampton, Shawn Robinson and Prospect Meadow Farm, Roberta Wilmore and Children's Equitation Center, Ben James, Oona Coy and Town Farm, Ben Wood and Sarah Bankert.

FWP thanks Rhonda Thomason and Teaching Tolerance at Southern Poverty Law Center for the grant that supported our first retreat, the Northampton Education Foundation for probably a dozen small grants over the years, and NEF board member Ellen Nigrosh, who let us use her farm house in Hawley for FWP retreats. We also want to thank the Highlander Research and Education Center (formerly known as Highlander Folk School) in Tennessee for welcoming us, and Highlander founder Myles Horton for inspiring us. Thanks to Risa Silverman for giving me *The Long Haul*. And thanks to Sue Thrasher, a former Highlander organizer, who, when I asked her if she'd be willing to talk with me over coffee about Highlander, said, "I will talk with you about Highlander anywhere, any time."

Special thanks to two good friends, Kim Gerould and Don Wheelock, and my daughter, Mairead Blatner, who read every word of this book and gave me such useful feedback. As a cofounder of FWP, Kim was part of all the Families with Power activities in this book and ensured historical and linguistic accuracy, with the assistance of her "in-house advisor," Dr. Roberto Irizarry. Kim was incisive in pointing toward what to highlight and what to trim. As a formal poet and musical composer, Don provided an indispensable outsider perspective. He asked hundreds of clarifying questions and pushed for precise and concise paragraphs and sentences. Don was equally demanding and encouraging—just what this writer needed to persevere. Thanks to my daughter, Mairead Blatner, who read, edited, and provided a mountain of technical assistance and waves of encouragement.

Thanks to all the teacher educators who still encourage student teachers to teach for social justice, think outside the box, and imagine what could be possible. Thanks, most especially, to the student teachers and new teachers like Hailee C. from Northern CA, who write me handwritten letters and emails: I hear you. Keep writing. I will keep listening and writing back.

Cuatro Gatos

In Puerto Rico, there is a saying: "*Somos cuatro gatos*," meaning, "How can we do anything? We are just four cats." *Miaou.* *

In K–12 education, in the era of No Child Left Behind, we often heard, "How can we close the 'achievement gap'?" In other words, if our students' parents speak little or no English, often lack formal education, and are strained by poor health, violence, inadequate housing and transportation, and the related stresses of living in poverty, how can teachers be expected to bring those students up to speed with their peers? *Miaou.*

In 2007 in Northampton, Massachusetts, some caregivers and educators found a way to change the question: *How can educators and community support the grassroots leadership development and organizing efforts of low-income caregivers to help our children succeed?* Together, we learned to roar.

I taught at Jackson Street School, the largest and most diverse of the four elementary schools in Northampton, a small, liberal city of about 29,000 in western Massachusetts. Thirty-seven percent of Jackson Street's students received free or reduced lunch. About half of my students' caregivers were service workers in area restaurants, hotels, colleges and universities, nursing homes and hospitals, or did agricultural, landscaping, or factory work. Others worked in various professions, from law and medicine to the arts. Some of my students lived in subsidized public housing and others lived in $500,000 homes. Some were homeless, staying in shelters or living with relatives.

Although approximately 24% of students in the Northampton district were children of color and about 25% were low-income in 2007, there were still no people of color on the School Committee or City Council. Each school's Parent Teacher Organization (PTO), civil rights committee, and school council were active organizations; their participants were generally college-educated, middle-class, White, and native speakers of English. This

---

* This prologue is based on the article "Learning to Roar" by Mary Cowhey, reprinted with permission of Learning for Justice, a project of the Southern Poverty Law Center. https://www.learningforjustice.org/magazine/fall-2009/learning-to-roar

was a district that thought and talked about multiculturalism, inclusion, and achievement for all students. It was also a district where many low-income caregivers of color felt like outsiders in their children's schools.

THE LONG HAUL

In 2007, two local parents, a colleague, and I started Families with Power/ Familias con Poder (or FWP), a grassroots effort to empower low-income families to take action to help our children succeed. We were inspired by *The Long Haul*, the autobiography of Myles Horton, founder of Highlander Folk School in Tennessee. Before I read *The Long Haul* in the summer of 2006, the main thing I knew about Highlander was that it was where the NAACP sent Rosa Parks for organizer training, before she sat down on the bus.

Horton was influenced by the Danish folk schools he visited in 1931. He noted some characteristics of these schools that he wanted to apply in the United States:

- Students and teachers living together
- Peer learning
- Group singing
- Freedom from state regulation
- Nonvocational education
- Freedom from examinations
- Social interaction in non-formal setting[s]
- A highly motivating purpose
- Clarity in what for and what against.

(Horton et al., 1998, p. 53)

For a decade, my colleague, Kim Gerould, and I used critical pedagogy and involved parents of all demographic backgrounds to volunteer in our classrooms, to chaperone field trips, to attend potlucks and performances. But after I read *The Long Haul*, I realized: It was always our party. By the summer of 2006, Kim and I saw that "our party" wasn't enough. For years, we'd served on our district civil rights committee where there were endless discussions of disaggregated standardized test scores and the "achievement gap." When a white, educated parent on the civil rights committee asked, "Why don't *they* come to our meetings?" I wanted to scream. When I read Horton's characteristics of the Danish folk schools, it made me realize that our meetings were exactly the opposite of what he described. No wonder caregivers of marginalized students weren't interested in coming. That made Kim and me feel that a radically different approach was needed. We wanted

Figure P.1. Kim Gerould, educator, parent, and cofounder of Families with Power, leads a bilingual writing activity at FWP's Family Writing Project at Casa Latina (2010).

Photo: Andrea Raphael

Meet Kim

Kim and I met in 1996 when she was the bilingual teacher in the classroom where I was a student teacher at Jackson Street School. In 1997, she was the bilingual teacher in my 1st-grade classroom and the parent of one of my students. For the next two years, we cotaught a looping, bilingual combined 1st and 2nd-grade classroom. When bilingual education was outlawed in Massachusetts, Kim became a 3rd-grade classroom teacher. Kim had been involved in political activism, community organizing, and adult education in Boston and Holyoke for 20 years before becoming an elementary school bilingual education teacher. Kim was my mentor and first ally at Jackson Street School and has been my colleague and co-conspirator for decades.

to shift the dynamic. Instead of teachers being the empowered ones, inviting parents to volunteer in educational activities at school, we asked: What if caregivers had some way to organize their own activities (educational, cultural, or social) in the community and perhaps sometimes invite educators to volunteer at those activities, if they felt like it? What might that look like? These questions pushed Kim and me to step farther out of our classrooms into the community to engage in popular education.

TOMANDO CAFÉ (DRINKING COFFEE)

As I contemplated where to begin, I remembered that in 2004, when my class organized a voter registration drive, Juan's mother, Eneida, came in

Figure P.2. Eneida Garcia, parent, community leader, and cofounder of Families with Power, at FWP's Family Writing Project at Casa Latina (2010).

Photo: Andrea Raphael

Meet Eneida

Eneida grew up in the rural village of Barrio Pozas in Ciales, Puerto Rico, one of 15 children. She moved to Río Piedras to attend university. She stopped attending university when she married at 24 and later gave birth to her son Freddy. Eneida and Freddy moved to Massachusetts in 1993 in order to find better medical treatment for Freddy. Eneida continued to learn English and earned an associate degree at Holyoke Community College in early childhood education. She volunteered at Casa Latina, the only Latinx-led organization in the Pioneer Valley at that time (the region of western Mass where Northampton is located). She joined Casa Latina's staff and became its codirector in 2001.

I met Eneida in 1995, when I moved to Hampton Gardens, where we lived across the courtyard from each other. Her youngest son, Jorge, and my daughter were born just a few months apart. I taught Jorge and his brother Juan in 2nd grade.

and told the children about the first time she voted. Eneida also described her first impression of a community organizer who came to her village when she was a girl in the 1960s to rally people around hurricane preparedness. Eneida remembered the organizer's patience as he spent time connecting with every family, drinking coffee from one house to the next, "He was able to bring people together through those small conversations they were having during the time they were having coffee." Eneida called this "*tomando café*." Eneida's father was part of the team who organized neighbors to get running water for their village. The grassroots model Eneida described sounded like what we were hoping to develop.

I talked with Eneida about Highlander and Horton's popular education ideas, which appealed to her too. She agreed to help and said we should talk with Maribel Abrego, whom I first met on a home visit when her son was in my class. Maribel had been trying to organize Spanish-speaking parents of students in special education.

"I'LL *MAKE* THE TIME TO DO SOMETHING *WITH* MY KIDS"

Maribel, Kim, Eneida, and I met to brainstorm. Eneida said, "I'm a single working mother. I don't have time to go to meetings at school to hear why someone thinks my kids' test scores are low, but I'll *make* the time to do something *with* my kids that will help my kids."

We knew from our experience with the Civil Rights Committee that inviting parents to an evening meeting at school, to talk about a bigger meeting, wouldn't be an effective way to recruit people. So Eneida said, "I got an idea! Maribel, are you free on Friday? After work, we feed our children, give them showers and they put on pajamas. Everyone comes to my house. Cowhey, bring books, Spanish and English. We read stories with the kids. And then, we have *chocolate, y galletes con queso*." I thought to myself, "Hot chocolate with cheese and crackers?" The combination of cheese and chocolate sounded unappetizing to me, but luckily, I remembered this was not my party and kept my mouth shut. I was privileged to be in the conversation. Eneida continued. "Okay, then we serve the *merienda* [snack], and that's when we talk with everyone about our idea, see who wants to make the next reading party, and who wants to come to the retreat." Maribel said it sounded good. "Wait," Eneida said. "Aurea has a bigger living room. We should do it at Aurea's." That was that. No checking Blackberries or pocket calendars.

"¿Quien quiere leer?" (Who wants to read?)

That Friday night was frigid, about zero degrees. Steam had frozen on the inside of Aurea's storm door windows. I shivered as I rang the bell. I wondered if anyone would come.

Children ranging from preschool to high school and their parents already filled the apartment. A *telenovela* (Spanish language soap opera) played loudly on the television. In the corner of the living room, I saw Aurea's daughter, Veronika Hean, my former 1st-grade student, now in high school, doing chemistry homework. We talked about her classes and cheerleading, and she mentioned the Friday night basketball games. I asked: Why wasn't she cheering at the game that night?

Veronika looked at me like I had a screw loose and said, "Because *this* is more important."

Eventually Eneida arrived, pushing her 18-year-old-son, Freddy, in his wheelchair, followed by her sons Juan and Jorge in their pajamas, bathrobes and snow jackets. Jorge spread out the Spanish and English picture books we'd chosen from the school library that morning. More families arrived, filling the sofa, the kitchen chairs brought to the living room, and every inch of the carpet.

Eneida shut off the television, looked around the room at her friends, smiled and asked, *"¿Quien quiere leer?"* (Who wants to read?) It was quiet. Then one of the parents, Mayra, smiled as she recognized a title in Spanish and reached for it. As she straightened up on the couch and held the book to show the pictures, her twin sons leaned in close to look. In a voice as confident as any teacher's, Mayra began to read.

After about 45 minutes of caregivers reading aloud, Aurea announced that it was time for *merienda*. Eneida wisely did not assign me to bring the hot chocolate, because I would have brought packets of powdered cocoa to mix with boiling water. Aurea had slowly warmed a gallon of milk in a large pot and had stirred in *Chocolate Cortes*, made of Caribbean cocoa. As Eneida finished arranging a plate of saltines and cubes of American cheese, she asked me, "What do you call this? Comfort food?" I must have looked confused. She continued, "When I was a little girl in Puerto Rico, the government gave us commodities, *galettes y queso* like this. It reminds me of my childhood, my family in Puerto Rico, and makes me feel good."

I was learning that it was better if I didn't say every little thing that crossed my mind. I was learning to not be in charge, to be quiet: to talk less and listen more. Aurea handed me a mug of *Chocolate Cortes* and Eneida dropped a cube of cheese into it with a smile, "That makes it even better." I took a sip, and it was like drinking velvet.

Veronika sat with Maribel's 4-year-old daughter, Jazmari, on her lap at the table. She took mini-marshmallows from a bowl, one for each letter as she spelled Jazmari's name. She held Jazmari's hand as they tapped each one and counted up to 7, then counted again as they dropped each one into the hot chocolate. Technically, Veronika, who was Cambodian and Puerto Rican, was not a blood relative of Jazmari, who was Panamanian and Irish, but they clearly had an important relationship that was invisible to the school.

Irma said she would host the Family Reading Party the next Friday. Eneida's idea was working, and we were on our way.

CHAPTER 1

Introduction

In the ninth year of my teaching, I became obsessed with Myles Horton's ideas of popular education, grassroots leadership, and "an out-of-schooling situation" (p 140), as discussed in his autobiography, *The Long Haul* (1998. I had just published *Black Ants and Buddhists: Thinking Critically and Teaching Differently in the Primary Grades* (2006) about what critical pedagogy looks like with 1st- and 2nd-graders.

I first heard of Paulo Freire's critical pedagogy work in Brazil and the popular education movement it spawned when I returned to college in 1994 as a "nontraditional" student after 14 years of community organizing. In my first education class, the professor asked us to write a "response paper." I didn't even know what that was, so I did the reading and "responded" by writing a story about organizing a "Survival English Class" among undocumented Guatemalan car washers who were beaten and fired when they asked for their tips; the class was taught by Puerto Rican welders who had been fired when they asked for a raise. The professor asked me when I'd read Paulo Freire's (1970) *Pedagogy of the Oppressed*. I said I'd never heard of it. I had a tuition scholarship but could not afford to buy books. The college library's only copy of it was on the reserve shelf. I had a work study job at the library and slowly labored through my first reading of *Pedagogy of the Oppressed* over many weeks, noting some big ideas that resonated with me. They became the foundation of my pedagogy as a 1st- and 2nd-grade teacher. It was hard for me to imagine Freire—if he talked the way he wrote—talking with illiterate peasants in Brazil or the car washers and welders I'd been organizing in New Jersey. Here are a few of Freire's ideas that I understood and used daily in my teaching:

- "Education is a political act." (Freire, 1998, p. 63)
- (Students and teachers) "both are simultaneously teachers and students." (Freire, 2018, p. 72)
- "Dialogue cannot exist without humility." (Freire, 2018, p. 90)
- (Critical thinking) "perceives reality as a process, as transformation, rather than as a static entity—thinking which does not separate itself from action." (Freire, 2018, p. 92)

As I read *The Long Haul*, I began to see a web of connections, similarities and differences between the work of Freire and the work of Myles Horton. They were contemporaries who knew of each other's work and met at conferences but had their first deep conversation with each other when they were in their seventies. Horton's work felt more familiar to me, with its emphasis on grassroots organizing and connection to both the labor and the civil rights movements in the United States. My obsession with Horton's ideas led to the creation of Families with Power/Familias con Poder (FWP), a voluntary grassroots organization of multicultural low-income families with children, experimenting with educational projects to support each other and help our children succeed. Our members defined success as their children reaching adulthood, being happy and connected strongly to their families and community, and able to support themselves and their families.

From the start, FWP was a group of families and educators engaged in a social education experiment outside the system, with what Horton might have called "out-of-school learning" (Horton & Freire, 1990, p. 202). I read *We Make the Road by Walking: Conversations on Education and Social Change* by Myles Horton and Paulo Freire (1990) a few years after we started FWP. That book was the result of their decision to "speak a book" (p. x) in a week of conversations at Highlander in December 1987. Many of Horton's ideas resonated with me and other members of FWP. We had started with a simple *what if?* question. Horton advocated thinking outside of conventional frameworks, saying, "Most people don't allow themselves to experiment with ideas, because they assume they have to fit into the system . . . the socially approved way of doing things and consequently don't open up their minds to making any kind of discoveries" (Horton & Freire, 1990, p. 40). He went on to say, "You experiment with people not on people. There's a big difference. They're in on the experiment. They're in on the process" (p. 148).

After I read *The Long Haul* in the summer of 2006, I remembered that Sue Thrasher, whom I met when she had interviewed me 5 years earlier, had mentioned that she had worked with Highlander. (I later learned that Sue helped organize the 1987 conversations that became the book, *We Make the Road by Walking*.) I was wrestling with Horton's ideas and was trying to get a grip on how to start. I asked Sue Thrasher if she'd be willing to meet for coffee to talk about Highlander. She said she'd talk to me anywhere anytime about Highlander. I told Sue it didn't seem authentic to try to recruit a group of parents from western Massachusetts to go down to Highlander. She said that we didn't need to go to Highlander, that we could "make our own Highlander" right where we were. Sue encouraged us to start ourselves, believing that we could organize our own Highlander-style residential workshops. Horton said, "The way you really learn is to start something and learn as you go along. You don't have to know it in advance because if you know it in advance you kill it by clamping this down on the people you are dealing with. Then you can't learn from the situation, can't learn from the people" (Horton & Freire, 1990, p. 40).

This book shares a collection of stories about Families with Power and our popular education approach to family engagement. It also describes my journey as an educator, as I began to look more critically at the school I loved and started to recognize the ways it excluded some families. On that journey, I built relationships with families as we learned from each other, over many years. What I learned through Families with Power transformed not only my work as an individual teacher but the culture of my school.

Freire distinguished between "systematic education which can only be changed through political power, and educational projects, which should be carried out *with* the oppressed in the process of organizing them" (Freire, 2018, p. 54). Recalling when I first imagined FWP, I was probably imagining changes in systematic education, maybe more representation on the school committee and school councils as a way to address bias and discrimination and create more equitable policies. But we did not "clamp this down on the people." We listened, asked questions—and found a refreshing willingness to experiment boldly. Because the families had felt excluded and invisible for years, they had no feeling of needing to conform with "the socially approved way of doing things" (Horton & Freire, 1990, p. 40). They had the humility to learn from mistakes and a great openness to making new discoveries as FWP organized educational projects.

Clearly, not every story will be familiar or replicable, because naturally your life, your students, their families, your school, and your community are unique. I hope some themes that emerge will resonate for you, raising particular questions and different dialogues with families, imagining unique experiments and educational projects.

WHO AM I TO WRITE THIS BOOK?

I am an educator, organizer, parent, writer, and lifelong learner. I am a White, Irish American, lapsed Catholic, cisgender woman who lived more than half my life in poverty. And 55 years ago, I was the really skinny, quiet kid in your class with bags under her eyes wearing hand-me-down clothes that often smelled like mildew. I am not an academic or an expert on critical pedagogy or popular education, but I work hard to understand these ideas and use them in my teaching and organizing.

My father was the first in his family to graduate from college; he earned two master's degrees, accruing a mountain of educational debt. A brilliant, funny, and explosive man, he hoarded and suffered from mental illness. His modest salary as an elementary teacher provided for our family of eight on Long Island, NY. We couldn't afford fuel oil for our poorly insulated house most of the winter, which meant we had to shut off the water to keep the

Figure 1.1. Mary Cowhey, as an infant, with her father, Bob Cowhey, at home.

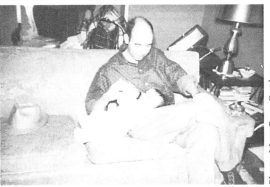

Photo: Mary Rose Cowhey

pipes from freezing. We often lacked enough food. My father's friend loved to fish in the ocean. He sometimes dropped off mako shark or striped bass. We ate a lot of fish and potatoes.

My father said never to tell anyone what happened in our home. As conditions in our house grew more extreme, we had fewer visitors, and then he allowed no visitors. As a teenager, I felt desperate and depressed. My mother said she thought that, with good grades, I could finish high school early. I graduated at 16, got a scholarship and went away to Bard College, where there was heat, hot water, and unlimited food. I got myself out but felt guilty for leaving my mother and younger siblings behind as things at home got worse.

While in college in the 1970s, I learned that poverty was systemic, not the result of shameful individual flaws. I did temporary and farm work. I developed more of a class analysis and wanted to learn how to make change. I squatted in an empty house and later lived in a tent in the woods. My father disowned me. I was too proud and frightened to go home.

I sought internships (with room and board) in education or community organizing. I carried a knapsack with a bedroll and journal and traveled by Greyhound bus. During our first semester, my roommate and I had gotten to know three sisters who worked in the dish room of our campus dining hall. Their abusive stepfather had abandoned them at a state psychiatric hospital even before they started school, saying they had severe cognitive disabilities. They lived there for more than 50 years before being released into the community in the mid-1970s as part of a deinstitutionalization effort. They wanted to learn to read and write. I thought an internship in a kindergarten would help me learn how to teach them. My first winter internship was in a New York City public school on the Lower East Side. At 17, a handful of racist, classist teachers there frightened me. To me, they seemed too grown up and powerful to change.

The next winter, I did community organizing with a settlement house in North St. Louis. I organized in the neighborhood where the failed Pruitt-Igoe subsidized housing project had been imploded, leaving a vast urban wasteland. One summer I applied for an internship as a community organizer in Maine, but the foundation assigned me to teach swimming in the frigid waters of an isolated fishing island in northeastern Quebec. Later, I organized seasonal workers in the Pacific Northwest. Then I stopped going back to college. I spent the next 14 years doing organizing work.

By the time I gave up full-time organizing at 33, I was burned out, banged up, and in rough physical and mental health. A single mother with a toddler, I had never earned more than minimum wage. I returned to Long Island, where my mother, now divorced from my father, and my siblings offered to help us as best they could. My sister Jane and her husband let my son and me stay with them until I found a job and could rent a studio of my own. They babysat one evening a week so that I could go to a support group and therapy.

A year later, I moved to Northampton, Massachusetts, with a scholarship to the Ada Comstock Scholars program at Smith College. I always worried that someone would tap me on the shoulder to say they just found out who I really was and that I should leave. I studied education and had a variety of work-study jobs including being a lunch aide and a library aide at the Smith College Campus School. I did field placements as a volunteer tutor at Jackson Street School. Perhaps because of my background as an organizer and my experience as a low-income parent, I developed a special interest in family involvement practices.

I graduated from college and began my career as a teacher at 37; it was my first job that paid more than minimum wage. I taught elementary school for more than 2 decades and have been organizing for more than 4 decades. I don't expect that your life story and mine are similar; they don't need to be. As I share bits of my story throughout this book, I hope it prompts you to think how your life shapes your teaching journey and to share it with others.

When I think back over the best teachers I had in my life, none of them "matched" my identity in all its intersectionality. One was Irish Catholic like me; others were Jewish, Muslim, Puerto Rican or African American. Some were male. They came from different economic backgrounds. Their effectiveness didn't depend on us sharing the exact same racial, economic, religious, linguistic and cultural background. They saw me, even when I tried to hide. They heard me and nurtured my voice.

The majority of elementary teachers in the United States are White, middle-class, female native speakers of English. The growing majority of K–12 public school *students* in the United States are not White. It is powerful for ethnically and racially diverse students to see educators who look like them. For that to happen, districts would need to prioritize the recruitment, hiring, retention, and promotion of a more diverse educator workforce, with better pay and more supportive school climates. We need every teacher we can get who has heart, a willingness to think critically, a passion for life-long learning and teaching. Those qualities aren't the exclusive property of any single racial, ethnic, linguistic, or socioeconomic identity. Teachers of all backgrounds can learn to develop trusting relationships with families and communities in order to make learning more powerful.

Whoever you are, especially if you are in the process of preparing to become a teacher, welcome to the struggle. I am so glad you're here. This book includes reflections on recognizing my White privilege, biases, and con-tinuing journey to become antiracist. Anti-Blackness, classism, and many other forms of bias cut across racial and ethnic groups. We can all benefit from continuing to educate ourselves and recognize our own biases. This is hard stuff, and it is lifelong work. I hope I can keep learning, admitting my mistakes, and evolving over time.

Part of that evolution is remembering that in a group like FWP I am only one member, not the group. For example, early in my career I was vehe-mently opposed to standardized testing, which I perceived as a racist policy, and I assumed that fighting this testing would be a burning issue for FWP. To my surprise, it wasn't. In fact, some FWP members said they thought a standardized test score was a "more honest number" than a teacher's assur-ances that their child was "doing fine." Throughout the history of FWP, I have reminded myself that I am one member; I am not the group. This work is not about me or my agenda. I remind myself to listen more than I speak. I try to balance that tension.

I did not give up the fight against standardized testing, but I pursued it instead through the progressive caucus within the state educators' union. FWP has focused attention and energy on actions and programs at a manage-able scale that caregivers felt would help their children and families survive and succeed. The FWP definition of success is more about happiness, family, and community connection, and has nothing to do with raising standardized test scores or college graduation rates.

For more than 2 decades, I taught elementary school. For 12 years I was a 1st- and 2nd-grade classroom teacher. When I shifted to part-time teaching to accommodate taking care of my mother, who had Alzheimer's, the superintendent at that time would not allow me to job share. Instead, she reassigned me as a math specialist. My new assignment challenged my understanding of what teaching for social justice looks like.

Ten years later, in June 2019, I retired from full-time teaching. I now tutor children in math. Until March 2020, I continued to volunteer and substitute at Jackson Street School. In 2020, I also became a worker-owner in Riquezas del Campo, an immigrant-led cooperative farm. But I still re-member the nervous excitement of preparing for the first day of school and the exhaustion at the end of a long week. I remember waking in the middle of the night replaying a difficult conversation with a colleague or parent, trying to rewrite what I wish I'd said. I know the satisfaction of creating a math problem that might nudge a student to make a developmental leap. I know how hard it is to teach. Even as I learn to teach one thing better, I keep setting new learning goals for myself.

During the 15 years I was a caregiver for my mother until her death in 2018, I took a one-year family leave and taught part-time another year. Other than that, I taught full-time and raised two kids with my husband. For all of us in FWP, our time and energy were always limited by caregiving responsibilities for children or elders and our physical and mental health. For many FWP members, that balancing act was further challenged by the motivation to achieve personal goals, such as learning English, attending college, buying a home, getting a driver's license or U.S. citizenship. I know how stressful teaching is and how little time and energy are left after teaching all week. Some people recharge by being alone. Other people, like me, are energized by the time we spend with others. Most of us struggle with balance and never get it quite right, as changes force us to constantly readjust.

NOTES ON TERMINOLOGY, LANGUAGE, AND VOICE

When I started teaching in 1997, my principal, Gwen Agna, guided educators to use the phrase "parents and guardians" to replace the narrower term "parents" or the exclusive "moms and dads." More recently, we replaced that with "caregivers." In the media, the term "caregivers" is often used for those who care for people who are sick, disabled or elderly, either in a paid or unpaid capacity. Throughout this book, I use "caregivers" as a more inclusive term for the adults who love and care for children. When I describe individual members of FWP, I may use a more specific term like "mother" or "parent" if it accurately describes the person.

When I write about Families with Power/Familias con Poder, I often use FWP for short. When we speak about FWP, we interchangeably use the Spanish and English names, Families with Power or *Familias con Poder*.

In this book, you will read the words of educators and caregivers whose children attended Jackson Street School between 1997 and 2020. It is a racially, economically, culturally, and linguistically diverse public elementary school in Northampton, a small city in western Massachusetts. It has about 350 students from kindergarten to 5th grade. Many students and caregivers were proud to be identified by name. Some have moved from the community, state, or country and could not be reached for permission. Others, for reasons of privacy, chose not to be identified. In both of those situations, I used a pseudonym, which is indicated with an asterisk* the first time they are introduced.

Many of the caregivers quoted here learned English as a second or third language or spoke a dialect other than standard American English.

I transcribed their words as faithfully as possible, without the constant insertion of [sic]. Note that many of these caregivers have continued their study of English since these quotes were recorded. If you met them today, you would find their English more developed. In consultation with the interviewees, we edited some quotes for brevity or clarity. Words in other languages are italicized, followed by their English translation in parentheses. The Arabic words are transliterated.

I am grateful to the FWP members and colleagues who agreed to be interviewed for this book, so that I could capture their words as accurately as possible. They speak for themselves as individuals. They do not speak for their class, race, religion, or ethnicity. I hope their words will be springboards for conversations in your school and community about these and other issues. I hope what they say provokes you to wonder what caregivers in your community would say.

Note that Paulo Freire wrote *Pedagogy of the Oppressed* in 1968 in Portuguese, which is a gendered language. The first English translation of it appeared in 1970. The modern reader may notice the extensive use of male pronouns and examples, which was typical of that time period.

A NOTE ON METHOD

The stories in this book about FWP occurred between 2007 and 2020. Some projects or programs continued across that period at varying frequency and size. For example, Family Reading Parties went from weekly to monthly as we increased other activities, and then to seasonally in later years. Morning Math Club started twice weekly with 15 kids and eventually grew to about 50 kids and switched to once a week; it ran for 10 years. Some 6-week programs ran for 1 to 3 years. The Afterschool Reading Club was fun, but there was more energy for the Morning Math Club, so Reading Club faded after one semester as Math Club grew. Some FWP activities became annual traditions, like the *parranda* (a Puerto Rican cultural celebration that occurs between Advent and Three Kings Day), the Love Your Family Dinner every February, and the weekend retreat every June. There was never a time when all the different programs described in this book were running simultaneously.

FWP created programs in response to widely and deeply felt problems and needs. Authentic interest, volunteer energy, and commitment powered these programs and naturally shifted in response to issues in the school or community and the life challenges of students and adults. Honest discussions about our individual and collective capacity guided our decision-making and growth.

I have auditory processing disorder, which created a lifelong habit of taking notes as a way to process what I hear. In addition, Freire describes a process of recording details in notebooks, "including the apparently un-important items" like language, idioms and lifestyle (Freire, 2018, p. 111). I often took notes in notebooks; at our annual retreats, we took notes on chart paper in Spanish and English. In 2015, I recorded and transcribed in-terviews with many FWP members. I often took photographs, as did Andrea Raphael, another FWP member. Sometimes when I returned from a Family Reading Party or some other FWP meeting or event, I immediately wrote down what had happened, trying to capture what people said and how it felt. In writing this book, I pieced together those notes from notebooks, charts, agendas, interviews, and photographs Andrea and I took. Given the limitations of book length and memory, some descriptions are less detailed. Kim read the entire manuscript and Eneida, Josefina, Elba, Rania, Pallavi, and other FWP members reviewed much of it to ensure accuracy.

A NOTE ON THEORY

The ideas and work of Paulo Freire and Myles Horton inspired the work of Families with Power. I read Freire's *Pedagogy of the Oppressed* (1970) on my own in 1995. In 1999, I read Paulo Freire's *Teachers as Cultural Workers: Letters to Those Who Dare Teach* (1998) in a course with Dr. Sonia Nieto while working on my master's degree. She asked us to write him a "Dear Paulo" letter in response; I found many connections between his text and my teaching. (Sonia included my letter in her 2008 book, *Dear Paulo: Letters From Those Who Dare Teach*.) The opportunities to reflect on Freire in writing and in class discussion helped to deepen my understanding. In 2006, I read Myles Horton's autobiography, *The Long Haul*. I list these three books by Freire and Horton that I read in the dozen years before we started FWP in 2007 in order to be completely transparent; I was a curious teacher, not a scholar. In the years following 2007, I revisited these books and read some others, including *We Make the Road by Walking: Conversations on Education and Social Change* (Horton & Freire, 1990) and Mariana Souto-Manning's *Freire, Teaching, and Learning* (2010). These deepened my under-standing and gave me perspective, often in retrospect. In writing this book, I refer to the work of other scholars whom I may have read or heard about, often in dialogue with other educators, *after* the FWP work described in the story. I include these references because naming something can help us reflect on it. I hope this can point you to resources if you are interested in learning more.

In January 2020, after I retired, I took a graduate course with Western Mass Writing Project on Teaching for Racial Justice, in which I read *How to Be an Antiracist* (2019) by Ibram X. Kendi. While I have wrestled with questions regarding the intersection of race, class, and gender for more than 4 decades, Kendi's book profoundly shifted my thinking and offered me new frameworks for understanding race, racism, and antiracism. He critically examines his own experiences and thinking, identifying ideas that could be categorized as segregationist, assimilationist or antiracist. Kendi is also the author of *Stamped from the Beginning: The Definitive History of Racist Ideas in America* (2016), winner of the National Book Award. He traces the roots and persistence of racist ideas and the emergence of antiracist ideas. Jason Reynolds wrote a shorter and more accessible "remix" for young adults and students, called *Stamped: Racism, Antiracism and You* (Reynolds & Kendi, 2020).

The other members of FWP and I hadn't read Kendi and weren't familiar with his ideas when we started back in 2007, or even in 2019. Throughout this book, I refer to Kendi, especially his definitions of space racism, class racism, gender racism and behavioral racism, which I find useful, even in retrospect, in reflecting on educators engaging with families and communities. There are lots of great scholars—essayists, poets, novelists, historians, and others—writing important work about race. I continue to seek out their work to keep learning about these critically important and complicated issues.

HOW THIS BOOK IS ORGANIZED

I decided not to tell the stories simply in chronological order. Instead, I tried to categorize the stories in ways that would be useful to readers. Chapter 2 brings you into the culture circles and action plans from our first residential workshop. Chapter 3 dives into home visits and reasons why some people find them a scary idea. Chapter 4 describes how I began to look critically at family engagement in my school, at who was included and who was not.

Chapter 5 focuses on FWP activities and programs related to literacy, including Family Reading Parties and Family Writing Projects. Chapter 6 focuses on bilingual Family Math Nights. Chapter 7 describes the evolution of Morning Math Club. Chapter 8 describes an FWP program on financial literacy and family workshops about how children learn math.

Chapter 9 considers our beautiful scars, recognizing caregivers' trauma and the need for self-care, including programs like self-defense and meditation. Chapter 10 explores healthy eating from school gardens to farmers markets and community gardens You will see that we changed our responses to specific concerns over time. These chapters focus on FWP members supporting each other in our physical and mental health and the interconnection between public health and education.

Readers might wonder why I included health topics like caregivers' trauma, depression, diabetes, exercise, and food security in this book, since they may seem less related to academic achievement than Family Reading Parties or Morning Math Club. I included these because they were a central and substantial part of FWP's caregiver-generated agenda, which intuitively understood that a child's success depended on the whole family's physical and mental well-being. FWP's work in these areas received statewide recognition in 2011, with a Massachusetts Excellence in Agricultural Education Award and a Frontline Award from the Massachusetts Public Health Association. I hope these stories will help promote more education, agriculture, and public health partnerships.

Chapter 11 features cultural organizing. It looks at our *plena* singing and drumming program and annual traditions like our Love Your Family Dinner and *Parranda*.

Chapters 12, 13, and 14 all focus on aspects of immigration. Chapter 12 describes How Schools Work, a mutual support group for immigrant families. Chapter 13 illustrates the language and culture clubs that grew out of How Schools Work, especially the Arabic Community Club. Chapter 14 spotlights building solidarity to stand with immigrant students and families and fight for immigrant rights.

Chapters 15 and 16 explore the challenges and benefits of working with other community organizations and educator unions. The Conclusion of the book reflects on what we've learned.

So let's dive in and meet these families.

CHAPTER 2

"I Used to Be an Outcast, but Now I Am a Leader"

In April 2007, Families with Power/Familias con Poder (FWP) held our first weekend retreat designed to cultivate leadership, inspired by the principles of Highlander Folk School as described in Myles Horton's book *The Long Haul* (1997). We knew we wanted to do a Highlander-style residential workshop using a popular education approach, where people gather together to learn from each other. At the time, it seemed inauthentic to bring a group of Latina mothers and grandmothers from Massachusetts to Tennessee. I sought the advice of Sue Thrasher, who had organized at Highlander decades earlier. She said, "You can make your own Highlander here. It's not about the place."

We used grants from Teaching Tolerance at the Southern Poverty Law Center to rent an arts camp with a dorm and dining hall (about 20 minutes away by car) for a weekend in early spring. We invited the caregivers who had emerged as leaders through the Family Reading Parties we had been holding for a few months. Caregivers organized childcare and FWP provided stipends for it. When I asked Nydia Canales, one of the caregivers, if she had any dietary restrictions, she looked at me suspiciously, then said, "Waaaaaaait. Is someone else gonna cook for us?" I said yes. Nydia said, "And we're gonna bring our toothbrushes? Like sleepaway camp?" I nodded, and she broke out in a grin, "I never been to sleepaway camp before!"

The effort it took for each family to arrange childcare, time off from work, postponement of normal weekend errands and chores, and the carpool logistics all signaled how momentous this retreat was, and the sacrifice and commitment each of us made to participate. Our first activity, once we had put our bags in our rooms, was to meet in a circle to share what each of us had needed to arrange in order to be there. Following Horton's observation of folk schools, all participants got to know each other in the less-formal activities as much as in the workshop activities. On a cold evening in April, we bundled up and built a bonfire outside; the next day we walked together in the snow. I was struck by the universality of gathering

Figure 2.1. Eneida (center) and other adults and children take a walk together during the FWP retreat in Hawley (2013). Daily walks, dancing, music making, singing and active *dynamicas* helped all participants get to know each other in less formal ways.

Figure 2.2. Elba and Kim prepare breakfast together at the retreat in Hawley (2013). Everyone took turns cooking, serving, and cleaning up. Members planned the menu together to include healthy, culturally appropriate and kid friendly foods. Meals were served family style, with tablecloths and fresh flowers to make everyone feel special.

around a fire: The women from Uruguay, Panama, Uganda, and Puerto Rico all said that the fire reminded them of home. All these years later, I still have a vivid memory of Doña Lucas, the great-grandmother of a 2nd-grader in our school, standing in the firelight telling us the story of how she fell in love with her husband: She sang the song he had sung to her, *Dame tu Mano, Paloma* (Give Me Your Hand, Dove).

CULTURE CIRCLES

In her book, *Freire, Teaching, and Learning: Culture Circles Across Contexts*, Mariana Souto-Manning describes culture circles: "Culture circles start from the very issues which affect participants' everyday lives. Generative themes, which are common experiences across participants' lives or relevant to participants' realities, serve as starting points to problem posing. As problems are posed, participants engage in dialogue, considering a multitude of perspectives, and seek to move toward problem solving. As the group engages in collective problem solving, it charts a course for action at the personal and/or societal levels" (2010, p. 9).

As we planned the retreat, Kim proposed that we use Paulo Freire's culture circles. She created simple drawings in black marker that we could use to generate themes, such as a sign saying "PTO meeting Wednesday Night at 7pm," a picture of a student of color sitting outside a principal's office, and a drawing of another wearing a graduation cap and gown.

We spread the drawings out on the floor for everyone to examine. Each of us was invited to take a drawing and sit in the circle. One by one, each participant showed the drawing she picked up and talked about it in Spanish or English. These drawings (we could have used photos) and the dialogue they sparked generated our themes. For example, Maribel chose the drawing that said, "Family Center, Parent Hour Wednesday 9-10:00am." She said she had gone there once, to check it out. The parents there had been discussing what they felt to be the best summer camps and places for music lessons. Maribel and her husband worked as cooks at a sleepaway summer camp and brought their children with them to camp each summer, but she didn't feel comfortable mentioning this.

The next afternoon, Maribel needed to buy something at the store after work. Even though she was sweaty and a little greasy from working at her food service job, she didn't have time to drive home to shower, change, and drive back to the store, only to drive home again, so she stopped on her way home from work. She saw a parent she'd met at the Parent Center the day before and stopped in the aisle to say hello. "It's like she didn't even see me there as a person, like she looked through me, or didn't want anyone to know she knew me. She didn't speak, just kept going." Other participants talked about similar experiences when they felt invisible, excluded, out of place. Our practice of culture circles may not have been textbook perfect, but it felt immediately relevant, authentic, and honest.

"THERE WAS NOBODY THERE LIKE ME"

Every caregiver in the culture circles expressed some variation on this theme: "I went to a meeting once, and there was nobody there like me." Let me say here that my school had a Parent Teacher Organization (PTO) that was wonderful in many ways. As a teacher, I appreciated many things it did. The PTO raised thousands of dollars each year through grant writing and fundraising, for field trips, a new playground, musical instruments, physical education equipment and teaching supplies. It organized popular annual events, like field days. It was full of creative, energetic, generous, high-powered, efficient parents who, historically, were mostly White, middle- or upper class, college-educated, articulate native English speakers, who had steady family incomes that enabled them to own houses, smartphones, computers, and cars. Most of these parents would describe themselves as liberal and antiracist, and they valued the multicultural character of our school. Yet the class divide in our school was a gaping crevasse.

"I tried going to meetings at school. These people do all the talking and sound all educated," said Nydia. "If I try to say anything, I don't know how to talk right. I ain't going to a meeting that's gonna make me feel stupid. I can stay home and feel stupid by myself."

Here's how Josefina described attending her first PTO meeting. "I felt like a bowl of white beans and having a black bean just in the middle, that everybody is pointing to you. Probably not everybody is pointing to you, but you feel like everybody is looking to you, seeing your movements, so that you want to be invisible, because you feel like you don't fit in. I felt like I didn't understand the language they were talking about because it was so sophisticated. And the way they act different: just listening to the person who is in charge of the meeting. I feel like it is not equal. I can't be there just sitting without saying what I think. I think my voice has power. I might say something really interesting. Everybody's voice is valuable. It felt really, really weird to be in that position. And I didn't come back." (See Figure 2.3.)

CREATING CRITICAL MASS/RESISTING DILUTION

As each caregiver at our first retreat echoed these feelings, I began to see our PTO and school activities from a different perspective. Maribel said that she had recently attended a PTO meeting where they were planning their big fundraiser, a silent auction for adults. They needed someone to run a dessert table. Maribel is an excellent baker, so she volunteered. Now she

Figure 2.3. Josefina Rodriguez reads her writing at the FWP Family Writing Project at Casa Latina (2010).

Photo: Andrea Raphael

Meet Josefina

Josefina Rodriguez was born and raised in Jarabacoa, Dominican Republic, and came to Massachusetts in 2002. Josefina is a widowed single mother who raised two sons, Reneury and Joseury. Josefina became involved with Families with Power when her oldest son was in kindergarten. She first attended, then hosted a Family Reading Party, then the Family Writing Project and quickly became a leader in FWP. Josefina has since graduated from Holyoke Community College. Her younger son, Joseury, is now a high school senior, applying to colleges. Josefina works as a personal care attendant and serves on the board of Northampton Survival Center.

felt uncomfortable, like she'd be the only person of color at the event, but she didn't want to break her promise and let them think she was unreliable. Sylvia, another workshop participant, said, "We'll all come with you, and then you won't be the only one!"

This was the start of what we came to think of as creating a critical mass, which has been a solid support for families of color negotiating unfamiliar and previously White-dominated spaces. None of the FWP members had attended the silent auction before. Some thought PTO members might wonder why they were there. Maribel proposed the idea that everyone should wear something that would let people know we were there together, as Families with Power. The event was less than a week away; we didn't have time or money to print tee shirts. Maribel proposed we make FWP buttons. I had a few dozen buttons left over from an event; we printed "Families with Power/ Familias con Poder" on white circles of paper, then cut and pasted them onto the old buttons. Perhaps the event organizers assumed Maribel would be standing alone at the dessert table, but at the Silent Auction a week after our retreat, there were ten FWP members with her, proudly wearing home-made bilingual FWP buttons, and when the music started, they ruled the dance floor.

A PTO member pulled me aside to ask what Families with Power was. I explained that it was a voluntary grassroots community organization of multicultural low-income families, many immigrants and people of color, that we'd just started the month before with Family Reading Parties and had our first retreat. She said she thought that was great and wanted to join. Awkward. This parent was an affluent White upper-class professional. I explained that this was an organization that low-income families had just started for themselves, to create a space where they could organize activities they felt would support their kids and their families. She asked again how she could join. I finally said, "You can't join as a member, but if you want, FWP can let you know when we need volunteers to help with a project." That request from an affluent White parent to join FWP was fol-lowed by others, including a professor who wanted to send undergraduate students to "mentor" FWP caregivers, as a community service project. No, thank you.

Kendi's ideas about *space racism* illuminate the integrationist tension in this incident. Kendi writes,

> Whenever Black people voluntarily gather among themselves, integrationists do not see spaces of Black solidarity created to separate Black people from racism. They see spaces of White hate. They do not see spaces of cultural solidarity, of solidarity against racism. They see spaces of segregation against White people. Integrationists do not see these spaces as the movement of Black people toward Black people. Integrationists think about them as a movement away from White people. They then equate that . . . with the White segregationist movement away from Black people. Integrationists equate spaces for the survival of Black bodies with spaces for the survival of White supremacy. (2019, p. 175)

FWP's work was not informed by this theory, but the FWP impulse and insistence on creating our own spaces with community-based activi-ties illustrates this voluntary gathering of low-income people of color in cultural solidarity, against racism. Our priority was to create and nurture that unique space, not to accommodate affluent White liberal parents (how-ever well-intentioned) pressuring us to "integrate" FWP immediately. We faced pushback for FWP's stance on this, but that early insistent practice of creating spaces as the movement of low-income people of color and im-migrants toward low-income people of color and immigrants was critical to our survival.

We talked about this within FWP. Members thought it was interesting that people who had never personally invited them to anything, who nev-er even seemed to notice them, were suddenly inviting themselves to FWP.

White, educated, English-speaking families already controlled the PTO, school council, civil rights committee, school committee and City Council. Members felt FWP was new and still figuring itself out; for the time being, members decided to keep it located in the community (in living rooms and community rooms), not in the school, and to hold it as a space for low-income families with children of all races and cultures, who had no other space or organization, who were developing as their own leaders. From the beginning, FWP members reserved the right to invite educators or other community members to participate or help out for specific projects or activities, or not. Some of those parents from the Silent Auction did help with book collections and transportation later.

ACTION PLANS

We finished our first retreat with a "head, hands and heart" evaluation. Each person filled out three sticky notes, jotting down something they learned (head), how they felt (heart) and one thing they would do (hands) and shared it with the group as they put it on a poster. We generated individual and organizational action plans. For example, Maribel's action plan had been to attend the PTO Silent Auction.

Another action plan from our retreat was to grow the Family Reading Parties. Eneida, Nydia, Irma Lucena, and a fourth parent, Janet Namono, committed to becoming Family Reading Party coordinators for their neighborhoods, running events every Friday night, rotating among their four neighborhoods. FWP ran a book drive to collect baskets full of books, which served as informal lending libraries in each neighborhood. Irma said, "We are not just *cuatro gatos* anymore. We are like the four pillars that hold up the house."

ONLY TEN MINUTES

Another action plan that came out of that first retreat was for FWP to speak before the School Committee. We weren't aware of low-income parents ever coming to the School Committee or speaking there in Spanish. (We recently learned from Sonia Nieto that a group of Puerto Rican parents did address the Northampton School Committee in Spanish and English regarding what they wanted for their children in the bilingual program, back in 1978—nearly 30 years earlier.)

The day after our retreat, I emailed the superintendent to request that FWP be added to the agenda of the next School Committee meeting. The superintendent reluctantly put us on the next agenda but repeatedly said we were only allowed 10 minutes. Eneida, Maribel, Nydia, Janet, and Irma

Figure 2.4. Irma Lucena, a founding member of FWP, coordinated Family Reading Parties in her Florence Heights neighborhood (2010).

Photo: Andrea Raphael

Meet Irma

Irma Lucena was born and raised in Lares, Puerto Rico, a mountain town once famous for its coffee and a rebellion against Spanish colonial rule. She met her future husband, Carmelo Vega, when they worked together at a shoe factory in Puerto Rico. In 2005 they moved to Northampton, MA, with their two sons, Mike and Alex, who attended Jackson Street School. Irma met Eneida through Casa Latina. She began to attend Family Reading Parties and participated in the first FWP retreat in 2007. Irma was part of the group of FWP members who spoke at the Northampton School Committee and attended the Highlander Homecoming. Her family was especially active in Family Reading Parties, Family Writing Project, and annual retreats. After Mike and Alex graduated from high school in Northampton, the family moved to Springfield.

waited patiently for more than 20 minutes while a group of White high school students presented a slide show of their spring break tour of Spain, which, they explained, was the only way they could have had the opportunity to converse in Spanish with *real* people. They all left before FWP members spoke, in Spanish.

FWP members were so nervous about speaking in public that many of them were trembling when they each came up to say a few words about the project and what it meant to them. Eneida interpreted for the Spanish speakers, and in her anxiety she simply repeated the words of the first speaker, Irma, until Maribel nudged her and whispered, *"¡En ingles!"* Three more participants spoke, ending with Nydia, who said, "If you saw me before, I was always alone. I used to be an outcast, but now I am a leader." The testimony of these speakers was so powerful that some of the school committee members wept.

After speaking, we gathered in the hallway outside the meeting room. The excited and proud family members in the audience *por apoyo* (for support) came out to embrace the FWP speakers. Suddenly the door opened, and a school committee member walked out. We thought she was going say we were too loud. Instead, she handed Eneida a $50 bill and said, "Your organization is doing what the schools should be doing. I support you."

The next week, some FWP members visited the Northampton Education Foundation board, to thank them for supporting FWP. After Eneida and Janet spoke, Ellen Nigrosh, a board member, offered to let us use her family's summer home for weekend workshops whenever we needed it, for free. We started to bring entire families, cooked and ate meals together, shared

Figure 2.5. Janet Namono and her son, Mwalye Martin, at FWP's Family Writing Project at Meadowbrook Apartments (2008).

Meet Janet

Janet was born in Entebbe, Uganda, and moved to Massachusetts in 2003 with her son, Mwalye. In 2004 they moved to Hampshire Heights in Northampton and Mwalye began to attend the preschool at Jackson Street School, where she volunteered. Gwen Agna invited Janet to apply for a job as a teaching assistant at Jackson Street School, where Janet and I met and became friends. I invited Janet to the first FWP retreat in 2007; she became the coordinator for the Hampshire Heights neighborhood where she lived. She went on to earn a master's degree in social work at Smith College and now works as a child therapist in Springfield, MA, where she recently bought her first home.

chores, and provided organized childcare on site, as a way to cultivate youth leadership. For many years, we organized a weekend "retreat" there each spring, with members leading the popular education training activities.

CHARACTERISTICS OF POPULAR EDUCATION

Five months after our first retreat in 2007, I learned that Highlander (now called Highlander Research and Education Center) was hosting a Homecoming for its 75th anniversary. During a Family Reading Party, I brought this up, asking if anyone would be interested in attending. Every hand went up. We scraped money together and began planning; Eneida, Maribel, Irma, Doña Lucas, Janet, and I flew to Knoxville. Sue Thrasher was also attending the Highlander Homecoming and gave us rides in her rental car, where we sat on each other's laps. We all squeezed into a hotel room together. I remembered that just a year before, I thought it would be inauthentic to bring caregivers from Massachusetts to Tennessee, but now, it felt just right. As we walked to the first workshop at Highlander, Doña Lucas said, "It feels like we are walking on hallowed ground." We attended workshops and met grassroots organizers from all over the world. The Highlander Homecoming taught us new skills and placed our work in a much larger frame than we'd imagined.

We participated in a Highlander Homecoming workshop on popular education. Below are some of the characteristics I recorded in my notes that day. We incorporated these into FWP's practice, especially in our retreats:

- **Get personal:** Popular education is from the heart; it's of, by and for the people.
- **Get active:** Get out of your chair and encounter each other.
- **Share the microphone:** Talk and listen; honor the people in the room.
- **"Drink from our own wells."** Give ourselves time and space to tell our own stories instead of always listening to stories in the media that aren't about us and our lives.
- Ask, "What **languages** are in the room today?"
- **Nurture horizontal vs. vertical relationships.**
- **Use the tools the community already has.**
- **Understand the situation and change it.**
- **Relevant education leads to collective liberation.**
- **Popular education is an old tradition,** with roots in the Highlander Folk School in Tennessee and Paulo Freire's work in Latin America and Africa.
- **We learn and share together.** Participants vocalize their questions and concerns and brainstorm alternative visions.

When we began our first retreat, the terms "grassroots organizing" and "popular education" were new to many FWP participants but gained meaning as we shared excerpts from *The Long Haul*. Yet in the course of the weekend, the activities themselves sparked memories for many. Some remembered attending community meetings with similar activities with their parents in Puerto Rico, Uganda, Panama, and Uruguay to discuss issues such as potable drinking water, agricultural methods, and hurricane preparation. I learned that the practice of popular education (if not the terminology) was culturally familiar to many FWP members who did not grow up in the mainland United States.

In 2007, our first year, FWP members spoke at the Civil Rights Committee and at faculty meetings and presented at educational conferences. Roque Sanchez, another FWP member, summed it up best. "Sure, they were nervous at first, but now they are like lions!"

"BUT NOW I AM A LEADER"

In June 2009, the Jackson Street School Civil Rights Committee invited FWP to a meeting with the superintendent. Beforehand, Nydia called the members and assigned each to a different portion of the agenda. When it was time, Nydia adjusted her glasses and gave her report about the recent FWP retreat. She called on other FWP organizers to speak about the programs they coordinated. Janet described the Family Reading Parties. Josefina described our Family Writing Project and gave a copy of our *Escribiendo Juntos* (Writing Together) anthology to the superintendent. Irma spoke about the *plena* drumming group (a traditional Puerto Rican style of drumming and singing). Eneida described our support group for families of kids with ADHD. As I watched Nydia confidently facilitating the agenda, I thought about what she said two years before: "I used to be an outcast, but now I am a leader."

CHAPTER 3

Home Visits

In my 2006 book *Black Ants and Buddhists* I describe my practice of making home visits to my students, to meet their caregivers and family members and to answer their questions. Student teacher readers of the book have asked me about this practice more than about anything else I talk about. They ask me, "What if I am not welcome? What if I don't speak their language? What if it's awkward? What if they don't want me to come in?" To answer these, I'll tell you a story.

The August sun beat down on me as I walked from one garden apartment to another, making home visits to my new students just before the start of the year. I had connected with nearly all of the parents by phone or email to arrange a time to visit that coordinated with their work and family schedule.

One family on my list had no email or phone. An Albanian refugee family who had just arrived from Kosovo, they did not yet speak any English. They had four children, including three who would be attending our school. The daughter, Bashirah,* would be in my 1st-grade class; one brother would be in 5th grade, another in kindergarten. I didn't know a word of Albanian, and I didn't know any Albanian speakers in our community. But it would be unfair not to visit this family. So I knocked on the door.

A man with graying hair answered the door cautiously, opening it just partway. I spoke slowly, saying, "My name is Ms. Cowhey. I will be Bashirah's teacher at Jackson Street School." I pointed in the direction of the nearby school. "I came to meet Bashirah and your family before school starts." He gestured for me to wait, or maybe just to stop talking, walked into the apartment, and spoke with his wife while, one by one, the children crept into the living room to spy on the sliver of me they could see through the barely open door. I baked on the small concrete patio, sweating profusely as I waited for the verdict.

A few minutes later, the man returned and gestured for me to enter. The children sat on a tired couch, ranged from largest to smallest. A fan whirred in the window. He sat in a chair and his wife, Betime,* came from the kitchen, balancing a tray of tiny glasses with gold edging. As she set the tray on a small table, I

---

* Names with an asterisk in this chapter are pseudonyms.

caught a whiff of steaming mint tea. She gestured to the tray and said something I didn't understand. I nodded and gingerly picked up the cup by the rim, trying not to grimace as it burned my fingertips. We all said our names, several times actually, as we practiced saying each other's names. They spoke Albanian slowly. I spoke English slowly. We latched onto cognates and used a lot of gestures. Every time I finished my tiny glass of tea, Betime refilled it. I could smell bread baking and learned that Betime baked her own bread. I learned that the father, Flladim,* worked at the supermarket. They told me the name of the village where they had lived and their gestures told me that it had been destroyed in the war. Betime cried. They said some angry things that included the name of Milosevic.

Betime showed me letters from the school with the class assignments for each child, so I knew they understood I was connected with the school. I underlined each teacher's name and taught them how to say them. The children proudly showed me some new pencils and notebooks. I smiled, nodded, and admired the pencils and notebooks. I did not say that the school would provide all the materials the students needed, that they hadn't needed to buy them. I understood Betime and Flladim wanted their children to attend school, that they valued education, that they were prepared to sacrifice for it.

I thought about how hard it was for me to leave my son with his kindergarten teacher on his first day of school a few years earlier, with a teacher who shared my ethnicity, language and religion. Imagining how frightening it would be to escape with my children from a war, then have to leave them at the door of a school in a new country where no one shared my ethnicity, language or religion, I struggled to keep from crying. When I left, Bashirah and Betime hugged me.

Yes, it was awkward, and yes, I was nervous about not being able to communicate, but in the end I felt a kind of tender joy. The benefits in understanding, empathy, and connection, and opening a relationship with this family, were more than worth my momentary angst.

How did I come to make these visits? What inspired me? In July 1997, I was hired to teach 1st grade in a class of mostly bilingual children. Over the summer, I took two graduate classes in teaching English as a second language. In one class, I read about a teacher making home visits to her students. I brought it up with my principal, Gwen, that August, saying that I'd like to do the same. After a pause she said, "I think it's a great idea, but it might upset some people. Just don't let anyone else know."

I was naive. I didn't perceive the problem or understand her hesitancy. I asked if I could get in touch with the families to set up the visits. She said yes, and I was off to the races. I had my list of students. I looked up their families' contact information and mailed a letter of introduction to each, saying that I would love to meet them and their child, that I would be making home visits the following week. I included my email and phone number and asked them to contact me if they'd like to schedule a time that would work for them. I scheduled visits with most of the families this way. Some parents shared complications having to do with divorce. They asked me to schedule at a time when the other parent could also be there, or if I would be willing to schedule two separate meetings in different homes. One family was living in a homeless shelter and asked the director for permission to let me visit them there.

I had to be flexible and creative in making visits possible. One student had a sibling in the intensive care unit. Her parents took turns talking to me on a cell phone in the hallway of the ICU, so the other could remain at the bedside of the sick child. They were grateful to be able to invest some time and attention toward the needs of the child who was well, as they shared their concern that, by necessity, they had to spend a huge amount of energy and attention to meet the needs of the chronically ill child. I was thankful to hear from the parents about this powerful family dynamic that had a huge emotional impact on my student.

"WHAT IF THEY DON'T WANT ME TO COME IN?"

My father was a hoarder. I grew up in a White working-class suburb on Long Island, in a house that lacked heat and running water in winter, that had mildew on the walls and rats in the basement. If any mandated reporter ever set foot in our house, my siblings and I would have been removed in a heartbeat. Even in the summer, the stacks of newspapers, magazines and books, the obstacle course of tools, car parts and general chaos inside would have been a red flag to any visitor.

No teacher ever called and asked to do a home visit when I was a child. When I decided to do home visits, I asked my mother how she would have responded, since I can only think of a handful of non-relatives who were allowed inside our house after I was ten. My mother said she would have assigned my big sister to mow the lawn around the old cars in the yard. We would make a pitcher of iced tea and fancy it up with fresh mint leaves. My mother and I would wait outside for the teacher, so we could greet her enthusiastically and walk her over to the picnic table to chat. We would never invite her inside.

In some phone conversations with parents, I recognized anxiety over potential visits. In those cases, I would casually say, "I know this is a crazy time of year for all of us. We could sit on the steps or in the yard for a few minutes, just so your child and I can meet each other before school starts." That reduced the anxiety, leading to many friendly conversations on stoops, patios, or porches. I never asked to go inside or use the bathroom. I made hundreds of home visits over the years, and hesitation about a home visit (likely related to hoarding issues) came up less than ten times, across socio-economic classes. The small number of times this situation arose, it happened to be with White families. Hoarding is a challenge I grew up with; I can relate. I focus on my students and their families, not their housekeeping. Simply put, don't judge.

Many of the families I visited lived in my neighborhood, in the apartment complex where I lived, or the one next to mine, or the two across the street. I was able to visit those on foot. I was able to bicycle to many others. If I didn't hear from a family, I knocked on the door when I was in the neighborhood to do a quick visit on the spot or to schedule one for a better time. Some of these homes were apartments, like where I lived. Some were two or three times the size of my little home. Some families consisted of a child and parent, and others were blended, extended and intertwined.

MY FIRST COFFEE

Of course, I did not expect anyone to offer me anything when I visited, but I learned, even before becoming a teacher, that I should accept what was offered.

When I was a young organizer in Trenton, New Jersey, in the early 1980s, I worked with a group of Puerto Rican welders who were fired when they asked their boss for a ten-cent raise. We filed an appeal because their unemployment cases were denied. There was a tight deadline to gather signatures from all the workers. Javier, the leader of the welders, took me from one worker's house to another's on a Saturday to gather signatures.

It was a summer morning and already hot in the city when we arrived at Pablo's house. We were sitting in the living room, chatting, when out of the corner of my eye I noticed Pablo's son running up the street of row houses. The conversation was completely in Spanish, and I only understood a little of it. I was impatient, wondering why Javier didn't just ask Pablo to sign the paper so we could go to the next house. Javier and Pablo kept talking. Minutes later, I saw Pablo's son running back, then heard the back door slam. I caught a glimpse of the breathless boy in the kitchen holding a partial bag of sugar. Pablo's wife, Camila, patted him. Soon she emerged from the kitchen with steaming cups of milky coffee. Camila stirred a generous spoonful of sugar into the first cup and handed it to me.

This was awkward. I had not asked for coffee and did not even like the smell of it. Javier smiled at me expectantly and nodded encouragement. I thanked Camila, and I drank my first café con leche. After we all had coffee together, Pablo signed the papers. Javier stood up and stretched, signaling it was time to go to the next house, after having gently taught me valuable life lessons about loosening my uptight grip on both my sense of efficiency and my personal preferences. As I learned that day and again over the years, this wasn't about me.

I never forget: It is a privilege to be welcomed into someone's home, especially when I am culturally different. I don't know what is culturally appropriate in every home. I proceed with humility, knowing I might make mistakes (and willing to laugh at myself when I do). But I learned that if I said "No, thank you," to the frosty bottle of tamarind soda, the steaming cup of *café con leche* or the gold-rimmed glass of mint tea, I would be rejecting a generous offer of hospitality and undermining our budding relationship. So I always say, "Yes, thank you!" (or *gracias*, *shukran*, or *merci*) and try all sorts of things that I wouldn't ordinarily try because what we really thirst for in this moment is trust and acceptance. My preferences about caffeine and corn syrup are insignificant.

"Do you want to hold Rodrigo?"

I learned to become open to unexpected lessons and opportunities. When I visited Isabela Rivera Santiago and her mother, Lourdes Santiago Campos, Isabela asked, "Do you want to hold Rodrigo?" Hmmm. I knew Isabela was the youngest child in her family. I didn't see or hear any babies in the apartment. Isabela seemed enthusiastic about Rodrigo as she bounced up and down.

"Who is Rodrigo?" I asked. Isabela just smiled. Lourdes, sitting beside me on the sofa, turned to her left, reached into a large cage I hadn't noticed, then faced me again, smiling as she held out what I learned was a leopard gecko. I like cats, dogs, and chickens. Reptiles and amphibians, not so much. In some homes, due either to asthma and allergies or apartment rules, family pets are amphibians, reptiles, or birds.

Rodrigo seemed active but friendly; in fact, he seemed to be smiling. I couldn't see fangs or claws. I said, "Sure." He climbed up and down my arm, with his dry, bumpy skin and weird suction cup feet. I noticed that he had five toes on each foot. I asked if I could take a picture of his feet to help me teach about ways to make five. Isabela was delighted.

AN INTENTIONAL CONVERSATION, NOT AN INTERROGATION

When I visit, I don't have a big agenda. I want to meet my students and their families and learn to pronounce their names correctly. I want to give them a chance to ask me questions and show or tell me whatever they'd like about their lives. I make it an intentional conversation, not an interrogation or evaluation. The goal is to build our relationship. I am listening for the experiences of the caregivers and my student. I try to understand what they want (or fear) and why. I lean in and make eye contact, without staring, unless that seems to feel uncomfortable for the person for cultural, neurological, or other reasons. I acknowledge their feelings and experience. I am sensitive to the fact that some students and caregivers may have been removed from their home or family or been investigated by child protective services and may be suspicious or uncomfortable with an unfamiliar visitor. I try to make it clear that I am there as a friendly teacher, not as a social worker.

I am humbled by the trust that families extend on these first visits, some-times sharing stories about fostering or adoption, trauma, illness, or death. Some families share stories of divorce, incarceration, or struggles with addiction. Some share news of impending births or a parent returning to school.

Families share what they see as the strengths of their children, maybe that they love cooking, chickens, or drumming. They mention challenges, or what past teachers have said were challenges. They might acknowledge the child is very active and that they thought the previous teacher had unrealistic ex-pectations for young children to sit still for so long. I listen without judgment and ask if they have any suggestions for me. Sometimes they share tips they know will help their child, such as taking a movement break, keeping a family photo in their cubby, or bringing a transitional object. They may tell me to let the child go to the bathroom immediately because they've wet their pants at school before—a simple piece of advice that can save a child from humiliation in front of their peers.

Some caregivers share a detail that anchors a family's story, such as when a parent survived cancer before the child was conceived, or when the child was premature and barely survived. These stories give breathtaking meaning to a child's name, like *Angel Gabriel*. Sometimes a caregiver shares some trauma background that gives context and compassion for that child in a way that places us all on the same team, instead of educators getting frustrated and upset with what seems like irrational or unsafe behavior.

I notice body language, how the child might climb onto the lap of an adult or sibling, or whisper into their ear, and how that person responds. I make an effort to learn the names of everyone I meet, not only the student and their caregivers, but siblings, pets, and extended family. It's important to know the constellation of people who love each student. These folks and our relationship will build a solid foundation for that student's happiness and success.

If a family is new to our school, I give basic information about arrival and dismissal, school supplies and lunch. I tell them that they do not have to buy any special supplies, that the school will provide what the children need but that a backpack and labeled water bottle are useful. I explain to every family how the free and reduced breakfast and lunch program works, and the paperwork they will receive about this on the first day.

As a classroom teacher, I always ask and enter on my class list how each child will get home from school. I have a poster with dismissal information near the classroom door so I (or a substitute or student teacher) will know exactly who goes to the afterschool program on which days of the week, who goes out the front to catch a bus and who goes out the back to meet a family member. If there's a call from the office with a change, I stick a bright-ly colored sticky note on the poster and the clipboard so that I can't forget it. This is an extremely important detail. I don't expect families to appreciate all the days we do it right, but I know they'll be justifiably upset if we get it wrong. This seemingly small detail is a priority for me on every home visit. I let the parents know how to communicate changes in the routine to me. It is an important first step in building our mutual trust and starting the year on the right foot.

Sometimes a small compliment opens up a larger conversation. On my very first home visit, I said, "Cool photo," when I saw a framed picture of my student holding a gavel with his two moms and a judge standing behind him. His mothers told me his adoption story. They offered to do a read-aloud in our upcoming family unit and help classmates understand both fostering and adoption. They also invited me to a workshop for educators about adoption issues. This made me realize I had no idea how to teach about fostering and adoption. I was extremely grateful for the support they offered.

In another home, I complimented beautiful handmade quilts and learned that a parent was passionate about quilting. In this way I recruited many parents more skilled in crafts than I am to set up sewing centers, help with math units that use quilts to teach geometry and fractions and sew clothing for teddy bears.

By noticing flowers out front or tomatoes ripening on a kitchen table, I found caregivers willing to volunteer with our school garden. I met family members replacing the brakes on a car, fixing a bicycle, drying out a tent from a recent camping trip, collecting eggs from backyard chickens, or repairing a porch. On the one hand, this helped me discover important resources, connections, and skills to help with classroom or school projects. More importantly, though, these conversations taught me about what Norma González, Luis Moll, and Cathy Amanti (González et al., 2005) called "funds of knowledge."

Every family, no matter their vocation or educational level, brings skills and life experience that we cannot see or even imagine when we look at any individual student in our classroom. I find that being in a student's home often pops these funds of knowledge into 3D focus. It helps me learn what a child might be passionate about, so that I can shape curriculum to build on those interests.

"Meet Our Families, Our Partners in Education"

I always ask if I may take a photo of my student and all the family members (and pets) who want to be included. I print these photos and make a display of our families, including mine and the student teacher's, at the classroom's doorway, with a heading like, "Meet our families, our partners in education." In moments of frustration, it helps me to look at the family photos, to remember this child (who might be driving me crazy that day) is loved and that the circle of people who love this child will likely be my first and best allies in finding a solution together.

A few years after I started my family photos practice, our principal, Gwen Agna, began a project of family photos for the whole school. Our PTO hires a professional photographer and sets up a screen behind a sofa in the cafeteria on Open School Night. Families patiently wait in line to have their photos taken together. One copy becomes part of a "Meet our JSS Families" display in the hallway outside the Parent Center, near the office. The other copy is sent home, where many families frame it or use it for holiday cards. Many caregivers say that these photos of diverse families (single parent, blended, multiracial, foster and adoptive, multigenerational, LGBTQ+ and more) make them feel that they will fit in at our school.

SPACE RACISM

Teachers sometimes worry not merely about feeling uncomfortable, but about feeling actually unsafe in what they imagine are their students' "sketchy" neighborhoods. These fears arise from our beliefs about race and class, beliefs that we were unconsciously steeped in our whole lives. Kendi (2019) introduced me to an idea that I never had a name for: "space racism." With this term, we name and can critically observe the stereotypes we may harbor about certain neighborhoods and our comfort level with being in them. Kendi writes about what a racist and misleading idea the "dangerous Black neighborhood" is. While people avoid Black neighborhoods for fear of crime, they may desire wealthy White neighborhoods, where they may live next door to white-collar criminals. Kendi writes that the FBI estimates that losses from white-collar crimes are near $600 billion per year.

When we can unchain ourselves from space racism, Kendi argues, "we will find good and bad, violence and non-violence, in all spaces, no matter how poor or rich, Black or non-Black" (2018, p. 169). He points out that we tend not to feel nervous about the disproportionate number of White males who engage in mass shootings when we visit a white neighborhood. The over-resourcing of White neighborhoods and the under-resourcing of Black neighborhoods creates a racial hierarchy of space that elevates White spaces and condemns Black spaces. Kendi points out that racist housing policies are more likely to concentrate poor Blacks into high poverty, under-resourced areas. White poverty tends to be scattered; that was the case in my childhood, where we managed to blend in, attend good public schools and take advantage of public libraries and other resources.

I believe that educators' feelings about neighborhoods matter a great deal. Neighborhoods are the soil in which our students grow. If educators disrespect or fear these neighborhoods, our students and their families feel that. It may be unspoken, but children learn it just the same. Recognizing our bias is a first step toward overcoming it.

Redlining

How did we come to have such differences between neighborhoods? To problematize the taken-for-granted idea of a "bad" neighborhood, Kendi (2019) reminds us to look at history to see how intentional government and corporate policies and practices shape the racial dynamics of who lives where and who owns what in the United States. Kendi cites statistics like the median net worth of White families being ten times that of Black families. Kendi constantly pushes us to examine the policies that create these conditions. Let's look at two examples of such policies: redlining and the GI Bill. I hope that these very brief descriptions will inspire other teachers to learn more about these policies and others that continue to inform the racialized nature of space in the United States.

For many years, the practice of "redlining" was official policy in the United States. Redlining was a discriminatory lending practice in which banks refused to give mortgages or loans to repair homes, especially to people of color, in certain urban neighborhoods deemed "hazardous." These neighborhoods were literally outlined in red on paper maps. Homeowners in redlined neighborhoods saw their property values decline instead of increase. Redlining practices contributed greatly to the wealth gap that exists today between White and Black families.

The GI Bill was a package of benefits to subsidize education and housing for GIs returning from World War II; it excluded most Black GIs. Debby Irving, in her book, *Waking Up White: Finding Myself in the Story of Race* (2014), writes about the GI Bill, "The federal government underwrote $120 billion in new housing, less than 2 percent of which went to people of color. America's largest single investment in its people . . . gave whites a lifestyle and financial boost that would accrue in decades to come while driving blacks and other minority populations into a downward spiral. . . . From the perspective of Americans excluded from this massive leg-up policy, the GI Bill is one of the best examples of affirmative action for white people" (Irving, 2014, p. 35).

Did you have a parent or grandparent who benefited from the GI Bill's educational or housing subsidies, or were they excluded from it? If they benefited from it, did wealth that accrued from that education or house get passed down to the next generation?

I grew up breathing the polluted air of racism in this country. I can still hear my father's voice saying, "Lock your doors!" when we drove into New York City. It isn't productive to feel guilty about stereotypical images or concerns that pop into our minds unbidden when we imagine Black, Brown, or low-income neighborhoods. It is more useful to be aware of our biases and learn how to check them. For me, learning about the history of racist policies such as redlining and the GI Bill is a corrective counterweight to the prejudice I grew up with. Kendi urges us to identify racist policies (like current zoning laws) and work to change them. With Kendi's framework and a better understanding of U.S. history, I can see that certain neighborhoods were deliberately under-resourced and that others were just as deliberately over-resourced.

DOING THE BEST I CAN

I believe that the caregivers I meet, like me, love their children and are trying to do the best they can. Of course, as a parent of a young child, I knew that stability was better than instability, but by the time my son was three, we had lived in six different places in three different states, none of them particularly "stable." I share my story here because it might help you to be open-minded about the stories of your students and their families and the maybe not-so-great choices they had to make to survive.

When my son was born, I was technically houseless; I had been couch-surfing for years. A minister who was going to visit her family in Puerto Rico let me stay at her house for 2 weeks when we left the hospital. While my

Figure 3.1. My son, Robeson Cowhey, walking in our Philadelphia neighborhood (1993).

son and I lived in Philadelphia, two brick buildings on our block collapsed onto the sidewalk. We often heard gunshots. There were rats in the alley and basement. There were crack vials on the sidewalk. Most importantly, however, we were part of a community that loved us and that we loved.

When I decided to leave Philadelphia, I had no resources to make a move. Back on Long Island, my mother was living in a small apartment with my brother, who had just returned from military service. Our old family home, where my father had been living, had been condemned and demolished. My sister Jane and her husband took us in, got us a used car, and helped me get back on my feet. Not everyone has family, and even if they do, other family members may not be in position to help.

I moved to a place I could afford with my minimum wage job: a basement studio for $600 a month, including utilities. Working full-time, I brought home $625 a month, received $80 a month in food stamps and a childcare subsidy. Without sick pay or health insurance, my toddler's 3-day fever threatened financial disaster. Between lost wages and the cost of a doctor's visit, I had to borrow money to pay my rent.

As a minimum wage worker and single mother, it was hard for me to imagine a way out of poverty and debt. I considered going back to college, but it would have taken me 8 years to finish up the 16 courses I needed, while working full time and accruing more debt. It would mean working all day, with my son in day care, and then asking relatives to watch him while I went to class at night. A friend told me about the Ada Comstock program at Smith College in Northampton, Massachusetts, for "non-traditional" students. In 1994, I applied and received a full tuition scholarship to Smith.

My friend Emma* and I drove up with my son to look for an apartment there. We pitched a tent at a campground and made calls from a payphone on the street to rental listings in the newspaper. On the rare occasions I spoke with landlords, they asked if I had children. When I said I did, they said they couldn't rent to me because the apartment might have lead paint. The law was designed to protect children from lead poisoning, yet it seemed a handy way for landlords to deny rentals to families. I filled out applications and was placed on waiting lists.

I was getting desperate. Emma agreed to drive me back up to Northampton. I left my son with my sister for the weekend. I had to use a realtor and pay his fee. He showed us a small one-bedroom on the second floor of a house on a busy street, a mile and a half from the daycare and my job. I didn't mention my son, and the realtor didn't ask. No one mentioned lead paint, which the old house surely had. I never met the landlord, who never knew I had a child.

After I moved in, I realized that lead paint might be the least of our problems. The freight train ran, loudly and often, just behind the houses across the street, and police cars and fire trucks from the nearby stations raced up our street at all hours with their sirens wailing. The dumpster overflowed because the landlord didn't pay for a large enough container for the two buildings that shared it. My fellow tenants, who were White, had been de-institutionalized after the state psychiatric hospital had recently shut down. Every night I unfolded a futon and slept on the floor of the living room, five feet from the door to the hallway, where my neighbor and her boyfriend argued loudly when he was drunk. He was often passed out in the foyer downstairs, blocking the exit. When my son and I tried to leave for school in the morning, I often had to push him out of the way. Perhaps I hadn't chosen wisely, but we had a roof over our heads.

A year later, I got a call from the rental office of an apartment complex, saying my name had come up on their waiting list. I had been approved for a Section 8 rental subsidy (a federally funded program to help low-income renters afford decent housing). I made an appointment to see the apartment the next day, fortuitous timing since I had an appointment that afternoon with the social worker who supervised my food stamps and childcare subsidy. I shared my good news. The social worker startled me by saying, "I wouldn't move there if you paid me. Everyone knows that place is dangerous. It's just not safe." I thought, *How bad could it be?*

I visited the apartment complex and sat at the playground for an hour as my son played with Latinx, Asian, Black and White kids from the neighborhood. It was late afternoon, and I could see people coming home from work, some relaxing in the shade in front of their apartments. I noticed some shopping carts and understood that some of the residents, like me, couldn't afford a car. There were no buildings collapsing, no rats or gunshots, no thundering freight trains or wailing sirens. The buildings did not have lead paint.

When I signed the lease on the 2-bedroom apartment, I felt like I won the lottery. Thanks to the Section 8 subsidy, at the age of 34, it was the first time in my life I had my own bedroom and, more importantly, rent that only took 30% of my income, instead of nearly every dollar of it. My son was 3 years old. It was the sixth place we lived, but it was safe and affordable.

In contrast, my daughter was born two years after I graduated from college, married, and joined the middle class, with two modest teacher salaries that were stable enough to get a mortgage. My husband and I bought the shell of an old summer cottage and fixed it up. My daughter had the privilege and stability of living in the same house for 20 years. Was it because she had a "better" mother than my son, who, through no fault of his own, had the disruption of moving six times by the age of three? Of course not. When my income increased, I had the resources to make better choices to provide for my family.

I believe that, just like me, the parents of my students are trying their hardest, doing the best they can to provide the safest and healthiest homes they can afford. Every parent has made mistakes, sometimes when they were between a rock and a hard place. I don't judge where families live. I show unconditional positive regard and acceptance, assuming all caregivers want to do what's best for their children.

I think critically about the priorities and policies of our capitalist society that value gentrification and soaring home prices as signs of progress. As a result of urban renewal—read urban *removal*—my old neighborhood in Philadelphia is now considered desirable. Single-family homes there sell for close to a million dollars; all our old neighbors are gone. I wonder how "desirable" a community is if the people who work there, who make its coffee, clean its offices, and harvest its food, can't afford to live there.

"WHAT IF I SEE SOMETHING I SHOULDN'T SEE?"

Student teachers have asked me about home visits, "What if I see something I shouldn't see?" When pressed for an example, they may name drug use as "something I shouldn't see." In doing hundreds of home visits over many years, I never saw drug use or anything else on a home visit that needed to be reported as a sign of abuse or neglect. Remember that whatever families share is a privilege, and most of what you see will be beautiful. Why might a teacher assume, on the basis of knowing only a student's name and address, that they might see something inappropriate?

Kendi defines "behavioral racism" (which can afflict members of all races) as "making individuals responsible for perceived behavior of racial groups and making racial groups responsible for the behavior of individuals" (2019, p. 92). When we notice ourselves making assumptions about students and families we've never met, based on their name or address, we can check ourselves and think how we can shift toward becoming a behavioral antiracist.

Kendi describes a behavioral antiracist as "One who is making racial group behavior fictitious and individual behavior real" (2019, p. 92). In the context of home visits, this means approaching each family with an open mind to engage with the individuals and situation that are actually there, rather than what one might have imagined that one would find. Because child abuse is real and serious, we as teachers have certain responsibilities as mandated reporters when we encounter such abuse. To be a behavioral antiracist in this context is to be aware that abuse can occur in any home or neighborhood, in a family of any race or class—not to expect it to occur in any particular kind of home or neighborhood.

MISTAKES

Student teachers ask me, "What if I make a mistake?" It's not *if* I make a mistake, but *when* I make a mistake. When I am new in a community or culturally different than the people I am visiting, the stakes feel higher. I've made many mistakes over the years, but I will tell you the most epic-fail cultural mistake I ever made in someone's home.

Figure 3.2. The seasick author off the coast of Quebec (1979).

When I was 18, I volunteered with a non-profit to be a community organizer in rural Maine for the summer. During our orientation, I learned they were sending me to teach swimming in a remote fishing village off the coast of Quebec.

Over the next two days, other volunteers and I took three planes, each smaller than the last, finally landing on a sandy strip on the Quebec coast. From there, we rode with a silent fisherman with thick glasses, a ruddy face and wild red hair in an open outboard boat over rough water for more than an hour. As we hurtled into a wall of fog, I hung on for dear life and tried not to puke (Figure 3.2).

When we arrived at the island, we got out at the wharf in the center of the harbor. We pushed our gear in wheelbarrows along the boardwalks that linked the forty or so small wooden houses that wrapped around the harbor.

I met the family with whom I would eat my meals, along with the other volunteer assigned to the island, a middle-aged American named Dick.* I was an ardent young feminist from New York. The women scientists I had befriended during the orientation and journey would be working on another island, but would join us for meals on weekends when they visited ours. Dick called me "baby" and the women scientists "girls." Our host was a widow named Ann;* her husband and his brother were fishermen who had drowned. She had two older sons who were fishermen and two younger children.

The islanders were descendants of British colonists. To my ear, they sounded like pirates, ending many sentences with "mate" or "maid." The small island, which had gotten electricity only in the last year, seemed far removed from Quebec and indeed from Canada.

I quickly learned that the spheres of men and women on the island were strictly divided. Only men became fishermen and piloted boats. Most women married young and cared for their homes and families. The fishermen went out at 3 a.m. and came home for dinner at noon. My first evening on the island, we sat down for a lunch of crab and bread buns. Ann led a short blessing. Soon there was shouting as two young men came staggering in drunk. Ann instantly tensed. "Warren,* mind yourself. Our company is here," she said sharply.

"Oh, mother dear, I am so happy," Warren said, grabbing Ann by the shoulders and planting a messy kiss on her lips. She pushed him away, telling him to stop his nonsense and sit down.

A few minutes later, Warren said, "Did you hear? Luke kidnapped Laura, then he raped her! He took her to another island and has her captive there. He raped her again . . ." He was breathless with this news. This little island was surrounded by at least a dozen uninhabited islands, dotted with shacks that seal hunters used in winter.

I thought surely the other women would say something. The scientists were chatting earnestly with the younger children about puffins. In just five minutes, this idyllic little fishing village perched on a rocky island in an expanse of the frigid North Atlantic had become an inescapable nightmare. Everyone seemed at ease with the terrifying status quo, happily chomping their bread buns while some maniac was raping Laura.

I sprang to my feet, yelling, "This is crazy! We can't just allow Luke to rape Laura. We have to stop this. We have to find Laura right now!" My heart was pounding. I was petrified at the thought of jumping back onto a boat, shaking my guts as we pounded over the waves, searching from island to island to find Laura, but it had to be done. I didn't even know how to drive a car, let alone a boat, but we had to act immediately. I was standing, holding a crabby fork high above the table like the Statue of Liberty.

Warren and his friend broke out in such laughter that they almost fell off their chairs. Then everyone else started laughing at me. I wanted to run from the room, but the twelve of us were packed so tightly around the table that I couldn't get out. Ann was pulling on my arm to sit down, still laughing with tears running down from her bright blue eyes. "Oh maid, me maid!" she was gasping. "Oh, me maid, it's just the story. We all watches it at dinner."

I didn't understand. "It's a soap opera," one of the scientists clarified. "About a year ago, the island got television, but only one channel and only one show, an American soap opera they call 'the story.' It comes on at 12:30, when everyone is eating dinner, so everyone watches it." She raised her eyebrows in the direction of the loud fishermen. I sat down, sick with the feeling that everyone on the island would be talking about a new story by morning.

I made a first impression all right. The young fishermen thought I was ridiculous. However, although the women continued to tease me about it, the incident immediately won their respect.

HUMILITY AND COURAGE

Paulo Freire, in *Teachers as Cultural Workers: Letters to Those Who Dare Teach*, describes "the indispensable qualities of progressive teachers for their better performance" in his fourth letter. He stresses that these qualities are "acquired gradually through practice . . . in concurrence with a political decision that the educator's role is crucial" (1998, p. 39).

Two of these indispensable qualities are humility and courage. Freire writes, "Humility helps us to understand this obvious truth: No one knows it all; no one is ignorant of everything. We all know something; we are all ignorant of something" (1998, p. 39). Ever since I first read these words more than 20 years ago, they have guided me. They remind me to be honest about my biases, flaws, weaknesses, mistakes, and in those most difficult moments, to be open to learning. This learning is endless; to me, that is liberating, not daunting.

Another quality Freire cites is courage.

> As we put into practice an education that critically provokes the learner's consciousness, we are necessarily working against the myths that deform us. As we confront such myths, we also face the dominant power because those myths are nothing but the expression of this power, of its ideology. (1998, p. 41)

The idea of a teacher making home visits seems, at first, to be simple. In many ways, it is. Upon deeper reflection, the act of leaving our schools, where teachers automatically have a degree of authority and power, to venture into the community (perhaps less familiar parts of the community) may bring up biases that we may not have been aware of: space racism, class racism, and behavioral racism, to name just a few. If we remain humble and open to new learning, we can recognize racist beliefs as myths that are nothing but the expression of the dominant power's ideology. Freire writes that it takes courage to become a progressive teacher who educates to "critically provoke the learner's consciousness" (1998, p. 41). Equipped only with humility and courage, I decided to give home visits a try, and they quickly became one of my most rewarding teaching activities.

I made home visits at the start of every school year I was a classroom teacher. After I became a Title I math specialist in 2010 it became impractical for me to continue the practice as I had as a classroom teacher. We had an assessment and selection process, which meant that I didn't have a list of my students before the first day of school. I also taught several cohorts of children each year, with new students being added when students met their learning goals and discontinued. This meant that I could have more than 50 students per year. With the same goal of getting to know students' families, my workaround was to initiate contact through introductory phone calls, personally greeting families at our Title I meetings and math workshops, offering conferences, and getting to know families through Morning Math Club and other FWP activities. I was still always happy to make a home visit if invited.

HOME VISIT EPILOGUE: GETTING OUTED

I wrote that when I first asked Gwen back in 1997 if I could make home visits she said that I could, but I shouldn't tell anyone. She thought the union might object, that it might set a precedent and expectation that would be required of all teachers. When an excited parent asked me, "Will my other son's teacher come to visit too?" I had to say, "Uh, no, uh, this isn't standard, and please don't mention it to anyone." I did my best to keep it quiet.

In 2001, there was a flurry of activity at my school to prepare for an assembly with officials from the state department of education. Their offices were two hours away in Boston, and they rarely traveled out to the western part of the state. I was suspicious and thought they might try to use our school as a photo op to make an announcement about standardized testing. The morning of the assembly, I told Gwen that I planned to boycott the assembly, which seemed a waste of instructional time. She wore a pained expression and said I couldn't boycott, that I had to be there. I rolled my eyes and said okay. My students and I sat on the floor of the gymnasium, finishing up a read-aloud as the place filled.

The assembly began, and the guest speaker was talking about the Milken National Educator Award, trying to excite the crowd. One of my busiest students, Sadie, knelt next to me and idly patted my head. Just as the speaker was reaching his crescendo, Sadie whispered, "I think *you* should win the award, because your hair is so soft," and I cracked up. Suddenly everyone was clapping and looking at me, and photographers were taking my picture. Apparently, the speaker had just said my name. Gwen was gesturing for me to come up to the front. I went over and hugged her, whispering, "Do they know what I do?" She whispered, "I told the truth."

The next day, there was a story about the national teaching award on the front page of the local paper, written from a press release by the state department of education. In saying why I'd received the award, the article mentioned that I did home visits with my students. How do you like that? I was outed by the state department of education. No one gave me a hard time about home visits after that.

CHAPTER 4

Looking Critically at the School That I Love

It was my first Open House as a student teacher. Students started arriving, clutching the hand of a parent, trailed by an impatient sibling. Children excitedly tugged parents into the room to show them their desks, the monarch chrysalises, their projects. My cooperating teacher and I greeted families and introduced ourselves. Through the swirl of enthusiastic students and friendly families, I noticed something. Most of the students and families in the room that evening were White. All were English speaking, many with professional parents. But about half the students in our class were not White. Many were Latinx, mostly Puerto Rican, and lived in one of the apartment complexes in the area, including mine. Many of the students and their families were my neighbors, but I didn't see them. I walked out to the crowded hallway. A chunk of our school was missing. This was puzzling, and it bothered me.

As student teachers, we were briefed to appreciate our cooperating teachers and the schools where we were placed, *not* to criticize them. I was in the habit of questioning and thinking critically, but I was new to the school. I didn't feel like there was anyone I could talk with about my observations. This chapter describes critical observations of my school, largely drawn from my journal entries and response papers, in my first few years there. There were, of course, good things happening there too. When I started at Jackson Street School as a volunteer tutor, Gwen Agna was not yet the principal. Her first year coincided with my student teaching year. She made many changes there over more than two decades.

After my year of student teaching, Jackson Street School hired me to teach a 1st-grade class that included all the native Spanish-speaking—mostly Puerto Rican—1st-graders who would gain their first literacy in Spanish. I team-taught with Kim Gerould, a bilingual teacher, during our literacy block.

I told parents they were always welcome in my classroom. Sometimes Latinx parents walked their children into the classroom in the morning to give them a final hug, kiss, and *bendición* (blessing) for the day, or an admonition to be good, do their work, and listen to the teacher. *Bendición* is a tradition practiced in Puerto Rico and some Latin countries. Often said as a greeting to a parent or other respected elder (or when leaving the house, going to school, or going to bed), *bendición* is literally asking for that person's blessing. The parent or elder usually replies, "*Dios te bendiga*" (God bless you). I learned that some of my colleagues complained to the principal about this, saying she should make me stop allowing this. I was confused. What could possibly be wrong with this picture? The complaining teachers argued that if I allowed parents to come in the classroom and the other teachers didn't, it would make them look bad, so I should stop.

In the staff lunchroom, I was stunned by how casually, how comfortably, Mr. Henderson, a loud White teacher, told racist, sexist, and classist jokes and how easily the other teachers there, all White and mostly women, laughed along. He did "imitations" of students and parents and spoke disparagingly about "those people" who lived "across the street," referring to the apartment complex where many of our students, and I, lived.

During that first year of teaching (1997), I was taking a course about antiracism for educators, based on Beverly Daniel Tatum's book, "*Why Are All the Black Kids Sitting Together in the Cafeteria?" And Other Conversations About Race*, which had just come out. I was learning that, however uncomfortable it might be, if I wanted to become antiracist, I would have to stand up to Mr. Henderson and other White people, even if they were colleagues, relatives, or friends, to interrupt the cycle of racism. I had progressed from being a minimum wage worker to being a salaried teacher, so I now paid the full "fair market rent" for my apartment and still enjoyed living in my neighborhood. I said, "I live across the street. You're talking about my family, my neighbors, our students. I find it racist and classist. It's extremely offensive." There was a stony silence. After that, whenever I entered the staff room, I was met with icy glares and the conversation stopped on a dime. My friend Lisa and I started eating our lunch together in her classroom.

I learned that teachers who were "insiders" had graduated from Northampton High School and had attended either the state college or university or a nearby Catholic college. They let me know that I was an "outsider" and didn't understand "how we do things here."

When I joined the school Civil Rights Committee, I was part of many discussions about the need to diversify hiring, retention, and promotion in our district. Our district's low wages and relatively high housing costs were part of the problem. It became clear that "school climate" was a real issue too. I considered the bruising reception I got from some colleagues when I was hired, even being racially and ethnically similar to them. Mr. Henderson and the teachers who used to laugh at his jokes are gone now. Yet we still have racism in our school. New teachers still need a lot of support and encouragement.

HOW SAFE IS THE LANDSCAPE?

Being anti-racist is about constructing a landscape that is safe for dark people to inhabit. It is not about white people trying to prove they are "woke" by putting up yard signs. . . . But being anti-racist in this dangerous era is something they can do, by going out of their way to make non-white people feel safe.

—Shayla Lawson (2020)

On my first day of professional development as a new hire, I walked into a room of 1st grade teachers from across the district. Not seeing anyone I knew, I approached a table with an empty chair and asked if I could sit there. The teacher next to the empty chair said, "I don't think you want to do that. I'm pretty abrasive." She was not smiling. I awkwardly backed away. In 1997, my district was not a welcoming place to anyone who had not grown up in the community. I had "colleagues" who mocked my teaching methods during faculty meetings and told racist jokes. It was the opposite of a safe landscape, even for a White teacher.

Throughout my career, I was intentional about welcoming people who were new to our school community: teachers, student teachers, paraprofessionals, substitutes, food service, custodial and clerical workers. I learned names and said hello every day. Especially in the case of student teachers and teachers new to our school, I invited them to activities in the community and introduced them to others. We talked about family, research interests, and resources to share. I invited them to eat lunch together, to come with me to staff "tea" after school, or sit with me at faculty meetings. I was intentional about building genuine relationships with people of color in the Jackson Street School community because I wasn't trying to be "colorblind." I wasn't assuming that their arrival in our community was just as comfortable as that of a middle-class White person who grew up here. People say, "Black lives matter" instead of "All lives matter" because in the social and historical context of the United States, Black lives have been treated like they don't matter. I especially tried to welcome people of color, to express that I see you as another human being, and I'm glad you are here.

I was thrilled to have landed my first teaching job. I loved teaching in the community where I lived. But I was constantly reminded that in this mostly White, liberal, small New England city, racism and classism were alive and well. This racism looked different from the kind of racism I had lived with in Trenton, New Jersey, where the state's "Metro Task Force" and local "K-9" units regularly made violent raids on bars and front stoops in the majority-Black neighborhood where I lived and worked.

New England racism is more subtle than Trenton's blatant police brutality was in the 1980s. Yet the more I looked, the more I saw this "proper" New England version of racism at work in my school, affecting generations of students. One caregiver told me that when she was a bilingual student at our school years earlier, a teacher told her and other English learners to sit in the back and gave them coloring book pages to color.

When my kindergartener son, who attended Jackson Street School, playfully called me "homey cracker" one day in 1997, I was stunned and asked him where he learned to say that. He happily told me, "Mr. Henderson [his physical education teacher] calls everybody that, like a nickname." My husband and I wrote a letter and asked to meet with Mr. Henderson and the principal. Mr. Henderson said that he didn't realize that was an offensive term, that other basketball players used to call him that, that he'd been using it for years, and no one had ever objected (meaning I was being oversensitive and overreacting).

In Trenton, "cracker" was a derogatory slang term for Whites, usually poor and/or racist Whites. The term "homey" was short for "homeboy" and was used with a close and trusted friend, literally someone you had grown up with. I explained what those terms meant and why "cracker" was offensive and how using them together was contradictory and inappropriate, especially coming from a White teacher toward students of color whose names he didn't remember, and especially to a biracial boy. As the physical education teacher, Mr. Henderson taught every child in our school, so every student had heard him use this term in place of their names over the years. He agreed to apologize and tell all the students that he'd made a mistake and would not use that term again.

After I became a teacher at Jackson Street School, I started attending occasional school committee meetings and paying more attention to the business of our city council. The school committee members and city councilors were White and always had been. (Northampton elected its first Black city councilor in 2019.) My son started kindergarten the same year I started teaching at Jackson Street School, so I attended my first PTO meeting as a parent and a teacher. I noticed that every parent at the meetings I attended was White, although about half of our students were Latinx, Asian, and Black.

A DIFFERENT PERSPECTIVE ON THE FAMILIAR

It is often hard to see what is going on right in front of us because we have been so accustomed to it, having grown up with things that way. Yet when we go to another country where we consider the culture "foreign" we easily observe (and judge) customs and practices that differ from ours. In 2001, I was invited to attend the United Nations World Conference Against Racism in South Africa, with an NGO delegation of social justice educators from UMass, where I was a graduate student. I brought up the idea of making the trip at dinner. My 9-year-old son, Robeson, who had attended many graduate classes with me at UMass and considered himself to be a UMass student, asked, "Can we go, please?" Elena, one of his 4th-grade classmates, had previously lived in South Africa with her parents and was going to be with them on the trip. Robeson joined me, and my husband stayed home with our 2-year-old daughter.

I met Thembi, a law student who had worked as Elena's childcare provider when she had previously lived in Durban. On our first full day there, Thembi and I were walking with the kids to the conference and passed through a park, where there were crowds of houseless children begging. Thembi must have seen shock register on my face. Without missing a beat, she called me on it, saying matter-of-factly, "It shocks you to see children like this . . ." I nodded. "Because in your country," Thembi continued, "it's the elders you treat like this, right?"

Thembi had nailed something I hadn't thought of. Part of my brain scrambled defensively, thinking, *Not all our elders are houseless and begging on the streets*. Then I realized that not all South African children were houseless and begging either. How could I be shocked at seeing houseless children begging in the park in the middle of a school day, when the sight of "bag ladies" a/k/a "elders" sleeping and begging on the streets in the United States was considered normal? I had accepted houselessness and institutionalization of the elderly in the United States as "normal," in contrast to the South African model of elders being taken care of in the homes of their children and grandchildren.

I caught myself judging like this again and again while in South Africa, then realizing with a thud that I knew an American version of each of these scenarios in my school or community. I visited a formerly White public school with a breezy faculty room that overlooked the Indian Ocean. A Zulu woman served tea to the all-White teachers, including me. As we sipped tea, a White teacher who had studied some Zulu in college joked about having to teach Zulu to their now integrated student body. I was struck by the parallel to my school, where the faculty was also majority White and a Puerto Rican custodian cleaned our classrooms, bathrooms, and hallways each night.

When I returned from South Africa, I was determined to look at American culture in general and my school culture specifically as a foreign visitor might, from an outside perspective. I researched our demographics to find out the percentages of students on free or reduced lunch; of English language learners, of students with IEPs. Furthermore, what languages other than English were spoken and by what percentage of families? And of what racial, ethnic and other demographics did our community consist? While roughly half our students at that time were on free or reduced lunch (meaning their family incomes were below the federal poverty line) and roughly half our students were people of color, that didn't mean they were the same exact groups of students. In other words, there were families of color and White families of all incomes and educational levels. One cannot and should not make assumptions about anyone based on their race or class. As I got to know more families and attended typical school activities (assemblies, PTO meetings, Open Houses, and school committee meetings), I noticed more patterns. Parents at evening meetings usually had a partner at home who could watch their children, or they paid for babysitters. I noticed the time of each activity (such as an 11:00 a.m. assembly, in the middle of the work day, or an event that ran until 8:00 p.m.).

I noticed whether childcare was provided or whether students or their younger siblings were invited, whether food was served, whether transportation was provided, whether admission was charged. I noticed the race and native language of those running the event, and their class or educational level if I knew it. I noticed it was rare to see family members who were older or disabled. I looked at the demographic representation of those who attended these events and compared it to the actual demographics for my school. The overwhelming trend was that the vast majority of caregivers who attended school activities were White, middle-class, native speakers of English, and often college educated. I kept asking: *What groups are statistically overrepresented? What groups are statistically underrepresented? Why?*

I was learning that my school was a living, breathing model of institutional racism. There were not many overt racists, but the institutional disparities were pervasive. One example of this was the dramatic overrepresentation of children of color, English language learners, and low-income students in the special education program. I noticed teacher attitudes that devalued the children in the program. I remember a couple of weeks into my first year of teaching, at a meeting with my 1st-grade colleagues, we were discussing reading levels. A 1st-grade teacher with more than 20 years of experience referred to the group of her students with lower scores by saying, "I'm not worried about these; they're all SPED." She waved her hand dismissively, as if shooing away a fly. I felt as if a dumpster lid had clanged shut on the educational futures of those students who had landed in "SPED" (special education). There was no conversation about what specialized instruction they needed to get to grade level. That teacher obviously felt like she was off the hook.

I was a first-year teacher and knew I was not yet skilled in the teaching of reading and writing, so I asked for a literacy mentor who visited weekly. I observed Kim as she taught on the other side of the classroom every day, as she taught shared writing, reading groups and writing workshops. Kathy, the ELL teacher, also mentored me informally. I observed and was observed. We briefed and debriefed, studied student work, listened to student voices, learned what they knew.

In that first year of teaching, I also began to see the disproportionate number of discipline referrals for children of color in our school. If I stopped by the office during a prep period or my lunch break, I often saw students of color who had been sent there. Roughly half our student body was White, but the vast majority of those sent to the office were students of color, including many with disabilities. I didn't know all the reasons those students were sent to the office, but I knew that as a preschooler, my Black son had been suspended, twice, from his daycare for typical childhood behavior like pulling hats off other children in line.

When I started teaching in 1997, the language that I heard teachers use to describe children and families often implied fixed qualities loaded with value judgment. At that time, no one at my school was talking yet about neurological differences and the anxiety, sensory integration issues, and communication challenges that can accompany them. Likewise, no one in my school was talking yet about "adverse childhood experiences" (ACES), the effect of trauma on the developing brains of children, or the ways it might manifest in their behavior. Rather, I routinely heard teachers label students as "smart" or "low," as "good" or "bad," and their families as "involved" or "don't care." The majority of these labels fell along racial and class lines.

I bent the twig the other way, refusing to send any students to the office for discipline. I was determined to resist the tendency of some colleagues to prejudge young students based on their race, class, or language by quickly referring them to special education. Instead, I didn't refer a single child for special education evaluation. As a brand-new teacher, I did not have the language, research or teaching expertise to back that up, but I was excited to later find and read *Why Are So Many Minority Students in Special Education? Understanding Race and Disability in Schools* by Beth Harry and Janette Klingner (2005). In her foreword to the first edition, Lisa Delpit wrote, "Would it not make more sense, the authors ask, to just teach children what they need to know, to provide them with the assistance they need to learn without concern about labeling and categorizing, and to keep teaching them until they have learned what they need to know?" (Harry & Klingner, 2005).

HOLIDAYS: CELEBRATING OR EDUCATING ABOUT?

When I was a student teacher at Jackson Street School in 1996, the school still had Halloween parties in classrooms as well as an annual "Christmas Concert" with carols. Non-Christian children were expected to learn and sing Christmas carols, just as my Jewish classmates on Long Island had 30 years earlier.

There were some immigrant children who were unfamiliar with Halloween, and there was a significant cohort of Latinx students whose families were Pentecostal. They did not celebrate Halloween; they felt it was celebrating evil. It was upsetting for these students to come to school to see classmates and educators costumed as witches, devils, vampires, and more.

At that time, the school expectation was that families with these religious beliefs should just keep their children home on Halloween.

During my first October as a teacher, I met with my principal, Gwen, to let her know I planned to talk with my students and send a letter home to let families know that Halloween would be a normal school day in our classroom, with lots of fun learning for all students and without costumes or candy. She supported me doing that. Some caregivers wanted more information about this decision, and most had no idea that some students were being kept home. All agreed it was unfair that some students had no choice but to stay home because something that had nothing to do with the curriculum was being imposed on them and made them too uncomfortable to be in school. Some caregivers did object; some of the pushback was along the lines of "Why is this being changed now?" In some ways, this presented an advantage to a new teacher. I could say that when I learned about the status quo it seemed unfair, and ask what they thought. It was an opportunity to open a conversation about what had been taken for granted for years.

In my second year, I remember a new teacher talking with colleagues in the lunch room. She described how one of her students "went crazy" during their morning meeting, after she asked her students to describe their Halloween costumes. One student had said she'd be a witch. This upset another student who stood up and started yelling, so the teacher called for the counselor to remove the child for "going crazy." I asked her if she knew that we had students in our school who do not celebrate Halloween because of their religion. She was dismissive, saying, "That can't be true. Everyone celebrates Halloween."

I had more conversations with Gwen about holidays and schools. Together, we read material from the group Teaching Tolerance (now Learning for Justice, learningforjustice.org) that distinguished between *celebrating* certain holidays (elevating the customs of dominant culture) and *educating* about a variety of relevant holidays (https://www.learningforjustice.org/professional-development/religious-holidays). A year or two later, at morning meeting one day, Jack said he was excited that Halloween was coming up that week. Miguel said, "If you go trick or treating, you're gonna go to hell." Jack said, "No, I'm not. I don't believe in hell. My family is atheists. Plus, I like candy."

Hmmm. I said that different families had different feelings about Halloween, that some celebrated it and some didn't and that we would be respectful of different families' choices. I asked if anyone knew how the tradition of Halloween got started. There were a few guesses, that a long time ago some kids liked to dress up or eat candy, but no one, including me, knew where it came from. Part of our social studies curriculum was to learn about cultures and traditions relevant to our students. We decided to see what we could find out. We reasoned that Halloween seemed to be about death (ghosts, skeletons, tombstones) and that it was in the middle of fall, when frost killed some plants and leaves fell off the trees. We wondered if there were other cultures that thought about death in the fall.

We decided to study the New Yam Festival celebrated by the Yoruba and Igbo; Tsukimi, the Japanese moon-viewing festival; Day of the Dead, celebrated in Mexico; and Halloween. My 1st- and 2nd-graders researched these in small groups and shared their findings a week later, concluding that different cultures have different traditions of remembering their dead ancestors, and that some of these do occur in the fall or at harvest time. We explored similarities and differences. For example, students noticed that the Day of the Dead seemed friendly toward dead ancestors (visiting graves, having picnics in cemeteries and playful images of skeletons) while Halloween seemed more fearful of the dead, with scary images.

We talked about how sometimes we invite a friend from outside our culture to participate in one of our traditions at home or in the community (like inviting a friend to a Passover seder or a Three Kings Day community celebration) and that this is part of how we learn more about the cultures of our friends and understand each other better. I said that at our school we learn about different traditions that people celebrate at home or in the community.

Over time, with Gwen's leadership, the culture of our school continued to shift. Our annual concert moved to March. Most classrooms stopped having Halloween and Christmas parties. New teachers started to be assigned mentors, who helped them learn the increasingly multicultural nature of our school, in addition to the ins and outs of curriculum, routines, schedules, report cards, conferences, and everything else.

WHO PARTICIPATES AND WHO DOESN'T?

When I first started teaching in 1997, I noticed that most of our school activities didn't start until 7 p.m. and did not provide child care, transportation, food, or interpretation. If you had a partner who could stay home, watch your children, and put them to bed, and if you were a fluent speaker of English and if you read every piece of paper that came home with your kids, you were more likely able to attend. If you were a single parent who worked all day, needed to feed your kids dinner and get them to bed and couldn't afford a babysitter, you were less likely to be able to attend. If you didn't have much English or felt overwhelmed by the mountain of leaflets that came home in your children's backpacks, you might not even know about the activity at all.

The members of our PTO in those days were not deliberately trying to discourage parents like Nydia and Josefina from participating. They weren't trying to make them feel stupid or like they didn't belong. But, in a pattern that I have recognized in myself as a White person, they were prioritizing efficiency, getting through the business on their agenda as expeditiously as possible, assigning themselves to do the tasks they already had the skills to handle. If they were raising funds to support field trips, or Field Day, or the Principal's Fund (to help families in need) they were oriented toward doing it efficiently by raising as much money as fast as possible. That meant using their tried-and-true activities. One of these was to use fundraising companies to sell wrapping paper and candy bars at inflated prices. Low-income families didn't have disposable income to purchase overpriced candy and wrapping paper and neither did their friends, neighbors, and coworkers. This reinforced the pattern of low-income parents participating less in the fundraising and increased the dynamic of wealthier White parents gallantly carrying the "burden" of fundraising for projects that would enrich the experience of low-income students.

Similarly, other fundraising events charged admission that lower income families couldn't afford, especially if their families were large. This reinforced the status quo, that middle- and upper-income families tended to come to school events, even events like Open House that didn't charge admission. Lower income families tended not to come, often feeling uninvited and unwelcome.

The annual book fair was a particularly excruciating fundraiser. Each year, the PTO contracted with a large corporate children's book publisher who came and set up a book fair with shelf after shelf displaying glossy new books, as well as non-book swag like fancy pencils, posters, toys, erasers, and movie tie-ins. Teachers were supposed to sign up for a time for their classes to visit the book fair. Students from middle- and upper-income homes came with $10 or $20 bills. Most students from lower-income homes came without money and just watched their wealthier classmates buy books and swag, then returned to the classroom empty-handed themselves. This pained some teachers, who tried to figure out a better method.

Some teachers would have a paraprofessional take the students who had money to the book fair during the library period, asking the students to tuck their purchases into their backpacks before the rest of the students returned to the classroom. Some wealthier parents felt guilty that they could afford to buy books for their children while they were aware that others couldn't. They might send in $20 to $50 to the teacher, asking her to help the children who couldn't afford to buy a book. This was well meant, but it put the teacher in the awkward spot of having to discreetly ascertain who had money and who didn't, then divide up the $50 among those and try to guide those particular students to pick out a book at or below that price point. First graders don't really understand how money works or why I am trying to persuade them to choose a $3 book when they have their little heart set on getting the $5 book or $18 toy their friend is getting. This annual book fair was a happy tradition and big fundraiser for the PTO, but it was agony for many of us.

My time in South Africa for the World Conference Against Racism was part of what pushed me to start critically examining these taken-for-granted demographics and dynamics in my school. But one doesn't need to cross any oceans to begin thinking this way. Here are some questions that I found helpful in illuminating dynamics of race and class in my school community. I hope they will be a useful starting point for others.

Observing My School From an Outsider Perspective

What are the demographics of our student body? (racial, ethnic, socio-economic, linguistic, religious, where they live)
What are the demographics of students in special education?
What are the demographics of student discipline referrals?
What are the demographics of our faculty?
What are the demographics of our non-faculty staff?
What are the demographics of our school and district administrators, the elected officials of school committee, of the city/town council, the leaders of PTO/PTA and the school council?
What are the demographics of those who attend school committee, city/town council, PTO/PTA and school council meetings? (including family structure and educational level)

School Events:

What times are school events typically scheduled?
What logistical supports (transportation, childcare, food, interpretation, and so forth) are typically offered, and how?
What supports are not offered?
What are the demographics of the families who typically attend?
What are the demographics of the families who typically do not attend?

In this chapter, I shared stories about how I started to look at my school culture more critically, trying to view our status quo from an outsider perspective, not to criticize, but to figure out what needed to change.

My experiences as a student, a community organizer, and a parent all informed my perspective as a teacher. As I looked critically at my district, school, and classroom, I probed the dynamics of power, especially the dynamics of race and class. I looked to see who was present and heard and who was absent or silenced and why. These were the questions and ideas that were percolating early in my teaching career, long before we started Families with Power. I sought first to understand the culture of my school. Then I tried to figure out how to change it. In the following chapters, I will describe how Families with Power began to organize programs that, over time, changed the culture of our school.

CHAPTER 5

Literacy
Rebel Librarians and Reading Parties

In my third year of teaching, I was having a parent–teacher conference with Eneida. I had just finished my enthusiastic rap about the benefits of parents reading aloud to children daily. There was an awkward pause. Eneida leaned forward and said, "I listened and heard what you said. I trust you when you say that it will help Juan if I read aloud to him every day. But you need to listen and hear me when I tell you this 'read aloud' is not part of my culture. My parents had fifteen children. No one ever read to me. There were no libraries. I do not have this culture."

Eneida was right. Her concise early literacy history made me reflect on my own. Although my family didn't have money to buy many books, I remember going to the library with my mother and siblings, even as a very young child, to bring books home. In elementary school, I remember the pleasure of taking out one Louisa May Alcott book after another, week after week. I still have fond memories of Mrs. Horton, our school librarian, who was a gifted storyteller.

The enjoyment of literacy was part of my culture, the fabric of my childhood. In our experience, limited finances were not an obstacle to accessing books, because we had good libraries (which we took for granted) in the community and at school. My parents had the privilege of graduating from high school because they didn't have to quit in order to go to work. In the 1960s, when I was feeling the thrill of holding a Beatrix Potter book in my tiny hands, millions of Black and Brown children in the United States were legally excluded from "public libraries" in many states by Jim Crow laws. Even after those Jim Crow laws changed, millions of children, particularly Black and Brown children, continued to be excluded in the sense that the books to which they had access were largely missing any reference to the children's lives, cultures, and native languages.

When I was a child, all the adults I knew could read. When I left home, the sisters who worked in the college dining hall dish room were the first adults I met who could not read. I was struck by the injustice of their situation, that institutionalization had deprived them of what I assumed to be a right to education. As I organized across the country and back, I met many adults who could not read, often because they had to drop out of school to work or to move frequently. I could see the economic impact that had, how it often limited them to the lowest-paying jobs. When I stopped organizing, my interest in literacy continued to grow. This chapter begins with several stories about literacy projects I organized as a minimum wage worker in a bookstore, a daycare parent, and a neighbor, before I even began teaching. Those stories are followed by Families with Power literacy projects as it grew over the years.

When I moved back to New York in 1992, I offered to work in the children's section of the new Barnes and Noble bookstore where I was hired, because no one else wanted to. I read Jim Trelease's *Read Aloud Handbook* and taught myself to be a skilled "reader-alouder." I organized story times, inadvertently increasing the profitability of the children's department.

I learned workers could take books home from the store to read, in order to sell them better. I started bringing books to my son's day care center to read aloud to the children there early in the morning, on my way to work. The children loved the stories and the books themselves. They liked to smell them, and rub their faces on the smooth pages. Seeing their pleasure, I hated having to take the books back to work. As an organizer, I knew about constituency. I talked with my customers, mostly caregivers and teachers, and asked them to donate books to start a library at the daycare center. I organized workshops about the benefits of reading aloud to children. Over the course of the year, I set up libraries in every classroom of the center.

READING CIRCLE

After I moved to the Hampton Gardens neighborhood in Northampton in July 1995, I would sit on my front stoop with my young son after work and read aloud picture books in the shade of a maple tree. Other kids playing in the neighborhood frequently crowded around us, like moths drawn to a lantern.

That same summer, an organizer with Community Action asked me to lead a 4-week summer "reading circle" in Hampshire Heights, the public housing complex next to where I lived. The person who was supposed to lead it backed out at the last minute. It was awkward, since I was new to the neighborhood and hadn't designed the project. There were boxes of books that had already been purchased, in Spanish and English, and a small budget for snacks. I was told that parents were supposed to bring their children to a weekly afternoon reading circle in order to receive a free book. Parents in the neighborhood had not been consulted in the writing of the grant. The organizer didn't know any parents who were interested in it. I knocked on doors with my son in tow, telling parents about the program.

A parent named Daisy was interested and helped recruit her neighbors. We sat under the shade of a tree with our books and cookies. Some students in kindergarten, 1st, or 2nd grade attended regularly and most brought pre-school siblings and cousins. The books were mostly written at a 3rd- or 4th-grade reading level and had too many sentences per page to keep pre-schoolers engaged. Daisy read aloud (or summarized) the Spanish stories, and I read aloud (or summarized) the English ones. The grant stipulated that we were supposed to give the books to *parents*. But the children who came wanted the books, even though they weren't able to read them independently. Daisy and I gave them the books.

I learned a few things from my experience with the summer reading circle: Just because someone wrote a proposal and got a grant to fund it doesn't mean it's a great idea. Don't write a grant for a family literacy program without family input. Meet outdoors in a visible place to attract more kids each week. Offer books at a variety of reading levels and lengths to accommodate different ages and developmental levels.

REBEL LIBRARIANS DEFEAT LIBRARY DRAGONS

In the spring of 1996, the year before I became a student teacher at Jackson Street School, I volunteered there as a reading tutor, working with a 2nd-grader in the school library. He said his mother wouldn't allow him to borrow books from the school library because his little brother had drawn on one with a crayon, and his mother had to pay $17 for it. I started signing books out for him in my name.

One day I observed the school library aide refusing to check out a book to one of my neighbors, a Puerto Rican girl, saying she hadn't returned the last one. Without checking the shelf, the librarian yelled at her and ordered her to find it. While the tearful, retreating 1st-grader was still within earshot, the librarian turned to another staff person and said, "Her drunk mother probably lost it." The woman the library aide was bad-mouthing was my church-going neighbor who worked 6 days a week. The girl left the library without a book.

At the time, I felt powerless and said nothing. I had already gotten in trouble once, when a classroom teacher said it was "extremely inappropriate" for me to have had a conversation with my neighbor, who was the mother of another student I was tutoring. The mother had come up to me in our neighborhood, excited about the tutoring. She had asked me how her child was doing and how she could support her. I had said that reading aloud to her child in Spanish or English was beneficial. I was busted after the mother asked the teacher if she might be able to borrow some books to read aloud to her child at home. These observations got me thinking.

Summer, 1996. Bicycling home from work, my son chats on the seat behind me as I sweat in the afternoon sun. I turn at the break in the fence, stop just past the dumpster to pick up my mail and coast down the sidewalk to my apartment. Suddenly, I am surrounded.

"¿La biblioteca está abierta?"

"It's library day!"

"You gonna open up now?"

Half a dozen children are shouting excitedly. I lean my bicycle against the tree. Children jostle around me as I open my front door. Vivianette turns on the fan. Her older sister, Norelis, takes two cardboard signs with hand lettered messages, "La biblioteca está abierta" and "Library is open." She uses old twist ties to fasten them to the front railing. More children come from Hampton Gardens and Hampshire Heights, returning books. They browse through shelves and baskets of donated used books that crowd my living room; many of the books had been discarded from the Smith College Campus School library where I had a work-study job. Ten minutes later, with a pitcher of lemonade and stack of cups in hand, I go out to the stoop. The children sit in the shade of the tree, and I read aloud a couple of stories.

Arlen, a bilingual tutor from the school, arrives and reads a story in Spanish. Afterward, the children ask us to listen to them read aloud. Lisette, a 3rd-grader, reads haltingly in Spanish. She learned to read in English at school, but she wants to learn to read in Spanish. Arlen is teaching her. Lisette picks out a storybook in Spanish for her grandmother to read to her and one English and one Spanish picture book for herself.

Norelis takes down a small box which contains a collection of index cards. Children haggle with each other over popular books and ask to stamp their own as they clamor to check their books out.

"¿Tu nombre?" Norelis asks in an official tone, then finds their card in the box, assisted by Vivianette. Norelis draws a pencil line through the names of the books the borrower is returning, and they copy the titles of the new books they are borrowing beside today's date. Unless they ask to do so themselves, Norelis stamps the inside back cover with the date stamp for a two-week loan. Most books return in a few days, exchanged for new ones. The children make the rules: There are no late fines or fees. If a book is torn, Norelis will help you try to repair it.

When I became a student teacher at Jackson Street School in the fall of 1996, one of the 2nd-graders in my class stared at me for a long time. Suddenly she shouted, "I know *you*! You're the lady that lives in the *library*!" My cooperating teacher gave me a weird look.

Behind my apartment was a fence that separated Hampton Gardens from Hampshire Heights. One day I noticed there was a hole dug under it, large enough for children to slide through, instead of walking the long way around. I was pleased to see that the children had created a desire path for themselves, wearing the grass down to dirt to get to the neighborhood library. Norelis, Vivianette, and I continued to run the neighborhood library in my living room for three summers, until I moved out of the neighborhood and their family moved back to Puerto Rico and then to Florida.

Sometimes we made kitchen science experiments, like baking soda volcanoes on the sidewalk. Sometimes teachers from Jackson Street School came to read aloud and listen to the children, who were excited to see their *maestras* (teachers) in the neighborhood. Sometimes they ran home to bring their caregiver over to meet their teacher. I found that some teachers had been hesitant to come to our neighborhood. One teacher said, "I never felt like I had a place to go or a reason for being there before."

I have a special love for libraries and those who share literacy as liberation. We can find people like this throughout history, like Susie King Taylor, an African American nurse and educator who joined the Union Army with her husband during the Civil War and taught Black soldiers how to read in the camp by firelight. In 1902, Susie King Taylor wrote *Reminiscences of My Life in Camp*, the only Civil War memoir written by an African American woman. As an enslaved child in Georgia, she attended clandestine schools taught by African American women. According to Karen Chittenden and Micah Messenheimer (2019), she began her teaching career at the age of 14 and was the first African American known to teach at a freedman's school in Georgia.

During the Great Depression, the Works Progress Administration (WPA) created the Pack Horse Librarians of Kentucky, mostly women who rode by mule or horseback, like an early bookmobile. They rode through the hills and hollers of Kentucky coal country to bring books, magazines, newspapers, and handmade scrapbooks to borrowers, often reading to those they visited. The historical novel *The Book Woman of Troublesome Creek* (2019) by Kim Michele Richardson describes the work of Pack Horse Librarians. (For more information on these real-life horse-riding librarians, see https://www.smithsonianmag.com/history/horse-riding-librarians-were -great-depression-bookmobiles-180963786/.) Additionally, Jeanette Winter's picture book, *Biblioburro, a True Story from Colombia* (2010), tells the contemporary story of Luis Soriano, a teacher in northern Colombia who carries books to children in remote villages, with the help of his donkeys, Alpha and Beto.

There was the heroic *Librarian of Basra*, portrayed in a 2005 picture book of that title by Jeanette Winter. Alia Muhammed Baker was the chief librarian of the Basra Central Library. She defied orders from the Iraqi government not to move the books from her library when the

Americans invaded. She moved 70% of her library's collection to safety in her home, the homes of friends, and a nearby business before the library was firebombed.

Recently, I learned of the rebel librarians of Syria. Ahmad Muaddamani was a young man living in Darayya, a town just outside Damascus. He had attended a demonstration before President Bashar al-Assad besieged the town with barrel bombs, chemical attacks, and rockets in November 2012. While many fled, Muaddamani stayed. In 2013, his friends called to ask him to help them retrieve books from the ruins of a bombed home. They collected thousands of books together. They built a secret underground library, which was visited by about 25 people a day, as barrel bombs still fell. Their efforts are described in *The Book Collectors of Daraya* (2021) by Delphine Minoui.

Our neighborhood library is not to be confused with the Little Free Libraries created by Todd Bol in 2009. Little Free Libraries are wooden book exchange boxes with doors set up in front yards, encouraging passersby to take a book or leave a book. Some people love them and others criticize them as a mark of gentrification, as they often appear in affluent White neighborhoods.

Our neighborhood library in Hampton Gardens was all about community, attracting dozens of neighborhood children when it was open to exchange, read, and talk about books. The neighborhood children took great pride in making the rules and running the library themselves.

While Norelis and Vivianette Ocasio and their fellow neighborhood librarians didn't face conditions as dire as those in Iraq and Syria, I see them as part of the brave and beautiful legacy of rebel librarians. I recently reconnected with Norelis and Vivianette, more than 25 years after we started the neighborhood library. Norelis wrote, "Seems like yesterday we were kids checking out books from the library. Now I'm running a business and teaching others. Being around all those books as a kid made me a book worm. I'm obsessed with reading."

My early experiences with the reading circle and neighborhood library before I became a teacher informed my understanding of children and literacy outside the school setting. I came to see literacy as a communal endeavor. I agreed with Freire, who wrote that students and teachers "become jointly responsible for a process in which all grow . . . Here, no one teaches another, nor is anyone self-taught. People teach each other, mediated by the world" (2018, p. 80).

FAMILY READING PARTIES

Josefina Rodriguez (see Figure 2.3 and the Meet Josefina text box on page 22) has been a leader in Family Reading Parties and spoke to me about them.

Figure 5.1. Diana Soler reads to her daughters, Camila and Melissa, at a Family Reading Party in Josefina's living room, while Josefina's son, Reneury Rodriguez, reads on the stairs (2013).

Josefina Rodriguez on Family Reading Parties

The Family Reading Party is a special day where parents and children get together in one of the families' apartments. It is a free choice for the family to say if they want (to host) it. If I have the reading party, I am responsible to get the people. I invite the people by phone or face to face. We decided this is the most effective way. Before, we used flyers, but it didn't work. When you talk face to face or call directly, that person feel commitment with you, that you want her because you invited her directly.

We get together. Parents, children, grandparents sit down and read picture books for one hour. It can be in different languages. It is really interesting how the kids feel powerful, reading a book with the other people listening and paying attention to what the kid is reading. Every single time any one of us finishes reading a book, we applaud the person. This means you did a good job; you were brave enough.

After the reading finishes, we have a conversation and some refreshments: crackers, cheese, fruit and mainly, we have hot chocolate. Having the hot chocolate symbolizes that we have had the reading party. We create a connection one to the other, about issues happening to our families. Every time we do it, more than 10 people come. It is really fantastic. My neighbor came with two kids. [Then he asked,] "When are you having a reading party again? We want to go!"

The reading party is a stream, a river, to unite families, because at that moment that we are reading together, we all feel the same. It is not that the teacher has the power, or the parent tell the kids to do something. No, everybody is at the same level and not anybody judge the other one because he pronounce the word wrongly. No, everybody is equally treated.

Josefina summed up what made FWP Family Reading Parties unique and beautiful: kids feeling powerful, applause for each reader, bravery, conversation, connection, unity, non-judgment equality. While they shared certain characteristics, they evolved over time. At the first Family Reading Party, organized by Eneida and Maribel and hosted by Aurea, the caregivers were the ones who read aloud. By the second reading party, hosted by Irma, the children were quick to raise their hands when Irma asked, *"¿Quien quiere leer?"* After that, both children and adults were the readers.

Reading Role Models

In our early reading parties, all of the adults were women. At our first retreat, visitors from a group of parents of color in another town described how the fathers in their group taught astronomy and calculus classes on weekends. Eneida interrupted to ask, "What is the *class* of the families in your group?" When the visitor answered that most of the parents in their group were professors, Eneida said, "None of us are professors. Most of our families don't have fathers, but we have a lot of sons. I like your idea of men as role models." So FWP adopted that idea and started recruiting men of color to come to our reading parties as "reading role models." Irma's husband, Carmelo Vega, began to participate at reading parties. There was an

Figure 5.2 Reading teacher Linda Barca reads with Angela Robles at a Family Reading Party in Angela's living room (2014).

African American reverend, a Puerto Rican professor, an African American veteran, a Puerto Rican psychologist, a retired African American railroad worker, and a Dominican school counselor. The member who invited the guest introduced him; the guest took a turn reading and hung out for the snacks and conversation.

When a family hosted a reading party, sometimes their children invited their teachers, principal, or other educators to attend. It was a different dynamic for the teacher to be the guest (sometimes with their children or partner), without any expectations. It was an authentic way for the educator to learn more about FWP and the community, by being immersed in an activity. For some teachers, it was their first time visiting these neighborhoods and the homes of their students. Our Title I reading teacher, Linda Barca, attended many and always allowed us to borrow her books so that there would be a book for every level of reader.

At our first retreat, four members, Irma, Nydia, Eneida, and Janet, stepped up as "the four pillars that hold up the house," to be Family Reading Party coordinators for their neighborhoods. We began collecting donations of books from some of those middle- and upper-class families who had been so eager to help at the silent auction. We organized these into laundry baskets, which each coordinator kept in her home. When it was her turn to host the reading party, she brought out the laundry basket as a kind of mobile library. During the snack-time conversation, children picked books out of the basket to take home. They could return books to any basket at any reading party.

Efficiency Racism

While we started in four neighborhoods, we expanded to other neighborhoods, often in smaller apartment complexes or buildings. It was during this time of expansion, maybe 5 years into our development, when I made a serious error. Members were talking about scheduling future reading parties and who would host them. One active member offered to host a reading party at her home in a nearby city, about 25 minutes away. There was a pause. It was not my place to speak, but I thoughtlessly said, "That's kind of far." Another pause, and then a member offered to host one in Northampton instead.

If I could take back one mistake in all the years of organizing with Families with Power, that's the one. I spoke before thinking. I realized my mistake and apologized the next day, but the damage had been done. I later came to see this as a pattern of microaggressions frequently made by myself and other White educators and administrators. Kendi talks about space racism, and I think about this as a kind of "efficiency racism," as if I, as a White person, imagine I know best how time should be "spent" most efficiently. In that moment, instead of keeping my thoughts to myself, I disrespected that member, her family, and where they lived by implying that it might not be "worth it" to drive the extra 25 minutes in each direction for a reading party at her home.

Really, what would have been the big deal? Maybe we would have gotten home a little later that night. So what? On what stupid scale could I have thought that 50 extra minutes of driving, or a story or two, would have been more valuable than the participation and leadership of that member and her family? But that's exactly the problem. I did not think. I just spoke, because a lifetime of white privilege, further fueled by the relative power of my position as a teacher, conditioned me to believe that I'm smart, that my opinion is important, and that my way of doing things is efficient and good. In that moment, my white privilege silenced that member and broke a trust that we'd been building for years.

I am humbled to say that was not the last time I made a mistake rooted in efficiency racism. After all these years, I have gotten a little better at recognizing this bias of mine and at holding my tongue, especially when it's not my decision to make.

Inviting Elected Officials

Sometimes FWP members invited elected officials to a Family Reading Party. They introduced themselves like everyone else and took a turn reading aloud. During snack time there was plenty of opportunity for them to hear from constituents about issues of interest and concern. One city councilor learned about a neighborhood community garden and answered questions about next steps for getting a grant to finally build a playground at Hampshire Heights. A state senator listened to several members with concerns about immigration, which is a federal issue. She followed up by connecting the members with the U.S. Representative for our district, who was able to get a human to respond quickly and move the previously stalled cases forward.

The presence of elected officials, not as exalted guests, but as fellow community members, has helped FWP members, regardless of their citizenship or immigration status, understand that an elected representative is supposed to represent everyone in their district. We are all counted as whole humans by the United State Census, and our representation in government is based on that count. Sitting next to an elected official on the couch in your neighbor's apartment makes that person a lot more human and accessible, as well as accountable.

Polychronic Culture

I remember attending a training about Puerto Rican culture early in my teaching career. The trainer was Dr. Roberto Irizarry, a Puerto Rican psychologist who described "polychronic culture" as one in which it is normal and preferable for many things to be happening at once. He said that many

White teachers were bothered by this and viewed behaviors like talking while working on math problems, several people talking at the same time, or moving while listening to the teacher as problematic, even disrespectful. I was privileged to attend many Family Reading Parties and observed that they were often a celebration of that polychronic culture.

I am not a great photographer; my favorite photos of Family Reading Party are blurred because children are jumping up, or leaning in to shout a refrain or to smell the fruit in a picture. In the photos, one child is calling on another child or doing a little dance to express the delight of a character. There is little discernible "personal space," as teachers like to say. Instead, children and adults are continuous as they lean, cuddle, and curl across couches and carpets.

In the community or school: Does it matter where?

One uncompromising characteristic of Family Reading Parties is that they happen in the community, most often in the homes of members. I began to notice that whether or not members had transportation or whether an event was near their home or across town didn't determine whether families attended. Lots of families could have physically walked the two or three blocks to school for events but didn't, and yet they managed to get a ride to a Family Reading Party across town. It was challenging to organize rides and borrow car seats for young kids, but we always managed it.

I remember, in my early years of teaching, Kim and I organized some bilingual family literacy parties in the school cafeteria. We invited our students to bring a pillow or blanket. We ended the evening with Kim and me reading aloud a bilingual bedtime story in the corner of the cafeteria. Our students cuddled with their pillows and blankets on the floor, while caregivers sat at tables. It might sound a little like a Family Reading Party, but it felt completely different. It was on the school's turf. It was teacher-centered. Kim and I chose the books, planned the activities and refreshments. We were leading it, performing; caregivers were the audience, looking at and listening to *us* interact with *their* children.

I remember being at a Family Reading Party at Doña Lucas's home beside a new member who was there with her kids. It was only my second time meeting her, but she knew a few of the other women in the group since she'd been a teenager. At one point, her 2-year-old daughter started banging her on the knee with a board book of *Runaway Bunny*, saying, "Read me!" She tried to distract her, then tried to shoo her away, but her daughter was persistent. The mother finally took the book, opened it, then turned to me and whispered, "I can't read this, like that word," and she pointed to "their." I asked if she wanted to try and that I would whisper any word she kept her finger under. She said yes, scooped her daughter onto her lap and read aloud that way, to her daughter's delight. I was struck by both her bravery and her vulnerability. Years later, we talked about that reading party. I asked if she would have been as brave if we had been at school. She laughed, waved her hand and said, "No way!"

Before we started Families with Power, I knew a father who never attended any school events because he wanted his kids to be successful in school and thought that if they ever realized that he did not know how to read, they would quit school. The danger of being outed as illiterate, the chance that his child might say, "Read this!" was sadly too great.

As Josefina described, there is applause after every reader. At one reading party, a new boy of 9 or 10 had come along with some neighborhood children. He was teasing his 5-year-old cousin, saying, "Gio can't read." Gio's sister was fierce in his defense, saying, "Gio can *too* read. C'mon, Gio!" She picked up a copy of *The Little Red Hen* and prompted Gio to say the repeating parts. When they finished their reading to applause, she challenged her older cousin, "Now what *you* gonna read?" There was a moment of tension, a kind of standoff, and then the older boy reached for a board book about Clifford the Big Red Dog counting to ten. Silence, and then he read it, very slowly, with lots of self-corrections. The reading party exploded with applause, and he smiled.

At our first Family Reading Party, I had an assignment: bring some bilingual books, chosen from the classroom and school library with the help of two FWP students, Jorge and Samuel. Mostly, I was a fly on the wall. This was markedly different from my usual "performer" role in school. In my classroom, I expected everyone to pay attention to *me*, because I was the teacher, right? From time to time, FWP members asked me to do certain things, like make a leaflet and make some copies for a parent to use for making face-to-face invitations for the reading party. I carried a paper pocket calendar and was assigned to keep track of dates. Mostly, I reminded myself to listen more than I spoke.

In that parent–teacher conference, Eneida listened to what I said about the value of parents reading aloud to children. Then she asked me to listen to her when she told me that she did not have a culture of reading aloud. Other parents said that they had also been raised in countries without libraries and related to Eneida's experience of being unfamiliar with them. The Family Reading Parties were Eneida's idea. It was an honor to watch as she and other caregivers and their families developed their own authentic traditions to celebrate reading.

FAMILY FIELD TRIP

Josefina suggested that FWP make a family field trip to explore the library. She started going to the library because that's where she met with the tutor who was helping her prepare for her citizenship exam. By then we'd gotten FWP tee shirts, and members liked to wear them when we went places as a group. We told the library that we were coming but declined their offer of a guided tour. Instead, adults and children took turns showing off their favorite features of the public library.

Josefina showed us the small room where she met with her tutor each week. My son showed us the room with computers that kids could use and the big fish named Paco in the aquarium. Another family showed how to "rent movies for free." (This was back in the era of video rentals, before Netflix and streaming services, when people rented or borrowed movies on videotape.) We found the toys kids could play with in the children's section. One parent asked to see the Spanish picture books and expressed disappointment at the small collection. (At our next reading party, we wrote a follow-up letter, requesting the library expand the Spanish collection; they did.) Some members tried out the elevator with Freddy, who used a wheelchair. We filled the children's room where Doña Lucas's daughter, Lilly Pastor, Irma Lucena, and other caregivers read aloud books in Spanish and English. We went to the circulation desk and signed up for library cards. There were a lot of us, and we were not pin-drop quiet. No one scolded us or gave us the hairy eyeball. The library welcomed us, just as we were. In later years, we took more field trips to libraries, and librarians came to FWP dinners to sign families up for library cards.

FAMILY WRITING PROJECT

In our second year, FWP members considered the idea of engaging with writing, in addition to reading. We brainstormed how members wanted the project to be and wrote a grant application to the Northampton Education Foundation together. We proposed a 6-week Family Writing Project. We requested grant money to cover a light pizza dinner and snacks each week and a small stipend for the families. It was designed for whole families, from toddlers up to great-grandmothers, to participate bilingually. We brought all kinds of paper and writing materials, from crayons and markers to pencils and pens. We met in the community room of Meadowbrook, another apartment complex where we'd been doing reading parties, and sometimes we met at the Casa Latina office.

Kim led a bilingual writing activity, using the writing workshop approach familiar to our students. She started with a shared reading, followed by a shared writing. After that, families had independent writing time. Later, we shared in small groups and ended with a closing circle.

We focused on different genres for different years, like personal narratives one year and "how-to" books the next. Josefina, Maribel, Irma,

Figure 5.3. Janet Namono, a founding member of FWP, co-presented a workshop about the Family Writing Project at a Western Mass Writing Project conference (2008).

Carmelo, and their families collaborated to write a guide for how families could help their children with their homework, *"Ayudantes de las tareas escolares"* and sold it to *En Familia* magazine, where it was published in Autumn 2009.

The Family Writing Project ran for 4 years, from 2007 to 2011.We began to present at local conferences about our literacy programs. In 2011 the FWP Family Writing Project focused on journalism. We wrote, edited, and published *Families with Power Community News*, an eight-page newsletter, with articles by adults and children and photos about what we were doing that spring: our Morning Math Club, healthy eating, family dances, Family Writing Project, reading club, and Love Your Family dinner. Reneury wrote an article about an after-school reading club of about 10 kids that he and A.J. were then leading.

At the conclusion of each 6-week writing project, members invited guests to our bilingual celebration. Guests included students' classroom teachers and principals and the relatives, friends, ELL teachers, and tutors of the caregivers. Part of the ritual of these celebrations entailed the emcee calling up each family together, showing their published work and giving them certificates of recognition to applause. The words and illustrations they proudly shared were *their* stories. We applauded everyone.

Small neighborhood libraries, Family Reading Parties, laundry basket libraries, writing projects, and other community literacy activities can all be sites of creative resistance, to nurture literacy, cultivate leadership, and build community.

Figure 5.4. Elba Heredia with her children (left to right) A.J., Eliaz, and Angela, receiving their certificate at the conclusion of their first Family Writing Project (2010).

Photo: Andrea Raphael

Figure 5.5. Doña Lucas Garcia, a founding member of Families with Power, participated with FWP's Family Writing Project every year with her great-grandson, Raymond Heredia (2010).

Photo: Andrea Raphael

CHAPTER 6

Bilingual Family Math Nights

When I was a student teacher in the mid-1990s, I read a lot of research about the benefits of family involvement by Joyce Epstein, James Comer, Sarah Lawrence Lightfoot, and others. I learned that the majority of family involvement programs focused on literacy, while (and perhaps because) math remained an area of even higher anxiety among parents. I learned that many parents wanted to become more involved in their children's education, but they didn't know how. Research showed a positive correlation between parental involvement and achievement. Family Math was a program developed at the University of California (Berkeley) to promote equity in math education for all children and received good reviews, but the involvement of low income and minority families was weak. While student teaching, I received training at the Collaborative for Educational Services (CES) in running Family Math Nights, using the *Family Math* book (Stenmark et al., 1986). CES is a local nonprofit educational service agency that works with students, schools, districts, and educators, providing services that range from special education to professional development.

For my senior thesis, I asked my professor if I could do action research. I wanted to organize bilingual Family Math Nights at Jackson Street School, where I was student teaching. He said it would be more work, and none of the other students were doing that. I acknowledged that and asked again if I could do it. He agreed but seemed skeptical. My goal was to organize family engagement events with a curricular focus and demographically representative participation. Gwen, and some teachers, like Kim and Holly, were enthusiastic and helpful. Other teachers pulled me aside to tell me I was wasting my time, that no one would come. I thanked them for their advice, kept organizing, and succeeded.

In my first year of teaching, I was using the new Investigations math curriculum, which had just been published by TERC for first grade (https://investigations.terc.edu/the-curriculum/, with later editions published by Scott Foresman). It was constructivist and included math games to be played together in class. I had the instructions for all the games translated into Spanish so children could play them at home with their families. (It is now published bilingually.) Marilyn Rivera was the bilingual and bicultural paraprofessional in my class and my informal mentor. One day she told me that some of the Puerto Rican mothers said that I must have thought their children were stupid, since I was sending games instead of flash cards and work sheets for homework. I was stunned and saddened but appreciated that Marilyn had told me. She said I shouldn't take it personally, that it was cultural; the parents had received a very traditional education that was based on rote memorization of facts. These ideas of learning mathematics with understanding and being able to explain your strategy were unfamiliar. I asked her advice, and we talked about the bilingual family math nights I had organized the year before, when I was a student teacher. We could invite families personally, face to face, have bilingual materials and interpretation. Marilyn suggested having food and calling it a party.

I talked with my 1st-grade colleagues about the idea. Lisa Musante, who taught a class with a cluster of English language learners, was immediately on board. Two other 1st-grade teachers were opposed to the idea, saying it would be a lot of work and besides, the parents in their classes were "fine." I said that Marilyn, Lisa, Kim, and I would organize it and that their students and families would be welcome to attend. They did not invite their students and families, or even send home the leaflets I gave them. When the series of bilingual Family Math Parties was a success, they asked the principal to make me stop; they thought it was making them look bad.

The following year, I looped up to 2nd grade with the same students and families. Parents from my class organized the bilingual Family Math Parties themselves; the families who organized them were mostly White and middle-class, but the participation was demographically representative of our class. The following year, as a "neutral" workaround, the PTO decided to hire a consultant from the eastern part of the state to run the math parties, but the consultant backed out.

I was frustrated. As a student teacher and first-year teacher working with a handful of allies, I had demonstrated both the feasibility and effectiveness of demographically representative bilingual Family Math Parties. We showed these were a great way to introduce families to the constructivist curriculum and engage them in supporting their children's math education. But the opposition of a few colleagues resistant to challenging the status quo effectively stopped Family Math at our school for nearly a decade. Trying to keep positive, I shifted my attention to other aspects of my teaching.

FWP'S FAMILY MATH PARTY

At our first FWP retreat in 2007, one of the action plans was for FWP to organize a bilingual Family Math Party. Our members decided to apply our own organizing principles to create an event that would be welcoming and successful for our students and families. Nydia said she wanted to invite one of her neighbors. She said, "If I'm the first person she sees, she'll know she belongs." Nydia volunteered to station herself at the first activity, which was a graph on the wall just inside the door. She welcomed each person in Spanish or English, gave them a stick-on dot and asked them to place it on the graph to indicate how many siblings they had. She chose this as an activity that would be accessible to everyone, not intimidating. While Nydia wouldn't have described it this way, she engaged families in making observations, asking questions, and interpreting the data.

FWP members used bilingual invitations to invite families personally, saying they'd also be at the event and would see them there. All of the games and materials were available in Spanish and English. Bilingual FWP members were scattered at different tables throughout the room. They facilitated activities and discussions bilingually and in ways that were comprehensible to other English language learners. Whole families were invited, so that toddlers, teenagers, and grandparents, as well as elementary students and their caregivers, were all engaged.

FWP organized bilingual Family Math Parties in the spring of 2007 and following years as "critical mass" activities. This was a change: When I was organizing bilingual Family Math Parties as a student teacher in 1996, my goal had been to reflect the demographics of my school. Looking back, I think Kendi would call that an integrationist goal.

Kendi (2019) points out "the logical conclusion of the integrationist strategy: every race being represented in every U.S. space according to their percentage in the national population. A Black (12.7 percent) person would not see another until seeing eight or so non-Blacks . . . White (61.3 percent) Americans would always see more White people around than non-White

Figure 6.1. Brian plays math games with his mother, Nourdine, at a Family Math Night.

people" (p. 179). What we learned through the FWP idea of critical mass was that mere demographic representation (the goal of my early efforts) was not enough to create a sense of belonging strong enough to overcome years of feeling excluded.

Organizing for critical mass in all FWP activities was an effective and deliberate counterweight to decades of erasure and invisibility. Without fanfare, FWP's Family Math Party asserted FWP's presence in the school and demonstrated what an activity with critical mass looked like when FWP ran it. There was a shift. It was not organized by educators *for* or to include diverse families, like my earlier efforts had been. Freire writes, "Authentic education is not carried on by "A" *for* "B" or by "A" *about* "B," but rather by "A" *with* "B", mediated by the world" (2018, p. 92). Caregivers in Families with Power organized and led it. And nobody tried to stop it.

CHANGING ROLES

In 2003, I had invited my mother to move up from Long Island to live with my family in Northampton. She was in her seventies and had arthritis, high blood pressure, and heart problems. She had already given up her driver's license because of confusion. She often joked, "I'm tellin' ya, Mo, I'm demented!" She had worked in health care as a phlebotomist, a certified nursing assistant, and as an X-ray and EKG technician. She had worked with many patients with dementia. She was already recognizing symptoms of dementia in herself. I didn't want that to be true; I made excuses as long as

Figure 6.2. The author with her mother, Mary Rose Cowhey, after the Walk to End Alzheimer's (2011).

Photo: Ellen Cowhey

I could. By the time she was formally diagnosed with Alzheimer's in early 2009, she called it "the thing that starts with A."

In the spring of 2009, I often got calls at school and had to leave abruptly mid-lesson to bring my mother to the hospital for one medical emergency after another. My mother's doctor was asking us to make end-of-life decisions. I was not teaching at my best. I decided to take a year of unpaid family medical leave in order to take care of my mother at home. I was the primary breadwinner; my husband would continue to teach part-time. My 10-year-old daughter nervously asked if we'd be poor. I told her we knew how to do this, that we'd be okay. We sold a car and rode our bicycles. We froze and canned food from our garden and baked our bread.

I went through a weird sort of identity crisis: What was I if not a teacher? I leaned more into my other roles, especially as mother, daughter, caregiver, and organizer. FWP remained active all year, growing deeper roots in the community. I spent a lot more time getting to know my daughter. My mother and I went to doctor appointments, to chair yoga and balance classes at the senior center. We started a knitting circle of neighbors in her living room. She wasn't a knitter, but she liked serving the neighbors tea and cookies. My mother's physical health improved as her cognitive decline accelerated. She said, "I want to make a plan while I can still make a plan," and decided to move to an assisted living facility in the spring of 2010. I decided to return to teaching part-time in the fall of 2010 so that I could continue my caregiving responsibilities.

In May 2010, while bringing my daughter to school, I had a bike accident which resulted in a serious head injury. We postponed and then scaled back our annual FWP retreat that year. The superintendent decided at the last minute that she didn't want me to job-share as a classroom teacher, although I had done it when my daughter was born. She offered me a part-time job as a Title I math teacher at Jackson Street School. Title I, the largest federal aid program for public schools in the United States, started in 1965 as part of the War on Poverty. These federal funds go to schools with a certain percentage of children eligible to receive free or reduced lunch; the funds pay for supplemental services such as math and reading. Title I rules require parent involvement in every aspect of the program. I talked with Gwen and said I would do it on three conditions. I had to be able to

- build authentic family engagement in the school;
- develop an effective model for math intervention;
- work to change the inequity of over-referral of low-income students, especially children of color and English language learners, to special education.

I returned to my old school trying to figure out a new role. I was working without direction, trying to make myself useful and figure it out as I went along. I knew that students of color and English language learners were overrepresented in special education referrals. Title I had been considered by some as a waiting room for special education because a student couldn't get an individual education plan (IEP) until intervention had been tried without success. Often the "plan" leaned heavily on "accommodations" such as being given a calculator, a multiplication chart, extended time, and an aide helping them complete worksheets; they were often light on research-based specialized instruction to teach children what they needed to learn. Arriving at school with skills that are below what is typical for the grade level or scoring below grade level on a standardized test does *not* mean that a student has dyscalculia, a learning disability characterized by persistent and extreme difficulty in math, even with good instruction. I didn't want to project a remedial presence that would stigmatize my students.

When I started teaching 1st grade, there had been a Title I math teacher; she had a caseload of students who had scored below a certain point on an annual standardized math test. She cruised through my classroom most days for 20–30 minutes, observed my math lesson, and then brought boxes of counting cubes to the tables as students began math workshop, perhaps reading a story problem to them or plugging in smaller numbers before moving down the hall to the next classroom. She didn't do formative assessments with her Title I students and didn't have relationships with the students or their families. She didn't seem to do anything to develop mathematical skills or understanding. For many students in our school, after a year of this ineffective "service," an intervention box was checked on a form, and they were referred to special education.

For the last decade as a classroom teacher, I had been dedicated to teaching for social justice, especially through my teaching of language arts, philosophy, social studies and science. I wondered how I would teach for social justice as a Title I Math teacher. Could I tackle the systemic racism that was depriving many of our students of quality math education?

A new 2nd-grade teacher asked for my help, concerned that many of her students lacked basic 1st-grade math skills. She had four students who just arrived at our school who didn't yet have the forward counting sequence to twenty in Spanish or English and two who didn't yet have 1:1 correspondence. When they rolled dice, they didn't recognize the dot patterns as numbers. They added by counting all the dots. The teacher was also concerned about another group of students who were counting all their fingers for simple addition facts such as $5 + 2$.

I was used to having my own class, where we created our own classroom community, with our own norms and expectations. I was used to creating integrated curriculum with inquiry-based investigations from student-generated questions. Suddenly I felt neck deep in a deficit model. I was now expected to "fix the gaps" in the mathematical knowledge of students who mostly happened to be low-income students of color; some were English language learners, some new to our school.

As a classroom teacher, I knew how hard it was to try to teach a 2nd-grade math curriculum while bringing students whose skills were far below grade level up to speed. How easy it is for a professor or administrator to tell a teacher to "differentiate instruction." All teachers know that, theoretically. Doing it is another matter! Honestly, as a 2nd-grade teacher, I hadn't understood why 2nd-graders might still count each dot on a die or lack 1:1 correspondence. I didn't know how to help them learn these kindergarten skills.

One October years earlier, a student arrived in my 2nd-grade classroom. She was nine years old and lived in a shelter. She couldn't remember how many different schools she had attended; her records hadn't arrived. Her mother didn't know if she had an IEP. She did not yet have 1:1 correspondence. She could not yet read, write, or count above ten. Were her academic challenges the result of trauma, interrupted schooling, or a learning disability? What should I do? Model counting things? Have her count things? Slowly? And what to do with the other 25 kids in the class, many of whom were English language learners or had attentional issues, learning disabilities, or trauma? As the year went on, the girl worked hard; she became an accepted and respected member of the classroom community. She was engaged and excited about the projects we worked on. She made some progress in math but was still more than a year behind. I tried my best to help her "catch up," but I lacked the expertise. By January, she was gone, her family placed in an apartment in yet another city. I thought of her when I accepted the Title I math job. Perhaps I could help kids like her.

Café Begins

My new job as a math specialist came with a new classroom. I arranged tables, some with adult-sized chairs and some with smaller chairs for young children. FWP members liked the new room, saying that they didn't feel like they were in a children's room.

In the fall of 2010, FWP members spontaneously started a new activity simply called "Café." The classroom had a long back counter with a sink and an outlet where we set up two coffee pots (caffeinated and decaffeinated). We heated milk for *café con leche*. We pushed two or three tables together for adults and another two or three tables together for children, often joining all our tables together for our conversations. We gathered after school on Wednesdays, with some coming right at 3 p.m. and others arriving later as they got off work.

At first, the Cafés seemed purely social for FWP caregivers and children. I appreciated the company. My new job as math specialist was kind of lonely, without a consistent class of students and their caregivers. As themes emerged from our conversations, these Cafés began to function like informal culture circles. By then we'd been using culture circles for three years in our retreats and other workshops, so the approach felt natural. Conversations were fluid, with adults calling children over for their ideas, or kids climbing on their caregiver's lap or just pulling their chairs over to join the circle.

The Cafés weren't part of a deliberate strategy for family engagement. These two ingredients happened to come together: a group of empowered caregivers who were emerging as community leaders and the availability of a welcoming space with some adult-sized furniture that wasn't already occupied by an elementary class. With the addition of a couple of tag sale coffee pots, Café was born. No one called it the Families with Power Room, although members referred to it as "our room." People only called it Café when we were actually having Café. But FWP members would often look around the room, holding their arms wide, and say, "We could do it here." Somehow the availability of a space that FWP members identified with unleashed their collective imagination.

From early 2007, when Families with Power began, to that fall of 2010, nearly all FWP activities had taken place in the community, either in living rooms or the community rooms of apartment complexes. Only two events had occurred in the school (library and cafeteria) even though Kim and I had classrooms during those first couple of years.

The fall of 2010 and the start of Café marked a turning point. As you will read in the next chapter, FWP began to run activities in the school, in addition to activities in the community. The change had many effects. The regularity of Café made it accessible to invited guests, whether staff or community members. The physical space, the actual foothold in the school building, gave caregivers a sense of ownership. There was room for caregivers to bring things such as coffee, cups, dishes, and sugar, and store them there. The custodians moved an unused piano into the room because we found a graduate student willing to give free piano lessons to Elba's son, Elíaz, two mornings a week before school. The informal culture circles at Café posed problems and generated ideas to address them. FWP had a fertile space, and seeds were starting to germinate there.

CHAPTER 7

Morning Math Club

"I COULD TEACH 'EM"

The new 2nd-grade teacher asked if I could work with eight of her students on their addition facts. It was challenging for me to wade into their particular group dynamics for 30 minutes and make meaningful progress. I was putting more energy into behavior management than mathematics. One afternoon, some caregivers and I were planning to have a Café for Families with Power after school. I asked Elba, one of the FWP members, if she would come early, to help me with this group. Many of the students in the group were her neighbors, and one was her nephew. I hoped that she might be able to give me some insight into their dynamics and advice about working with them. Perhaps it was Elba's presence that settled the students that day. We played addition games, and the students made some progress.

After the lesson, I asked Elba to help me assemble a booklet. Using material from our curriculum's student handbook with information for parents in Spanish and English about how to help children learn addition facts, I had designed a little booklet for caregivers. Elba copied them for me. We talked as we collated and stapled them. Elba said she'd like to play the games we used with her own kids. I told her that was why I made the booklets, for the parents to learn the games.

Elba looked at the booklet, as though for the first time, then said, "Valentina wouldn't read it." (Valentina was the mother of Elba's nephew in the 2nd-grade group.)

"Why not? It's in Spanish."

"It's in Spanish?"

I pointed to the Spanish words on the cover. Elba squinted at the cover, then flipped through the pages. "What about you?" I asked. "Would you read it?"

Elba shook her head, "Nah. It's too. . . ." She gestured to the page. "It's too—mathy. Like, see all these numbers and boxes and arrows? I wouldn't read it either."

I was stunned. As someone who reads everything I see, it hadn't occurred to me that the booklets I had assembled to help caregivers access to math games would in themselves be completely unappealing and inaccessible to some parents. I thanked Elba for being honest with me. I stared at the booklets on the table. "What should we do with these?"

"No offense," Elba shrugged, "recycle them?" We did just that and started to make the *café con leche.*

Elba said she liked the games; they were fun and helped the kids learn math. She thought other parents would like to play them with their kids. I asked, "If math games help kids learn, but people won't read the booklets, how do we get parents to learn the games?"

Elba considered this for a minute. "I could teach 'em. The way I do reading parties at my apartment. We could invite the families, play math games, have some snacks and they could see how the kids learn."

Our Café was part Freirean culture circle and part social gathering. That afternoon, as Elba and I talked and set up, caregivers arrived with their children, who ranged from preschool through middle school. Edwin, father of a 1st-grader, warmed a pot of milk, then improvised on the piano. Older kids helped younger ones as they took snacks to their tables and pulled out large boxes of Legos. Kim arrived from her 3rd-grade classroom. Adults took *café con leche* and sat together, talking in Spanish and English. Elba told them the story of the math games and how she recycled the booklets.

Valentina said, "I do like this, for $8 + 8$, you put the 8 in your head." Here, she lightly slapped the side of her forehead, then continued, counting on her fingers, "Then you go 9, 10, 11, 12, 13, 14, 15, 16." Claribel demonstrated the same method for $9 + 9$. I thought about my 2nd-grade colleague who was exasperated that some parents weren't helping their children memorize addition facts—facts that I now realized many parents were counting on their fingers. I kept listening.

Edwin said, "I went to school until eighth grade in Puerto Rico. Since then, I've been working, always working. To be honest, I don't understand the math my daughter is doing in 1st grade. It's not the way I learned math. This is different. I can't help her. I want to learn."

Elba shared her idea to organize a math party at her home. Other parents were excited and eager to start, but Edwin objected, "No, this isn't fair. I *need* this for my daughter. You know I work nights at the factory. If you make a math party at Elba's house at night, I can't go, and I need to go." It got quiet for a minute. Then Edwin said, "I got an idea. The kids stand around outside school in the morning, and it's cold out. A lot of them come to school early for breakfast anyway. Let's make the math party here, before school. I get off work at 6 a.m., take a shower and pick up my daughter. I'll make the *café con leche*. It will be ready when you get here."

STARTING MORNING MATH CLUB

Simple as that, it was agreed. Parents called the kids over to make the plan: Tuesdays and Wednesdays, from 8:15 to 8:45 a.m., from mid-October to mid-May, because children should run around and play before school when the weather is good. Children could bring their breakfast from the cafeteria or from home. The kids named it Morning Math Club. They said it should be free, and it should be cool. And you can only come to Morning Math Club if you want to be there.

Families were invited to volunteer, regularly or occasionally, and to come to workshops and events, but they didn't have to. Whenever possible, we created leadership opportunities for students and caregivers. Parents would help the kids play math games and learn how the kids were doing math. It would help the kids learn more math if they had fun and did more of it. The kids wanted cards "like a library card" that said they had permission to come into the school building early. This proved to be an excellent idea when a hypervigilant staff person took it upon herself to interrogate children who were in the building early. With support from our principal, students flashed their neon-colored Morning Math Club cards; many chose to pin them to their backpacks.

And so we began. That first year, most of the kids came from Families with Power and Title I math, with an average of 15 students per session. We had eight caregiver volunteers. They were all FWP members and all English language learners. Most had not graduated from high school. Edwin and I were always there. Elba and Josefina came at least one day a week. Valentina came when she could. Panha, a Cambodian parent who worked swing shift at the candle factory, started coming regularly. She said, "I get up and get my kids off to school. I clean the house and make their dinner, then go to work. I am never home when they do their homework, but if we come to Math Club together before school, I can help them, and other children too."

At the end of the first year, the older students decided to organize a Morning Math Club "graduation." They invited special guests, family members and educators, to a special potluck breakfast. We distributed certificates and math prizes such as dice and play money to all the kids and a flower to each volunteer; it became an annual tradition.

Volunteers

Most of our founding caregiver volunteers from FWP participated regularly until their children moved on to middle school or they started attending adult ed or community college classes, or found employment at that time of day, or their health deteriorated. New students continued to join Math Club. Some of their caregivers and grandparents began to volunteer. Student teachers and community volunteers, including retired doctors, engineers, and teachers supplemented the ranks of our volunteers. Morning Math Club offered an opportunity to volunteer that was accessible to caregivers who worked evenings and overnight, as well as those who worked 9–5 jobs.

In the first few years, we had no formal training for the volunteers, although some always stayed to clean up and have another cup of coffee, which gave us time to talk about how that day's games had worked and what they noticed or tried. I observed parents naturally developing the ability to differentiate the math activities for the various skill levels of students.

Children tended to come to math club in groups of siblings, cousins, and neighbors. Their caregivers often told them to stick together, expecting the older ones to keep track of the younger ones. Often a 3rd-grader and her kindergarten cousin, or a 4th-grader and his 1st-grade sister, would sit down at the same table to play together. A favorite game was Coin Dice. There was a pile of fake coins in the middle of the table and kids rolled dice, added, and took that amount of money from the pile; then they traded low-denomination coins for higher ones so as to have as few coins as possible at the end of each turn. Elba often sat at the Coin Dice table, and she became skilled at differentiation. She brought a cup of different kinds of dice to the table, asking younger kids to add smaller numbers and older kids to add, subtract, or multiply larger numbers. She fine-tuned this as she observed them playing.

One day Pallavi, the mother of Pranav, a kindergartener who loved math, asked if I could add her to an email list for Morning Math Club families. Hmmm. I said that sounded like an excellent idea and that I'd heard of email groups. I was honest and said that I didn't know how to set that up, and I asked her if she could volunteer to do that for Math Club. In this way, I learned that Pallavi had a background in computers; technology is not yet one of my superpowers. Pallavi volunteered regularly, bringing her younger daughter, Dhuythi. Math Club was growing quickly, but I often didn't have the time to give as much attention to the volunteers as I would like. I asked Pallavi to be the volunteer coordinator for Math Club.

With Pallavi's help, we began offering a series of volunteer training sessions. These emphasized a growth mindset approach and lots of ways to differentiate game playing. I introduced "the zone of proximal development," a concept developed by the Soviet psychologist Lev Vygotsky; it refers to the distance between what a learner can do independently and what a learner can do with help from an adult or peers. I explained how children develop an understanding of the structure of numbers, a foundation for learning "math facts." I described our constructivist approach to math. It was important for volunteers to understand why we don't show kids "math tricks" or the standard algorithm in the early grades. We engaged in 10-minute Number Talks, in which participants solve the same problem different ways and then share their strategies with the group. These talks helped adults appreciate the cognitive benefits of sharing their thinking and realize that there's more to math than memorization of facts or completion of worksheets.

Creating a safe space

As you walk down the quiet hallways of Jackson Street School at 8:15 on a Tuesday morning, you start to hear a noise like humming. Rounding the corner, you notice a small backpack, maybe a rubber boot and the handle of a baby stroller poking into the corridor. An easel announces, "Welcome to Morning Math Club!" Approaching the alcove, you realize the 15′×15′ space is filled with drifts of backpacks, jackets, lunchboxes, and boots along a narrow pathway leading to the open classroom door. You can't resist peeking in at the busy students and adults, wondering, "What's going on in there?"

The core of Math Club members came from FWP and Title I students and their siblings, cousins, and friends. It had a critical mass of students and caregivers who were immigrants and people of color who felt seen, heard and appreciated. They could make friends and emerge as leaders. Caregivers were invited to stay and play math games with their children before work. Some stayed a little while, met others, and began to volunteer themselves.

As Morning Math Club became a friendly gathering space for families, there were more face-to-face opportunities to invite them to activities in the school and community. A caregiver might invite another parent to a meeting about community gardening or to a reading party at her home, or a meeting of the Arabic Community Club. Our counselor and teachers stopped by Morning Math Club for quick conversations with caregivers. Often teachers would pop in for 15 minutes to have fun with their students and learn the games we were using. Some teachers attended regularly, with many of their students. Caregivers and volunteers who first met at Morning Math Club later collaborated on other projects. For example, a retired engineer offered to tutor a parent in her community college math course. A parent and a retiree teamed up to offer an after-school class on computer coding.

Making math cool

FWP kids wanted math club to be cool. One of my personal goals was to destigmatize Title I math. Students called my room "Math Club." Whenever I entered a classroom to pick up my students for their daily small group lesson, other students would say, "Take me today! Please take me! Can I come?" I used to tell my students not to brag to their classmates because it would make other kids jealous. Students who first came to Morning Math Club through Title I often stuck around for the rest of elementary school, becoming strong Math Club leaders.

There was no stigma about coming to Math Club, which have might been the case if it only admitted students in special education or Title I math, or if it only admitted "gifted" students. Some kids in Math Club were 2nd-graders who struggled with adding 10 to a two-digit number. Others were 1st-graders who wanted to add fractions. Lots of kids were everywhere in between. Math Club didn't have a reputation as being for "dummies" or "geeks." Mostly I heard kids say that Math Club is cool, and that if you go to Math Club, you get smarter. As students shared strategies in math lessons, I often heard them say, "I learned that in Math Club."

Morning Math Club continued to grow and improve. By 2018, it averaged 50 children from kindergarten to 5th grade every Tuesday and Wednesday from 8 to 8:45 a.m., with even more coming for very popular activities.

SUPPORTIVE FAMILY-LIKE ENVIRONMENT

Unlike Family Reading Parties, which always happened in homes, Morning Math Club always happened at school. Yet Math Club had an unmistakable family atmosphere. For one, Math Club was multi-age: there were students from kindergarten through 5th grade, but many parents and grandparents also brought babies and preschoolers.

There were adults of all ages, from undergraduate student teachers to retired doctors. Our retirees were our most reliable pool of volunteers, rarely

Figure 7.1. Dhuythi Belur was one of many preschoolers who attended Morning Math Club regularly with caregiver volunteers. Dhuythi holds a mini-marshmallow on a piece of spaghetti during an engineering challenge to build a tower (2014).

missing a week. They were also consistently patient and kind, whether baking, playing checkers, or teaching how to tell time.

Elementary school staff are often majority female, but there was a regular group of male fathers, grandfathers, and retirees who came to Math Club. We had only a handful of male educators, but most of them came to Math Club at least once or twice a month, even if only for 15 minutes. Similar to the male "reading role models" at Family Reading Parties, these men—fathers, grandfathers, educators, and retirees—provided a positive presence that isn't felt in all elementary schools or in all families.

It is hard for one teacher in a class with 25 or more students to give everyone individual attention. Part of the beauty of Math Club, with its abundance of volunteers, was that there were caring adults in the lives of the 50 or so children who came to each session. These kind and patient adults noticed if a child was sad, tired, hungry, sick, or anxious and took the time to check in gently and bring concerns to my attention. Sometimes we could help by connecting the child with the counselor, nurse, teacher, or secretary to resolve the issue before class. Often that extra ounce of individual attention made the difference in a child having a good day at school.

Math Club was a culturally affirming multilingual space. As I circulated through the room during Math Club, I enjoyed hearing a caregiver at one table talking with her children and other students in Spanish. A mother might say goodbye to her children in Chinese. At another table, a father might be encouraging a child in French. And at yet another table, a mother

Figure 7.2. Mya Grant hugs her dad, Michael Grant, at Morning Math Club (2015).

might be brainstorming with her daughter and other kids in Arabic. The tables weren't organized by language, but children were exposed to multiple languages naturally this way. Children of different races and ethnicities could look around the room and see children and adults who looked and sounded familiar. This made it feel like an extended family learning environment, whether the children and adults were actually related or not.

Many students joined Math Club as kindergarteners and participated all the way through 5th grade. These "fifth grade leaders" were treated with great respect and often took on the role of responsible older siblings in relation to younger students. They led a group of children to the cafeteria to get their breakfast, or helped an anxious 1st-grader find their lost mittens. When an older child was going to bring their younger sibling or cousin across the school to the kindergarten and 1st grade wing, they gathered other youngsters and brought the whole group.

ENRICHMENT: PROJECTS, CHALLENGE, AND PLAY

Some visitors to Morning Math Club asked, "Is this a program for gifted and talented children?" Jackson Street School didn't use those labels or have separate programs. But the idea of Morning Math Club was that *all* children thrive with interdisciplinary project-based learning, challenge, and play. Math Club was also a conscious effort to give all children experiences that some take for granted, including baking, building things, and playing board games.

Project-based learning

Interdisciplinary project-based learning is best practice. Nationwide, higher income students and those in "gifted" programs are more likely to receive it, while lower income students are more likely to receive a remedial curriculum that is boring and skill-based. As a classroom teacher, I loved to design project-based units. With some redesign, I was able to bring some interdisciplinary projects to Morning Math Club.

One example of project-based learning at Morning Math Club was the UNICEF campaign. The participants in Morning Math Club were more diverse than the school as a whole, with many immigrants and others who didn't celebrate Halloween. Often these kids felt left out in the typical "Trick or Treat for UNICEF" campaign.

We started the campaign in Morning Math Club by showing a short video about UNICEF and the kinds of education, health, and other projects UNICEF supports for children around the world. A parent who had been a refugee child talked about attending a UNICEF school. We considered the costs of resources UNICEF provided, compiled a list of items students thought were important, then tallied the cost to set a goal for the campaign.

Some Math Club members celebrated Halloween and others didn't, but we could all work together on the UNICEF Campaign. We brainstormed the work to be done: distributing and collecting the orange boxes; organizing a bake sale to collect UNICEF donations at school; making posters and newsletter articles to advertise the bake sale and Trick or Treat for UNICEF. We scheduled the bake sale for the day after a Math Club.

There's a line in Lewis Carroll's *Through the Looking Glass* when the Queen says, "Why, sometimes I've believed as many as six impossible things before breakfast." She must have attended Math Club before a bake sale! We baked in school, to make it equitable, since not all families have a working oven or baking sheets and pans, and box mixes or scratch ingredients, and a caregiver with time to supervise. I had a mismatched set of baking supplies for Math Club, cobbled together over the years.

As children and adults arrived, we set up table teams with the ingredients and materials they needed, each with an adult or 5th-grade leader. All children got a chance to follow the recipe, break eggs, measure, and stir. In less than 45 minutes, we produced about 15 recipes. It was hectic and messy, but the children were proud of their efforts.

At the bake sale, we tacked up a student-made banner and set up a row of folding tables in the front lobby. Children who didn't trick-or-treat staffed the bake sale, using the money skills they practiced playing coin games to make change. There were up to 20 Math Club volunteers at a time, shoulder to shoulder behind the tables, enthusiastically serving customers, accepting money, and making change. As some children left to get breakfast in the cafeteria, others took their places. They earnestly explained what UNICEF donations can buy: a school-in-a-box, vaccinations, wells, tents, blankets, and soccer balls. They loved seeing cookies and muffins turn into money in the cash box.

Math Club leaders made announcements over the PA and in their classes to remind students who trick-or-treat to take their orange boxes home and to return them right after Halloween. I was surprised when one Math Club leader from an Ecuadoran family active in a Pentecostal church (that is, NOT a trick-or-treater) brought back a very full orange box. She proudly told me that her mother, who works as a housekeeper in a fancy hotel downtown, loved the idea, brought the box to work, and got more than $60 in donations from hotel guests and staff.

Children loved to count the UNICEF and bake sale money at the Math Club after Halloween. They loved to fluff up a pile of bills or to feel hundreds of coins streaming through their fingers. Amazingly, in about 45 minutes, from an anthill of activity, we arrived at a total, and the students cheered what our school community had done.

To be honest, our money counting was unnecessary. I could have just carried the unsorted coins to the bank to dump in their coin counting machine. (Ultimately, I would have to do that, so that I could obtain a certified check to mail to UNICEF.) It would be more efficient for Math Club to skip the counting, but that would be so much less exciting, not to mention less educational.

Over the years, especially when it comes to elementary students engaging in community service projects, I have learned that efficiency is never the point. My guiding criteria is that community service projects should be at "kid scale." Here's what I mean by that. When adults design and control community service projects, they often come up with something more ambitious, efficient, and complicated than children can manage. When children design their own projects, the results may be less efficient and "impressive" in a dollars-and-cents kind of way, but they learn from their experience, especially their mistakes, because it is their own project. When it is a recurring project, and when they are given an opportunity to reflect and debrief, they naturally come up with ways to improve their process. That's exactly how this UNICEF Campaign developed over the years.

Challenge: Hour of Code

Pallavi, our volunteer coordinator, excitedly told me about the first "Hour of Code" in December 2012 and asked if we could try it at Morning Math Club. I struggled to grasp what "Hour of Code" even meant, but Pallavi was enthusiastic and confident. I went to a short coding class at a computer store, which gave me a little "Aha!" moment about what coding meant. I learned it was another kind of problem solving. Not being a tech maven myself, I recognized a serious growth mindset challenge when I saw one. I had to be brave. It was a challenge for me to imagine 50 kindergarten to 5th grade children—including some who did not yet have literacy, English, or familiarity with computers—solving computer coding problems.

I talked with our technology specialist to figure out if we could bring laptops into Math Club to make this work. At the time, our school had 24 laptops on one cart. We spread out into the adjoining classroom with folding tables and set children up in pairs (often a reader with a not-yet reader or a bilingual student with a newly arrived English learner), sharing a laptop. The first time we tried this, after the initial panic of volunteers trying to open and log in to 24 laptops, it went well . . . for the first 10 minutes. Volunteers helped children navigate to the Hour of Code site and sign in to a particular challenge, like Star Wars. The coding instruction was given through a series of short videos.

Initially, with 12 tables in two classrooms and a pair of students settling in at each table as they arrived, it seemed to work. But soon, there were at least two pairs of children at each table, with 24 laptops all playing video instructions out of synch. It was loud and a little maddening. We sent volunteers to beg for headphones from nearby classrooms. Once we sorted it out, the children loved coding and wanted more. Soon children were teaching the adult volunteers how to code.

Pallavi brought in a bunch of great posters from the Hour of Code website, featuring Malala Yousafzai, Stephen Curry, and Shakira. When the technology specialist later introduced Hour of Code in classrooms, the Morning Math Club students stepped up as leaders to help their teachers and classmates. At that time, about half the students at our school had Internet access at home and at least one device they could use. The other half had neither. The advance exposure to coding and experience they gained by teaching other students and adult volunteers to code at Math Club allowed students without Internet or devices at home to become confident tech leaders in their classrooms.

Another Challenge: Engineering

Another example of enrichment was the Engineering "Design and Build" Challenge that Math Club offered each fall and spring, in cooperation with engineering students from Smith College. Tom Gralinski was a Smith College staff person who led the program and worked regularly with Morning Math Club for many years. He and his engineering students collaborated with us to decide on how to organize each challenge. Since Morning Math Club didn't have a budget, we appreciated that Tom and his students purchased and brought the materials for each challenge.

Figure 7.3. Angela Robles tests the marble roller coaster she made with her team at Morning Math Club (2014).

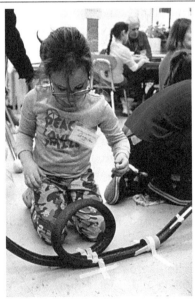

Multi-age teams of students, with an engineering student or another math club volunteer, reviewed the design process, listened to the goal of the challenge and the constraints of the problem. Together they made multiple designs, with the input of all team members. After agreeing on a design, they gathered materials and started to build. They continued the process of testing and refining their design during two math club sessions. Some favorite design and build projects were: Balloon-powered cars to travel at least 15 feet, cardboard houses for teddy bears, toothpick and mini-marshmallow towers, and roller coasters for marbles.

At the conclusion of each Engineering Challenge, we shared our results. Sometimes we took over the corridor, turning it into a race track to measure the distance each team's balloon-powered car could travel, or filming the trials of our marble roller coasters. Students were intrigued to see how other teams creatively solved the same problems they had encountered.

Play

Play is our brain's favorite way of learning.

—Diane Ackerman (quoted on a Jackson Street School tee shirt)

Classic Games. During a Family Game Night with FWP families, I noticed that many children liked to play UNO but didn't know how to keep score; they didn't realize that scorekeeping was part of the game. Similarly, I observed a game of Monopoly. A 3rd-grader said, "Deal out the cards." Everyone else nodded, not realizing players were supposed to buy or pay rent on the properties. While Monopoly unapologetically promotes capitalism, I found that playing it as a child helped me learn the meaning of rent, tax, mortgage, utilities, and more.

We decided to add "Classic Games" to the Morning Math Club rotation, playing Parcheesi, Sorry, Monopoly, UNO, Yahtzee, Connect Four, and others. Adults modeled pulling the instruction sheet out of the box and used it to guide students in how to set up and play the games. Many families started their own Family Game Nights at home.

One day I observed my colleague, Mary Bates, teaching her entire 1st grade class how to play checkers. I was impressed! She agreed to come to Morning Math Club, with all her checker sets and a squad of her 1st-graders, to teach everyone. Some of our caregiver and retired volunteers offered to teach dominoes and chess too. Soon, "Checkers Day" became one of Math Club's most popular activities, with children and adults dressing in red and black. One father always wore bright red pants. I was jealous.

From my teacher perspective, I noticed an added benefit to playing checkers: impulse control. Sometimes a player impulsively moves their piece, then realizes they've put it in harm's way. The player wants to cancel their move, but that's not allowed. We dramatically over-modeled holding on to your checker in the new spot to crane your neck and view it from multiple angles for danger before finally letting go. Sometimes, our hands or mouths are faster than our brains. Checkers can help students who make impulsive mistakes slow down and increase their self-checking behavior. Many kids started playing checkers at home too.

Coins and Clocks. When I was little, my sisters and I used to bake mud-pies and set up elaborate bakeries, using leaves for bills and small shells for coins. Everyone wanted to be the cashier; being the younger sister, I often had to play the customer. We haggled over prices and argued about getting correct change. We were playing; we didn't know we were learning.

Schools tend to assume that students possess more experience with coins, paper money, and analog clocks than they actually do. Nowadays many families pay with debit, credit, or electronic benefit transfer (EBT) cards instead of cash. There's less pocket change floating around, so children have less opportunity to practice counting coins or playing with them. So Math Club set up pretend stores, counted UNICEF money, and played Coin Dice and other money games.

Similarly, I noticed some students, even 4th- and 5th-graders, would look right at the clock and ask me, "What time is it?" when they wanted to know if it was breakfast time (8:30 a.m.). Digital clocks were ubiquitous in their lives and many never learned to tell time. We played with clocks and developed games and activities about reading analog clocks.

Math curricula treat time and money as merely minor topics in the measurement strand. They don't give children any more time on them now than they did decades ago when coins and analog clocks were everywhere.

On the one hand, some argue that making change or telling time on an analog clock is no longer a relevant skill. On the other hand, math curricula assume robust understanding of time and money. They rely on clocks as a model for solving elapsed time problems and teaching fractions, and coins as a model for decimals, percent, and structure to 100. Some kids get more exposure and practice at home. Other kids get almost none. Including playful time and money activities in Morning Math Club gave all children the experience to master these skills and confidently use these mathematical models.

MATH CLUB AS LABORATORY

Part of the fun of Morning Math Club was that it was a creative, innovative place. Sure, between 9 and 3, I might *look* like a mild-mannered elementary math specialist focused on the Common Core math standards. But from 8 to 9 a.m. on Tuesdays and Wednesdays, I was a math scientist in a bustling laboratory! I was inventing, experimenting, and playing around with mathematicians from 3 to 73, unbound by the constraints of curriculum, intervention, and standardized test prep.

Figure 7.4. Giada Rodriguez gently holds a chick at Morning Math Club (2015). Giada died in 2021 from complications of COVID-19. She was 13 years old, and she had hoped to study animal science at Smith Vocational High School.

We've had great conversations over the years in response to children asking, "Wait, is this math?" This is a good question for kids to explore: Where is the math in baking, building, hatching chicks, computer coding, reading clocks, learning how the brain works, or playing checkers? If you can make a good argument about where the math is, we'll try it.

Flexibility

The laboratory approach fostered flexibility. There was a boy named Kenneth who was drawn to Morning Math Club as a 1st-grader. He loved math and the opportunity to challenge himself beyond the classroom curriculum. He usually came with his mother or father, or sometimes with both parents and his younger sibling. I don't know if he was on the autism spectrum, but I observed that sometimes he had significant meltdowns. His parent was there to help him deescalate. Morning Math Club's crowded and busy setting could be challenging. One had to take turns, share materials, cooperate with others in a group and so forth. I was impressed that so many neurodivergent kids came to Math Club anyway and really seemed to enjoy the math and the friendships they made.

One morning I heard a distressed growling sound coming from the closet; I saw Kenneth crouched in there and his father nearby. I gave them space. Later, his father said that Kenneth had been hoping we would be doing a different activity that day. If Kenneth's father hadn't been there, I wouldn't have figured out the cause of Kenneth's frustration. I asked Kenneth's father if it would help to have a calendar for several months, so that Kenneth could see the planned activity and decide the night before if he wanted to come to Math Club that week or not. It took extra effort for children to come to school an hour early; they should have a choice. Kenneth's father and I agreed it was worth an experiment. The next week, we gave out the new Morning Math Club calendar, which everyone enjoyed. It became part of our routine and helped us all.

Differentiation

When we first started, we mostly played games from our *Math Investigations* curriculum, or variations on those. As I got more professional development in Math Recovery, I began to incorporate more of those games and routines. (Math Recovery provides professional development, which completely changed my understanding of how children learn numeracy (https://www.mathrecovery.org/). I started with *Teaching Number: Advancing Children's Skills and Strategies* (Wright et al., 2006). I learned to conduct individual diagnostic assessments and design research-based targeted instruction. My Math Recovery repertoire included a lot of bingo games that targeted certain families of addition and subtraction facts. I guided children to games, or ways to differentiate games, that matched their zone of proximal development.

I created many homemade "path games" that were generic enough that I could use them for a wide range of mathematical learning targets. They all followed the same simple pattern: 25 dots (made with dot stickers or a bingo marker) around the edge of an $11 \times 17''$ board, with every fifth dot being a special color, like red. If you landed on the red dot, you got to collect a card, which was a sticker on a small square of card stock. All the game boards were the same, but children got to choose the set of cards they'd collect. Each set of cards was inspired by students' special interests, with stickers of puppies, trucks, horses, fire fighters, bunnies, and other favorites. Students helped invent and name new games.

Depending on the learning target and their zone of proximal development, we offered different dice. They might roll a 0–9 die, then say how many more they need to make 10, or use a 0–20 die and subtract that number from 20, or roll two different dice to add or subtract. Four students at one table might be playing the same board game together at four different levels. They might move themselves up to more challenging levels with the support of more capable peers.

Morning Math Club promoted discussion of math strategies and curiosity about mistakes. The mathematical norms of math club affirmed effort, struggle, cooperation, and a willingness to challenge oneself. Others like it until they lose. Math Club taught most games cooperatively. For example, in a bingo game, the goal was to cover the entire board with your partner, not to block them.

Students often created new rules ("allowable cheats") for additional challenge, such as: If the sum you found in a path game wouldn't let your game piece land on a special dot, you could subtract them to see if the difference would let you do so. Another rule, to promote cooperation over competition, was that if your answer wouldn't get you to a special dot, you could give your move to another player if it would get them to a special dot, so that they could collect another token for the "team." These "allowable cheats" motivated students to solve more problems and use higher order thinking.

One favorite "cheat" is the "Wish Rule" in bingo games. Let's say you are playing a Multiples of 4 bingo game, you roll 3, say, "$3 \times 4 = 12$," but all of the 12s on your bingo board are already covered. You can call "Wish Rule!" You figure what number you'd like to cover to get a bingo, then solve for the missing factor to say what number you *wish* you'd rolled, like, "I want to cover 32, so I wish I rolled an 8, because $8 \times 4 = 32$." The players are happy because they are getting closer to making a bingo, and I am happy, because they are stretching from fact fluency to algebraic thinking ($4 \times \_\_ = 32$.)

You can only come if you want to.

In the 1990s, my sister Ellen taught at *Moo Baan Dek* (Children's Village) in Thailand. Their website (www.childrensvillagethailand.org) says that *Moo Baan Dek* educates "disadvantaged children whose rights have been violated." Following the model of the Summerhill school, its students have the freedom to control the terms of their own education, including whether or not they attend class. When she told me about it, I struggled to imagine how it could work. And yet, when the FWP children started Morning Math Club, they had one rule: *You can only come if you want to*. Math Club, from its inception, was an experiment in student freedom.

Whenever a caregiver asked if their child could come to Math Club, I asked the child why they'd like to come. Usually they said, "Because my friend says it's fun," or "I like to solve puzzles and play games." If the child didn't want to come to Math Club and the parent wanted before-school childcare, I referred them to the before-school care program. One reason Math Club worked is that every child in the room wanted to be there. Sadly, that's not the case for every student in every classroom.

In the 10 years that I ran Morning Math Club, the only discipline incident that arose was when a student named Barbara bullied another student. She whispered that he was fat, making him cry. Several volunteers and I had noticed that Barbara seemed disconnected, often drifting from table to table. If a volunteer observed her struggling and tried to work with her, she walked away. I privately asked Barbara if she liked Math Club. She immediately said no, because her stepfather made her come. I asked if she remembered our rule, that no one can make you come to Math Club, that you can only come if you want to. Barbara said her stepfather made her come anyway because her mom went to work early. She and her stepfather argued a lot. On the other days of the week, Barbara went to a resource room to practice a reading program she enjoyed on the computer. The resource room teacher and I talked with Barbara's parents and arranged for her to go to the resource room early every morning.

NORMALIZING FAMILY ENGAGEMENT

In the best of all possible worlds, caregivers and teachers would hold each other in unconditional positive regard, assuming good intentions on the other's part. We'd be able to listen, ask questions, even disagree while working together in the child's interest. In reality, it's not always like that. Some teachers get anxious about parent–teacher conferences, feeling defensive in anticipation of a "difficult" parent. Yes, some students, parents, and educators are difficult. There's a Buddhist expression that says that difficult people are suffering, like Barbara had been. As we get to know each other, we can see that is often the case.

Early in my career, I was frustrated with the district's lack of support for a student in my class with volatile behavior and complicated needs. After a meeting with his mother, my principal, Gwen, asked me to check in with her. She let me know that the way I had expressed myself in the meeting made the mother think I was frustrated with her child. I felt awful about it. I appreciated that Gwen took the time to set me straight. It taught me an important lesson about what matters most in a meeting. I had spewed my insecurity, frustration, guilt, and feelings of being overwhelmed without thinking about how that was received and felt. The mother wasn't interested in the departmental dysfunction that was frustrating me. She needed me to care about her child, and to see and hear her. With Gwen's help, I realized I had done neither. I vowed to do better.

Spending time together at Math Club always reaffirmed for other educators and me that parents are warm, funny, caring, kind, interested, and helpful. It gave parents a similar impression of educators. Through my involvement in Families with Power and Morning Math Club, I learned to approach caregivers more calmly and with compassion. I improved at listening to their concerns and working together in the best interest of the child.

Most caregivers who bring their children walk them all the way to the Morning Math Club room, even if they don't have time to stay and volunteer, just so they can say hello. For caregivers of my math students, I can make face-to-face invitations to upcoming workshops, meetings and events. This provides me with an opportunity for frequent, friendly conversation with caregivers, when they might share bits of family news about employment, health, and more. This regular, low-stakes interaction lowered the anxiety about caregiver–teacher communication, including conferences or special education meetings.

Over the years, I observed many caregivers who had not previously been engaged at school but who started to participate in Morning Math Club. Many immigrant caregivers from Math Club soon joined How Schools Work, a mutual support group for immigrant families, and later joined a language and culture club. Many came to a Families with Power reading party or participated in a math workshop. Some volunteered for hiring committees or started teaching a class in the after-school program. Morning Math Club became an organic point of entry for more than a hundred caregivers who became comfortable in school and gained the confidence and connections to engage in more opportunities at school. As they developed relationships with more students, caregivers, volunteers, and staff, a sense of belonging replaced a sense of feeling like "an outsider."

Incubating leaders

Morning Math Club and FWP are incubators for leadership. At one point, Gwen was looking for volunteers for a hiring committee. I recommended Edwin, one of the Math Club founders, to be on the hiring committee for a new guidance counselor. I pointed out that he worked 6 p.m. to 6 a.m., in the next city, so they would need to consider his work schedule. Gwen invited Edwin and arranged afternoon interviews that fit his schedule. Edwin said he liked the process, although he was a little nervous at first.

Edwin thought the best candidate was a bilingual/bicultural Latinx applicant. Another committee member said they thought he was a good candidate, but noted that his English "wasn't perfect." That member said that it would be an embarrassment for parents or other schools to see reports that might have errors in them. This angered Edwin; he said, "We are looking for someone who can speak both languages [Spanish and English], so the parents can speak and the children can be more free. We're looking for someone with experience working with people from the different countries, who knows how to talk and work with parents, with respect for the families. My English isn't perfect. I don't care if his English isn't perfect. He has many years of experience. I don't care what people think about a spelling mistake in a report. That's not important to the families here. He has heart. He is the best person for the job." Edwin prevailed, and we hired an outstanding guidance counselor.

Reflecting on his experience as the first FWP member to be on a hiring committee, Edwin said, "It's a good idea to involve us. We think a little bit different. They need to understand what we have in the heart for the child. I think as parents we have real power if we want (to be) involved in school activities."

WHY MORNING MATH CLUB WORKED

FWP's organizing is organic and doesn't follow a cookie-cutter design. We share our experiences to the extent that others can learn and benefit from our stories. Grassroots organizing and family engagement can look different in different contexts, but there are no shortcuts to building authentic and trusting relationships. Superficial imitation doesn't work.

At one point, another school decided to imitate Morning Math Club. Their administrator did not ask caregivers for their ideas. She had some grant money kicking around and low math scores on the state's standardized test. She assigned some paraprofessionals to come to school early to staff the computer lab, where Title I math students or students with math on their IEPs were assigned to come before school for "extra help." The paraprofessionals helped them sign in to their computers to play online math games. Caregivers and volunteers were not involved. The program was short-lived.

We hope other educators and caregivers might be inspired to organize a Morning Math Club in their school or community for reasons similar to ours: To make math welcoming, accessible, cool and fun for everyone, to cultivate youth and caregiver leadership, and to create a supportive and inclusive community, *not* because someone thinks it will be a silver bullet to raise standardized test scores.

Reflecting now on the evolution of my involvement with Bilingual Family Math Nights and the creation of Morning Math Club, I can see that Math Club as an ongoing institution, created more of an intentional community and safe space than can happen in a single event. Bilingual Family Math Nights can introduce parents to math curriculum, but they can be more performative and teacher-centered events with less personal interaction. Larger events tend to be more stressful and expensive to organize. They also tend to be less innovative because a flop is more public; the stakes are higher.

Morning Math Club was a sustainable routine for hundreds of families for a decade (2010 to 2020). It was part of the fabric of our school community. Caregivers and educators got to know each other as fellow volunteers in a relaxed and natural setting. Because of both the regularity and long-term nature of the caregiver involvement, it fostered robust leadership development. Every session of Math Club felt like part of an ongoing conversation; as such, it had a profound impact on student and caregiver attitudes about math.

Even though Math Club was a little hectic, with so many students and caregivers, I was not "teaching" the whole group. That freed me up to innovate and experiment, to circulate and observe compassion, creativity, persistence, curiosity, and leadership; these greatly informed my teaching with children and adults. Morning Math Club taught me to be a better teacher.

CHAPTER 8

Financial Literacy Project and Math Workshops

"I HAVE A RIGHT TO KNOW ABOUT THE MONEY"

FWP's educational projects all came from members' experiences and needs. One parent shared a story that inspired a financial literacy project. Her husband, the family's sole breadwinner, died unexpectedly. In the midst of her grief, she was trying to figure out a checking account, credit cards, and mail from creditors about debt she didn't know existed. With the help of another member, she planned and stuck to a budget; she learned to write checks and balance a checkbook, and how to restore her credit. As she spoke with other FWP members, she realized she was not alone. That allowed her to let go of the shame she had felt. "I learned from my experience. I will never let myself be in that position again. I have a right to know about the money in the family. You have a right to know; you have to learn."

FWP organized a 6-week Family Math Project to promote financial literacy. With the help of a grant from Northampton Education Foundation, and the cooperation of a local bank, we opened savings accounts for all participants and gave a weekly stipend of $3 for children and $5 for adults. We encouraged a weekly minimum $1 deposit in the savings account, but it was up to each individual to decide how much to deposit and how much to keep in cash. Adults and children announced personal and family saving goals at our first session. The majority of participants deposited their entire stipend in their savings accounts.

Caregivers who had been spending $1.00 for every money order at Walmart because they didn't know how to write checks learned how to write checks and keep a check register. They learned to calculate the cost of using credit. Many were shocked and disgusted to figure out the real cost of purchases bought on credit with exorbitant interest rates. Many developed a policy of setting goals and saving up for what they wanted, whether a vacation or a bedroom set, and paying for it in cash. Each family made their own monthly budget based on their expenses and income. Parents shared tips for saving money and low-cost fun activities for their families. Each

Figure 8.1. Josefina Rodriguez introduces a budget-making activity at one of the financial literacy workshops, while children play math games at other tables.

week, families shared new ideas they had tried for saving money. For example, a family with three kids calculated how much it cost to go out to a movie theater, buying tickets, soda, and popcorn. After the FWP family field trip to the public library, they started borrowing movies from the library for free, making their own popcorn and enjoying family activity together more often—and for less than 50 cents! They put the money saved toward their family vacation goal.

Caregivers developed a critical consciousness about consumerism in America. They questioned how advertising makes people want to have what they see on TV, how store credit at exorbitant interest rates affects the cost of furniture. Role-plays helped caregivers learn how to respond to pressure from their children to go to MacDonald's. Caregivers and children also learned to play math games together, with adults learning the mental math strategies our students used.

AUTHENTIC FAMILY ENGAGEMENT IN TITLE I

When I became a Title I math teacher in 2010, I was intrigued to learn that Title I regulations actually required family engagement. That was interesting, since I had never observed that in our district. I learned that in the past, it had been the practice to send home a notice about a meeting. The Title I teacher usually sat in a room alone for an hour and then went home. I researched and learned that parents were supposed to be engaged in the process of drafting a compact between school and families and that there was supposed to be an annual meeting with families.

Linda, the Title I reading teacher in my school, and I met with the administrator in charge of Title I for the district about increasing family engagement in Title I. We looked at the Title I budget and learned how much money was supposed to be allocated to family engagement and how we could spend it. We met with a group of parents to explain their rights and asked for their help in creating not only the Title I documents in Spanish, Arabic, and English, but more importantly, a vision for how Title I intervention services should work in our school and eventually, in our district.

Linda and I organized an annual meeting for Title I families with personal bilingual invitations, face-to-face or by phone. Those first conversations opened the door for parents to ask questions and share their concerns, such as, "Does this mean my child will be in special education?" and "Why didn't last year's teacher ever say there was a problem?"

We made the event accessible, just before Open House, with childcare and a light pizza dinner. This made participation feasible for all caregivers, including single parents and those just getting home from work. We discussed how students were selected, the research-based interventions we used in reading and math, and ways families could support children's learning. We answered questions, invited participation and signed families up for parent–teacher conferences, Morning Math Club, and family workshops.

We began having trainings for Title I teachers district-wide and soon shifted the culture and expectations for the program across the district.

HOW STUDENTS LEARN MATH WORKSHOPS

Some of the caregivers from Morning Math Club said they thought all parents could benefit from the training workshops we had done. Pallavi, the Math Club volunteer coordinator, and I organized a series of workshops called How Children Learn Math. For kindergarten and 1st-grade families we organized "How Children Learn About Numbers." The workshop focused on how children learn to say the forward and backward number sequence, read and write numerals, and begin to count objects with one-to-one correspondence. In "How Children Learn to Add" (for families of 1st-, 2nd-, and 3rd-graders) we explored how children develop conceptual understanding as they move from counting all to counting on, and then move to non-counting strategies based on their developing understanding of the structure of numbers. Eventually they develop conceptual place value that enables them to mentally add three-digit numbers. Each workshop consisted of Number Talks, discussion, and activities, with games, dice, and counters for families to take home.

I personally invited all the FWP and Title I families to these workshops. Title I funding provided a light dinner, childcare, interpretation, teacher stipend and take-home materials. Pallavi and I invited all the families from Morning

Math Club and the How Schools Work group. I asked teachers in the targeted grade levels to invite their students' families. The workshops were advertised in the school newsletter. I organized these as the math specialist, but they were open to and popular among many parents.

Growth Mindset

We developed a family workshop program focusing on growth mindset, something I had initially learned about through a math professional learning community (PLC) I had organized with colleagues. We started with Jo Boaler's book, *What's Math Got to Do With It?* (2008). We were exploring "assessment for learning," an approach "that gives useful information to teachers, parents and others, but it also empowers students to take charge of their own learning." (2008, p. 97). Our interest in assessment for learning led us to the concept of growth mindset and led us to engage with the work of Carol Dweck (2006). In Professor Carol Dweck's talk, "Teaching a Growth Mindset" at Young Minds (2013) (https://www.youtube.com/watch ?v=kXhbtCcmsyQ), she said that a fixed mindset believes that intelligence is a fixed trait, whereas a growth mindset believes that intelligence can be developed. One thing in Dweck's work that resonated with me was her emphasis on math anxiety. Some of my students as young as 5 and 6 years old already had a fixed notion of their intelligence, describing themselves as "bad at math."

After that PLC and our reading of Dweck, I started each new year by teaching my math groups and all the 1st-grade classes a lesson about how the brain works. We studied how we have billions of neurons that connect with each other to create pathways in our brains each time we solve a challenging problem, correct a mistake, and learn something new. We learned how everyone has the capacity to learn, and that we get smarter by making mistakes and learning from them. I always ended the lesson with a video of Janelle Monáe singing *The Power of Yet*, using Carol Dweck's phrase (meaning: "you can't do it" becomes "you can't do it *yet*"), on Sesame Street (2014).

My students and I brought growth mindset to Morning Math Club, and I included it in the training for Math Club volunteers. Pallavi was excited about growth mindset and suggested we develop a family workshop on the topic.

We started the workshop with a pair-and-share introduction, asking everyone to share with their partner "something you failed at before you succeeded, or something you had to work really hard to learn." Josefina offered some personal testimony of how growth mindset allowed her to accomplish challenging goals. This included passing the test to become a U.S. citizen, getting her driver's license, and starting classes at community college while working to support her family.

Figure 8.2. Morning Math Club volunteer Pallavi Bandalli holds her daughter, Dhuythi Belur, at a math club celebration (2014).

Pallavi Bandalli on Growth Mindset

"It's Not Just for Kids"

When I heard about growth mindset and watched the [Carol Dweck] video, I was really shocked. I was always thinking praise was a good thing, but I didn't see the after-effects of praising the kids. I came to know praising their effort is different than praising them, "You are trying so hard," instead of "You are so good at it." I used to say that. I could see the difference in my son. He felt he was perfect in it and didn't want to try anything he's not comfortable doing. I had to consciously change this because I'm so used to praising him rather than his work. I can see a big difference in my kids and in Math Club kids [because of] praising their efforts rather than them.

For me, in the culture that I come from [India], making a mistake is a horrible thing. I feel very low if I'm making mistakes, and learning from mistakes was hard for me. I see the same thing in my son, too. For him, making a mistake is a big thing, and he doesn't want to accept that. So through growth mindset, I really understood it's okay to make mistakes, and we can learn from it. It's not just for kids. I personally changed my mindset. It's a big thing, too.

In Morning Math Club, kids used to get frustrated with tangram puzzles. When we volunteers learned about growth mindset and used motivating words, praised their effort, they learned it's okay (to struggle). As volunteers, we encourage each other. We correct each other if we go back to the old way, so now we praise their effort.

[In the parent workshop on growth mindset]: When we gave the caregivers the engineering challenge to build a roller coaster for a marble, it wasn't easy, but parents tried. They didn't give up. They were having fun, though it was frustrating for them. At first, they couldn't get the marble to roll [around the loop], but they kept trying. There was good team work, and they didn't give up. We kept encouraging, by praising their efforts, not them. It kept them going. Some of them got good results and some didn't. They went around and looked at others' and said, "Wow! Yours came out really good." In other scenarios, people would say, "They got this output and I didn't." In this workshop, I didn't see that. People were encouraging each other, saying, "I like your idea of using this," motivating each other.

Josefina described the obstacles she had to overcome and how important it was that she shared these stories of struggle with her sons. She wanted them to learn how much effort was needed to accomplish her goals, so they wouldn't expect things to come easily. Josefina had only recently learned the term "growth mindset," but I asked her to share her story because it was a perfect illustration of it.

We watched a brief video of Carol Dweck (2013) explaining growth mindset, with clips showing researchers praising either the individual or their effort while they solved puzzles. (https://www.youtube.com/watch?v =kXhbtCcmsyQ. The research showing the puzzles is at 12:35.)

We saw how many of those who received praise for being smart gave up quickly when the puzzle tasks got harder. Those whose effort was praised were more likely to persist and to choose more challenging problems. Caregivers were intrigued by the idea of growth mindset, a new concept for many. Participants engaged in short role plays to shift from praising intelligence to effort, saying, "Wow! You really worked hard on that project," instead of "You're so smart!"

For many caregivers of all backgrounds, the principles of growth mindset were new. It was startling to realize how often they reinforced fixed mindset messages with common expressions like, "You're really talented!" and "You're such a good reader!" In our workshops, we brainstormed with partners about ways to change our language, using phrases such as, "You really challenged yourself by solving that problem. It was hard, but you didn't give up." Caregivers thought about how to increase curiosity about mistakes, and how to remove the stigma from failure by sharing the lessons they learned from their own experiences.

We shared a short clip of the "You failed!" scene from the movie *Meet The Robinsons* that celebrates failure as an opportunity to learn and "keep moving forward!" (Anderson, 2007). The workshop included games and picture books we used at Morning Math Club to promote growth mindset, like *Iggy Peck, Architect* (2007) and *Rosie Revere, Engineer* (2013) by Andrea Beatty and *Your Fantastic Elastic Brain* (2010) by Jo Ann Deak.

Pallavi initiated a regular Growth Mindset Day at Morning Math Club each semester, featuring games and puzzles in which effort and practice help you succeed, such as Rush Hour, Set, Rubik's Cubes, Tower of Hanoi, Tangrams, and noncompetitive Qbitz. Math Club students made posters for a schoolwide growth mindset campaign, with the quote usually credited to Albert Einstein, "It's not that I'm so smart, it's just that I stay with problems longer," and the Japanese proverb, "Fall down 7 times. Get up 8."

FAMILY ENGAGEMENT AND MATH: WHY DOES IT MATTER?

For me, the biggest takeaway about family engagement in mathematics is how vital it is for students to feel their agency and that of their families, in problem solving in school, at home, and in the community. I want them to see mathematics as an opportunity and learn that STEM fields need diversity to solve problems and achieve their goals. I want students and caregivers to see themselves as mathematicians and problem-solvers.

From my first individual diagnostic math assessment with a student, I ask them about their special interests, their families and what they like to do. For example, one student became animated as he told me about how he and his grandmother liked sitting together on her front porch. They each picked a color and counted how many cars of each color drove down the street. I asked him to invite his grandmother to Open House so that I could meet her. It is important to listen to children: One story can tell me so much about a child and his world. And I could see in the counting game my student and his grandmother played the starting point for a math activity.

We wrote and rewrote countless problems to give them meaningful and authentic contexts, like, "Grandma counted 38 red cars and I counted 43 blue cars. How many more cars did I count?" Sometimes those contexts were based on shared experiences, like hatching and raising chicks, "So far, thirteen chicks have hatched. Six are dry enough to move to the brooder box. How many chicks are still in the incubator?" Our problems often referenced engineering problems in Morning Math Club, "Alyssa's paper bridge held 51 pennies. Julie's paper bridge held 14 less pennies. How many pennies did Julie's bridge hold?"

I constantly asked students to make their own story problem for an equation, which increased their engagement while giving me a formative assessment of their understanding of the operation. It also developed their language skills and exercised higher order thinking skills.

Many caregivers, especially those who had interrupted or traumatic educational experiences, took the growth mindset message to heart. It is liberating to understand that an adult who may not yet know how to add and subtract, multiply and divide accurately is not "stupid" and is not considered "stupid" by their child's teachers. As I tell the caregivers of my math students, there could be many reasons a person may not *yet* be confident, accurate, or efficient in mathematics, but never assume that lack of capacity or intelligence is the reason. All children, and adults, can learn.

I must note here that there is a valid critique of growth mindset when it is used to put down people who have been historically oppressed. It is wrong to use the concept to blame people for "not trying hard enough" or not having enough "grit." Mindful of that critique, I write about growth mindset in this chapter because I have found it empowering for students and caregivers, as well as myself.

Rania, when asked to describe math education in her native country, summed it up by saying, "I learned math with a stick," meaning that she would be struck if she could not answer with a memorized fact fast enough. After years of volunteering with Morning Math Club and other FWP projects while studying English, she recently graduated from community college. She transferred to Smith College to complete her bachelor's degree; she plans to major in math.

A founding member of Morning Math Club decided, at the age of 40, that she wanted to get her high school equivalency diploma. She borrowed a preparation book from her niece and realized she needed to start with elementary math. She lives out of state, works full-time and is still raising teenagers, but she asked for weekly math tutoring by video call. Despite weariness at the end of long work days, family health issues, and other challenges, she is highly motivated and disciplined. In less than a year, with about 30 lessons, she has made great progress. Since participating in the Financial Literacy Project, she has maintained a family budget and plans to purchase a first home this year.

A Title I parent really wanted to help her 2nd-grade son in math. In a conference to discuss his progress, she said she had only attended school until 2nd grade in her country and solved math problems by counting on her fingers. She asked if she could come in after school once a week so I could teach her what I was teaching her son, enabling her to play the games with him for practice. In order to make this happen, she arranged for her husband to stop work by 3 p.m. on Wednesdays to watch the baby, drop her off at school, and pick up their son.

Individual adults have different personal goals for themselves as well as for their children. It helps to feel a sense of belonging in an environment where previously unlikely things are possible, where it is legitimate to have and even share a dream, where your goal finds not only encouragement, but support. When I attend the graduations of FWP members who have spent up to 6 years to complete community college, while single-handedly parenting, running a household, working physically demanding low-wage jobs and sometimes simultaneously becoming citizens and licensed drivers, I feel the pride their children feel. As someone who attended college as a single parent and low-wage worker and graduated at 37, I know how hard-earned and momentous these achievements are.

I am not suggesting that a teacher should take responsibility for the education of all her students' caregivers. That could be a recipe for burnout. But as an educator, I can listen to caregivers' stories and offer encouragement. I can connect them with community resources for adult basic education to earn high school equivalency, learn English, prepare for community college and find volunteer tutors. I can relate to and honor their struggles. As a teacher, I can create supportive spaces in school like Morning Math Club and family workshops about growth mindset and math. These are sites of possibility, encouragement, and support for adults as well as children.

CHAPTER 9

Taking Care of Ourselves and Each Other

BEAUTIFUL SCARS

At our very first residential workshop, I realized that most of us in Families with Power had at some point survived abuse or violence. To be clear: a culture circle is not group therapy. But culture circles are a way to think critically about our experiences, especially those we share in common with others, and to explore the dynamics of power and oppression related to those experiences. For example, for those of us who experienced abuse as children and were not listened to or protected, this had a large impact on learning as well as educational and therefore occupational outcomes. For those of us who experienced abuse or violence as adults, the brave decision to escape the abusive situation (with one's children) had a significant negative economic impact. The decision to escape, often without resources or time to plan, was like jumping off a financial cliff. Yet each of us had decided to buck the family, religious, cultural, and other pressures to suffer in silence, because we decided our own lives were worth saving.

Freire wrote that humanization "is the people's vocation . . . It is thwarted by injustice, exploitation, oppression and the violence of the oppressors, it is affirmed by the yearning of the oppressed for freedom and justice, and by their struggle to recover their lost humanity" (2018, pp.43–44). In my view, emerging from trauma is part of the struggle to recover one's lost humanity. In this chapter, I begin with my own story as a way in to understanding post-traumatic stress disorder in children and in caregivers and include examples of some FWP educational projects caregivers designed to transform the situation.

Hope Begins in the Dark

Hope begins in the dark, the stubborn hope that if you just show up and try to do the right thing, the dawn will come. You wait and watch and work; you don't give up.

—Anne Lamott (@ANNELAMOTT, 2013)

I pulled up to the stop sign at a T-shaped intersection, facing a park. I needed to get around it. I could turn right or left to go around the park and continue to my destination, but I froze with indecision. I tried to reason with myself, "Turn either way, right or left. It doesn't matter, just keep going." But I was stuck. A car pulled up behind me. I thought, "Okay, just turn right. It's no big deal. Just turn right." But I couldn't make myself do it. Now there were two cars behind me. I thought, "Okay then, just turn left. You'll get to the same place. Just move!"

I knew this wasn't logical, but I couldn't think straight. I couldn't move my body the way I wanted. My heart was pounding. The drivers behind me started beeping. I was short of breath. Someone back there was cursing. I wanted to jump out of the car, grab my son from his car seat and run away as fast as I could.

The night before, while I was making dinner, I froze up trying to decide whether I should make mac and cheese from a box or open a can of pork and beans. There were only two choices, and neither posed an earth-shattering consequence. I went back and forth, back and forth, as my son, a toddler, whined for dinner.

These panic attacks started after a traumatic event; they were happening more and more. I didn't know that these were a manifestation of post-traumatic stress disorder (PTSD). I thought I was crazy. I didn't tell anyone because I thought if anyone found out, I could lose my son.

I was unable to keep food in. When I ate, food went straight through me, running through my intestines like a subway train. I was still nursing my son and was losing weight fast, falling below one hundred pounds. A clinic doctor I had seen only once diagnosed it as irritable bowel syndrome and prescribed labetalol, which didn't help. I was depressed and could not focus or make a plan. I loved my son. I had to stay alive to take care of him. I didn't know what was wrong with me, but I knew I needed help.

My son and I left Philadelphia. My sister Jane and her husband let us stay with them on Long Island. I was a wreck. I found a women's resource center run by Adelphi University's school for social work; it offered free counseling and a support group every week. When the director did the intake with me, she said, "Nothing can undo what happened to you. Our goal is to make it so that it isn't the first thing you think of every morning when you wake up and the last thing you think of every night before you fall asleep." I felt like she could see through me, that she knew how this was for me.

Jane watched my son every Thursday evening so that I could go to my therapist and support group. I worked my minimum wage job and went to the women's resource center every week for 10 months. My focus was to heal, so that I could parent my son. My work was to become whole, so that I could be fully human again. I wanted to feel a range of emotions: joy but also sorrow, excitement but also fear. I needed to feel an emotion like sadness or fear in the moment without *becoming* that emotion.

Working with my therapist, I came to realize that what often triggered my panic attacks was the need to make a decision, because I still blamed myself for having once made a seemingly insignificant decision that had life-changing consequences. In my support group, I felt tremendous compassion for women who were blaming themselves for the violence that was done to them. It was obvious to me that none of what had happened to them was their fault. I had to learn to treat myself with the same kindness and acceptance that I felt toward others. I learned to step back and see my younger self and the decisions I made with compassion. I had made decisions that were driven by fight-or-flight fear and desperation at a time when I had no hope, no confidence, and no vision of a future.

I learned to recognize panic attacks and what could trigger them. I learned strategies to manage them so that I didn't have to live in fear of them. I stopped being afraid that if anyone looked at me for more than a minute, they would see me as irrevocably broken. I began to understand what it meant to become stronger in the broken places.

Most importantly, I learned I was not the only one who ever felt that way. The women in my support group were diverse in age, race, class, ethnicity. We did not identify as victims. We connected to each other, bound not only by our trauma but by our decisions to keep *living*, not crawling like frightened, shattered things, but as women who grew stronger and walked taller through collective healing.

TRAUMA COMES TO SCHOOL

On my first day of teaching, I gathered my 1st-graders on the rug for morning meeting. Just a few minutes into our greeting, one child turned to the student beside him and bit him on the face, without provocation. The child who was bitten burst into tears. The child who bit him seemed calm and smiled at the rest of us, without a trace of guilt. I couldn't figure out what had just happened. I comforted the child who was bitten, looked at his face, and asked another student to walk with him to the nurse's office. I told the child who had bitten him to take a time out, and pointed to a chair, which he sat in. Later, I replayed the morning, trying to figure out what I had done wrong: I had gathered the children on the rug for morning meeting, welcomed them, introduced our greeting, just like it said in my *First Six Weeks of School* book from Responsive Classroom. What happened? I couldn't make sense of it.

At lunchtime, I asked two other 1st-grade teachers for advice. One rolled her eyes and the other chuckled, then said, "Glad he's in your class," as though she already knew something about my student. As a brand-new teacher, I felt set up and unsupported. On the home visit, his caregivers told me that he came to them as a foster child when he was 2 years old. He had experienced trauma, although they didn't know the details of it. They had used the word *trauma*, but I don't think I registered what that meant. After our rough first day together, his mother told me that she didn't think I was a good match for her son, who she thought needed worksheets and to sit in a desk in a row, not on a rug or at a table with other children. She went to the principal to request that he be moved to the class of the veteran teacher, the one who had said "Glad he's in your class." I felt like a failure. I didn't argue with her. I cried in my classroom after school. I was so preoccupied that I made matters worse by not calling the family of the child who was bitten.

The next morning, the mother was back with her son, miffed that the principal declined her request to move him to the other class. She told me she had studied elementary education; I was intimidated. Not knowing what else to do, I invited her to volunteer in the classroom, so she could learn how I was teaching and help me learn about her son. She accepted my offer, and she taught me about trauma. Near the end of that 1st-grade year, the mother said she was going to recommend to the principal that I loop up to second grade. ("Looping" is when a teacher and her students go up to the next grade together as a class.) Gwen agreed and I spent another year with this wonderful, challenging, brilliant child.

The next year, a new student showed up on the first day of school. He hadn't been on my list, so I hadn't reached out for a home visit. Midmorning, he got frustrated and flipped his desk. When classmates invited him to play at morning recess and to eat with them at lunch, he screamed at them to go away, that he didn't want to be friends, that he had friends where he came from and was going home soon anyway. The guidance counselor stopped by at lunch time to tell me there was "trauma in his background." A few weeks earlier, there had been an incident with a SWAT team invading the home where he was with a parent. Now one parent was in a psychiatric hospital and the other was in a long-term drug rehab program. The counselor said he was in foster care, and there was no home for him to go back to.

In my first 2 years of teaching, I reacted to explosive behavior like biting, desk flipping, and screaming as "behavior" that I ought to be able to "manage" by separating the explosive child and trying to keep children safe. I didn't punish the explosive child, but struggled to understand what happened. At that stage in my development, I thought trauma in children always manifested as explosive behavior. I thought I was supposed to do the detective work to figure out the triggers and find strategies to de-escalate that behavior. I did not connect students' explosive behavior to the panic attacks or physical symptoms I had suffered.

In my third year of teaching, Kim and I team-taught again, with a double classroom of 1st- and 2nd-graders, including native Spanish speakers, native English speakers, and English language learners who were native speakers of other languages. As the year started, I observed some explosive behaviors from easily triggered children and was perplexed by some indoor playtime behavior when I observed children who had not yet developed a capacity for imaginary play. A child might put on a dress from the dress-up box and scream, "I'm the mother!" over and over while chasing other children around the room. Their play lacked both a story line and role playing. I was sorely tempted to shut down the imaginary play space; it was driving me nuts. But I knew that closing the space wouldn't resolve anything. Within the first 2 weeks, one family pulled their child out to attend a private school, saying they'd been on the waiting list. Another moved their child to a different classroom.

Kim and I weren't sure how to help. We invited our principal, Gwen, and Barbara Black, our early childhood coordinator, to visit and observe. It may seem counterintuitive, when your classroom is chaotic and out of control, to invite administrators to observe the chaos. But we had tremendous respect for Gwen and Barbara as early childhood educators and trusted their goodwill to help us re-establish our classroom as a safe and fruitful learning environment.

As a result of Gwen and Barbara's observations and our conversations, in 2000 Gwen, Barbara, Kim, and I decided together to pursue professional development in the field of "trauma-informed instruction." I could feel us make a shift. Instead of just looking from the outside at a child's behavior, we started to look from the inside. We learned about how trauma changes the brain. I started to see the connection between the PTSD that combat veterans, other adults, and I suffered, and the PTSD that children suffered. We learned that children who experience trauma are often hypervigilant, constantly scanning for danger. Some children who experience PTSD are frequently in fight-or-flight mode. This explains why they are easily triggered by things that seem insignificant to others.

I realized that I had been too quick to think a child was inattentive when it was just as possible that the child was hypervigilant. Every time I redirected and said, "Mind your own business," I hadn't realized that a particular child considered it not just his business but his responsibility to look up every time the classroom door opened, to see who was coming or going. For him, it might not be a matter of idle curiosity but survival for himself and his siblings. I had a 1st-grade student who ran to the classroom door every time there was a sound in the hallway. He'd say, "I think that's my brother. He needs me." His behavior became more understandable with knowledge of his home life. Imagine being 6 years old and needing to call 911 to get an ambulance for your bleeding mother after an abusive boyfriend attacked her; imagine being 6 years old and in charge of keeping your three younger siblings safe. Imagine there's no "off" switch to your vigilance.

ACEs: Adverse Childhood Experiences

Previously, I had thought of trauma as a traumatic event, like surviving a violent incident. I learned that an event could be an example of acute trauma, but that there is also chronic trauma (or toxic stress) that goes on day after day. Vincent Felitti, MD, of Kaiser Permanente, and Robert Anda, MD, of the Centers for Disease Control (CDC), used data collected by Kaiser Permanente, gathered from questionnaires filled out by middle-class patients with an average age of 57 who were invited to help researchers understand how childhood experiences might affect adult health.

Researchers asked 10 questions: if, before the age of 18, the patient had ever experienced emotional, physical or sexual abuse, or emotional or physical neglect, if they had ever witnessed their mother being treated violently, if they lost a parent to separation or divorce, if they lived with someone who misused drugs or alcohol or who was mentally ill or if they had a member of their household in prison. Felitti and Anda's study (Felitti et al., 1998) called these adverse childhood experiences (ACEs). For each yes answer, they assigned one point. Two-thirds of the patients had at least one ACE. Anda and Felitti correlated the ACE scores with the patients' medical histories as adults. They found that an ACE score of 4 doubled their risk of cancer or heart attack. An ACE score over 6 was likely to shorten their lifespan by 20 years.

According to the Centers for Disease Control (2021a), "as the number of ACEs increases so does the risk for negative outcomes," including addiction, chronic disease (cancer, diabetes, heart disease), mental health (depression, anxiety, PTSD, suicide), maternal health, infectious disease, injury, and opportunities (education, occupation and income). On its website, the CDC says, "Some children may face further exposure to toxic stress from historical and ongoing traumas due to systemic racism or the impacts of poverty resulting from limited educational and economic opportunities" (CDC, 2021b). According to the CDC, "ACEs and associated conditions such as living in under-resourced or racially segregated neighborhoods, frequently moving and experiencing food insecurity can cause toxic (extended or prolonged) stress . . . which can change brain development and affect such things as attention, decision making, learning and response to stress" (CDC, 2021b).

At the same time as we recognize this organic reaction to trauma in individuals, we must be cautious about expanding this concept to groups in ways that may be stigmatizing. Kendi makes this point in warning about the danger of what he calls the "oppression-inferiority thesis," writing, "There is a thin line between an antiracist saying individual Blacks have suffered trauma and a racist saying that Blacks are a traumatized people" (Kendi, 2019, p. 97).

Anda and Felitti's research increased public awareness of ACEs and demonstrated how common they were across all cultures and classes. However, not everyone who experiences trauma will develop PTSD. An ACE score is *not* destiny; it is a tool to understand risk and guide us to make changes.

The more I learned, the more I realized how many of my 1st- and 2nd-graders had multiple ACEs. One had nine. Still, the fact that a child has any number of ACEs doesn't mean that child is necessarily traumatized or suffering from PTSD. I became more sensitive to information that families shared, especially as caregivers talked about their own experiences. I reacted less impulsively toward what I earlier thought of as misbehavior, attitude or inattention. Instead of taking a student's behavior personally, I tried to balance the development of engaging culturally relevant curriculum, the cultivation of a respectful and inclusive classroom community, and the organization of a safe and predictable classroom environment. I collaborated with my principal and colleagues to increase our attention to social–emotional learning and to become a trauma-sensitive school that provides optimal learning conditions for all students.

Freire wrote, "The affective existence of countless children is . . . crushed, like broken glass" (1998, p. 50). In the letter I wrote for Sonia Nieto's book, *Dear Paulo: Letters from Those Who Dare Teach*, I wrote about a student, Elonzo, I taught in my first year. He struggled with learning, seemed inattentive and was frequently off task. One day he was paying less attention than usual and was disrupting the class. I noticed he was scratching and picking at his arm, which was red and swollen. Marilyn, the paraprofessional who worked with me, came over and offered to walk with him to the nurse's office. Later, she told me what had happened. His father was beating his mother and threw something at her, shattering a mirror that was hanging in Elonzo's room. He and his brother started crying. His father told them to shut up and get in bed. As he slid into bed, a thin shard of broken glass embedded itself in his arm. This 6-year-old had been attending school with a shard of glass under his skin for weeks as an infection worsened. The nurse called his mother, who brought him to the doctor, who cut open the wound to remove the broken glass, clean it, and stitch it closed. Elonzo never mentioned the pain. And I had been frustrated with his inability to focus on math and his disruption of my math lesson, while his existence was like broken glass (Nieto, 2008, pp. 14–15).

WHAT ARE YOU GOING THROUGH?

The love of our neighbor in all its fullness simply means being able to say, "What are you going through?"

—Simone Weil (2000)

At our first FWP retreat, as we shared our stories in culture circles, over meals, on walks, and around a bonfire, it became clear that most of us had experienced trauma and suffered from some degree of PTSD or depression that inevitably impacted our families and relationships.

One mother shared her story. She had suffered serious injury because of neglect as a young child. After being molested as a preteen, she dropped out of high school. She and her children later fled from her abusive husband. After living in a shelter, they finally moved into an apartment in a new city, where she enrolled the two older ones in school. One weekday morning, she was lying on the couch with the TV on. She couldn't bring herself to get up, wake the children, and get them ready for school. Eventually they woke themselves and came downstairs, hungry. She couldn't get up to feed them. They gathered around her, crying, but she couldn't respond. Eventually they started fighting, hitting each other and screaming, trying to get some kind of reaction from her. But her depression was so profound, she could not move.

As a teacher, I had sometimes felt frustrated with caregivers who didn't get their kids to school on time. I have heard administrators frustrated about attendance, in part because school funding from the state depends on it; this is especially important in less affluent districts where property taxes don't cover the cost of public education. But the story of this young mother, numb and paralyzed by depression in the face of her confused and crying children, resonated with me, as when I was paralyzed at the stop sign, unable to make myself move.

The action plans we produced at our first FWP retreat in 2007 didn't specifically address trauma, but it became increasingly clear that caregivers' trauma impacted not only their own physical and mental health, education, and opportunities; it could impact their children's educational experience as well. FWP members realized we had the power to support each other, no matter what we were going through. Freire wrote, "To surmount the situation of oppression, people must first critically recognize its causes, so that through transforming action they can create a new situation, one which makes possible the pursuit of a fuller humanity. But the struggle to be more fully human has already begun in the authentic struggle to transform the situation" (2018, p. 47). FWP members created a variety of educational projects to transform the situation while asserting their humanity and that of their children.

One of our earliest FWP projects was a support group organized by Eneida and Maribel for families of kids with attention deficit disorder (ADD). Eneida invited a friend from the board of Casa Latina who was a Latinx social worker and therapist to participate. It was different from the model of "parenting classes" in which an expert tells parents how to deal with children's behavior. Instead, families met weekly for four sessions and learned together about how the brain works. Kids talked about their experiences: how it feels when teachers and caregivers get frustrated and yell at you for not being ready, for not having what you need, for dawdling or needing to move or spin around, for daydreaming or not paying attention, for being more interested in something else. Caregivers listened, asked questions, and listened some more, then brainstormed with their kids about strategies that might help.

The FWP-organized support group opened up more conversations about learning differences. Eneida was a fierce advocate for families of children with disabilities and trained other caregivers to learn their rights and advocate for their children. Parents began to share stories of their own harrowing educational experiences as children: moving from school to school, being an English language learner, being separated from the rest of the class, feeling invisible. Not to mention struggling with reading, writing, and math. Finally, feeling stupid and dropping out.

In my classroom, I spoke more openly about having a learning difference myself. I have auditory processing disorder, which means that sometimes my brain can't fully understand what my ears just heard, that I can't process everything I hear. Sometimes I hear a word that rhymes with the word that was spoken, which greatly changes the meaning of the sentence. I need to see the speaker's face and expression, so that I can tell when what I think they've said isn't matching the expression on their face. If there's a mismatch, when, for instance, I think they said something angry but their face looks friendly, I have to stop and replay the tape in my head to think what else they might have said in that sentence. Naturally, this leads to me falling behind in the conversation. Long (and fast) talkers exhaust me. I love subtitles and sign language interpreters who clearly re-mouth the important words. It's almost impossible for me to remember email addresses or phone numbers that people say without carefully writing them down. I depend on lists that I always carry in my pocket. I can't hold on to anything that follows the first step when someone gives verbal directions. I get nervous about live interviews, especially rambling questions, because I fear that the long pauses while I process what has been said will make me look stupid.

In my classroom, I inform my students about this learning difference, how it is different from being hard of hearing or deaf, how I need to see their faces if they want me to understand them, how it helps me when there's not background noise, like pencil sharpeners. I emphasize that a learning difference doesn't make you less smart than anyone else. It just means that you have to work harder and speak up more bravely to tell others what you need to succeed. I find that people do respond by speaking up, sharing their differences, and saying what they need. When I share my story with humility, students and parents are more inclined to share what learning is like for them. That sharing increases my effectiveness as a teacher.

YOU GOTTA MOVE

Over the years, at Cafés and reading parties, we had many conversations about weight and how and what we ate, not from the standpoint of beauty or looks, but from the perspective of health. At one Café, a member said, "Look, I know I'm fat. I don't care what people think about how I look. The thing is, I want to feel better, to be healthier, so I'm here for my kids. I'm all they've got. I want to do something with them that's healthy and fun."

Another member said, "I wasn't like this when I was young. You know why? It's not just that I had kids. Before I had kids, I used to dance all the time. I never went to the gym, but I danced with my friends. Now with kids, I don't go out dancing. Who'm I gonna go with? Who's gonna watch my kids? I don't have any money to go out."

Many caregivers know, at least theoretically, that self-care is important. But the reality is that self-care requires some combination of time, energy, routine, childcare, and money. Especially for single caregivers who live in poverty, who may work long hours and struggle with trauma, depression, or other physical and mental health issues, self-care is a real challenge.

Elba suggested having a family dance party. "We could do it here after school on Friday." Gesturing to the tables and chairs in the room, she added, "We could push all this stuff out of the way and make a big space. Anabel could help me make a CD of good dance music. I'll ask Totty if we could borrow her boom box. We could get some healthy snacks and have water instead of soda. Then everybody come, and I'll lead it." These Family Dances were FWP's first self-care activity.

The first Family Dance attracted a crowd, about 75 students from pre-school to community college, caregivers, and staff: our principal, nurse,

Figure 9.1. Elba Heredia organized and led FWP's Family Dances for fun and exercise (2010).

secretaries, and student teachers. The room was packed. It was one of FWP's first school-based activities, and it drew lots of families, including many that were not in Families with Power. It was free, and it was fun. It created community and allowed the kids in FWP—and staff—to see Elba up front and in charge. Normally, Elba is pretty shy and quiet, but she loves to dance. Her own children came up front and stood beside her as she led the group. Then other FWP children came up front to help her lead.

Elba led FWP Family Dance Parties about once a month. Janis Totty, our physical education teacher, asked Elba if she would come lead a dance session in P.E. class. Next, Gwen asked Elba if she'd lead an all-school dance party on the day before December vacation. Elba set up in the gym from 11 a.m. to 1 p.m. Classes came and went, many on their way to lunch, staying for 20 minutes or half an hour. As a class in front departed, the class behind them danced forward, making room for more classes to fill in behind. It was a great way for the whole school to get exercise and to see Elba and FWP kids up front and in charge.

"MEDITATION SAVED MY LIFE"

Café conversations included health and body image, but other themes emerged too. The topic of stress came up frequently at financial literacy workshops. At a Café, people offered ways they coped with stress, including prayer, and one member said that the grief group she attended after the death of her husband taught her how to meditate. Around that same time, Jackson Street School was becoming a "mindful school" with mindfulness training open to all staff. Twice weekly, Gwen led morning meditation over the public address system. Many FWP members said they were interested in learning to meditate. We wrote a small grant to pay for the mindfulness teacher and childcare, to run a 6-week series of mindfulness workshops for caregivers.

FWP organized the workshops, which were open to all caregivers in our school community. At one session near the end of the series, we began with our usual check-in when Pallavi said, "This week, meditation saved my life." What? We leaned in. It was early spring, still cold out. She had been out for a walk around the park pushing her young daughter in a stroller. She was about a half mile from her car when she started to have an asthma attack. When she realized that she had left her pocketbook with her inhaler and her cell phone in the car, she started to panic. There was no one around to ask for help. She could no longer even get out words. She sat on a bench and parked the stroller beside her. She made herself breathe in and breathe out, slowly, in and out, focusing only on her breath, in and out. By meditating, she calmed herself and regained control of her breath. She was able to walk back to her car with her daughter and get home safely.

"NO! GET YOUR HANDS OFF ME!"

Many caregivers worried that their children, especially those with disabilities, would be bullied. Many were concerned that their children would be abused, like they had been. FWP members sometimes invited educators or community people to our Cafés. Elba invited Janis Totty, a physical educator, martial artist, and empowerment self-defense instructor. Caregivers talked about wanting to design a program to address teaching children to stand up to bullying and abuse. We came up with The Kime Project to teach whole families personal and collective safety strategies, and to recognize the protection skills they already had. Kime is focus, decision-making, and clarifying energy that we receive and offer in practicing movement arts, and in building community. Middle and high school students could learn to become trainers. We received a small grant to fund six weekly sessions.

We gathered at 5:30 p.m., ate a light dinner of pizza and salad, and warmed up together with some playful physical activities and community building. Then we moved into role-playing and learning physical skills like strikes and kicks. We learned to assess possible danger, trust our intuition, extract ourselves from unsafe situations, and use our voices and our bodies to defend ourselves.

Figure 9.2. Elba, Josefina, and Maria eat dinner and talk together in the Jackson Street School cafeteria at the start of a Kime Project workshop (2011). The Puerto Rican flag is part of the mural on the wall behind them.

Figure 9.3. The author practices a strike with Janis Totty, who led the Kime Project (2011).

Photo: Mairead Blatner

Figure 9.4. Maria, Janet Aalfs, Janet Namono, Elba, and Elba's son, A.J. Robles, practice strikes at the Kime Project.

Students and caregivers suggested scenarios based on what they'd experienced. These role plays were often intense, as a survivor, perhaps decades after an assault, gradually raised her voice to shout with new-found confidence, "No! Get your hands off me!" with a strike or a kick. Some were overcome with emotion as they relived that experience. This was so hard, but these caregivers were determined to give their kids the skills they needed to protect themselves. After the first session, we debriefed. Many of us felt an avalanche of rushing adrenaline, feeling shaken up, but brave and powerful at the same time. I silently wondered if they wanted to stop. One mother said, "We should reward ourselves for being so brave. We need a way to calm down after we do this."

The families' solution was not to stop the self-defense training. Instead, we added a period of moving meditation at the end of each session. Janis Totty's wife, Janet Aalfs, an integrative arts educator, came and led us in moving meditation (based in tai chi and qigong) at the next session, and we ended every session with it after that. At our sixth and final session, every family got their own copy of a CD with music to use for moving meditation at home. After the Kime Project, different members took turns leading the moving meditation at our annual retreats.

CULTURE CIRCLES

One of the most striking things about Families with Power is the organic way it developed programs in response to authentic concerns of members. The Cafés served an important and ongoing role, creating a family-controlled time and safe space within the school, where the conversations gravitated toward problems and then programs. Myles Horton describes how Highlander started by trying to go from the theoretical to the practical. After a few months, they realized that wasn't working, that they weren't reaching people, so they changed their approach. "Instead of coming from the top down and going from the theoretical to the practical, trying to force the theory on the practical, we learned you had to take what people perceive their problems to be, not what we perceive their problems to be. We had to learn how to find out about the people, and then take that and put it into a program" (Horton et al., 1998, p. 140).

In our annual retreats, we used a process of Freirean culture circles. The basic components of a culture circle include using simple drawings or photos as prompts to identify generative themes that are socially and culturally relevant to FWP members and our community, a recursive process of problem-posing, dialogue, and problem solving that leads to action at a personal or societal level (Souto-Manning, 2010, pp. 19–20).

However imperfectly we employed Freire's method of culture circles, our members internalized that process and used it naturally and informally in our Cafés to discuss themes including physical and mental health, stress, finances, and violence against women and children. This process affirmed our members' agency, resilience, resourcefulness, and strength in community. In relation to each theme, there was critical reflection about power dynamics and what created the conditions, or who profits or benefits from maintaining the status quo. Why are so many of us sick? Who makes money off us needing so much insulin? How come Walmart is full of so much unhealthy food? Is anyone making us buy it? Are commercials marketing unhealthy food to us? If you depend on food stamps, how could you afford organic vegetables? If farmers markets don't take food stamps, is that food just for rich people? Why didn't our schools teach us how to write a check, balance a checkbook, read a bank statement or a credit score? Do businesses that target us for ads and offers of "no money down" do it so they can make more money off interest than selling us a product? How does financial dependence increase the chance of being abused? Why does society act as if violence against women and children were normal? What media, what messages reinforce that?

Freire did not want his method to be imported or exported. In a conversation with Donaldo Macedo, Freire said, "Please tell your fellow American educators not to import me. Ask them to re-create and rewrite my ideas" (Freire, 1998, p. xi). I do not pretend to know or understand enough of Freire's theory or method to claim that our work in Families with Power successfully re-created Freire's ideas. I humbly cite Freire here and throughout this book to give him credit as an inspiration for our popular education work. I hope that these stories provide windows into our process of using dialogue and problem-posing in relation to specific themes relevant to our members to generate problem-solving action, which frequently led to some kind of transformation of caregivers, students, our school, and our community.

Instead of feeling isolated and ashamed about our debt, our physical or mental health, our bodies, our stress, our learning differences, and the violence we'd survived, FWP members found a way to think critically about these issues. We took action, creating programs as beautiful as *kintsugi*, the ancient Japanese art form that repairs broken pottery using a lacquer mixed with powdered gold to accentuate the veins that mend the piece, finding beauty in the imperfect and impermanent. These programs—meditation, financial literacy, family dance, self-defense—glued us together at our broken places with golden lacquer, making us stronger.

CHAPTER 10

Healthier Eating

A NOTE TO MY FARMER

In your email you wrote, "The flowers are done. We'll plow them under next week and start preparing the fields for fall." I understand the natural rhythm of these things, can visualize the decomposition of fallen leaves and stalks under the soil as the worms, microbes, and mycelium work their quiet, dark magic.

I know it is your field, that you chose the seeds from a catalog last winter as you nursed your infant, that you planted, watered, and weeded them with your baby bundled on your back, and that one soon September morning your husband will climb onto his tractor and plow those flowers under. But first, I have to tell you about your flowers.

My friend's husband was buried three weeks ago. Now she and her sons sleep together on a mattress in the living room, when they can sleep. She worries that they stay up under her like chicks, playing video games inside the apartment, and won't go out to play.

Last Friday, we were driving, and I asked if she'd mind coming to pick up my weekly farm share. She shrugged: Okay. After we got the vegetables from the farm share room and began to climb the dike to get to the fields, I noticed her gold plastic flip-flops, and felt stupid. When we got to the steep path down the other side, I apologized. She squinted at me in the sun and said, "It's okay. In my country, I live on a farm. This reminds me of my country."

After we picked cherry tomatoes, I took out scissors and said, "Now we can pick flowers." I asked her son his favorite colors. He said he liked black and blue.

"Do you like orange? These are tithonia," I said, pointing down the row. He looked them over and asked for just one. I raised my eyebrows as I offered him the baby-soft stem. He accepted two. I could see my friend ahead of us, alone, two rows over, picking flowers like a queen would.

"How about purple zinnias? Purple is kind of like black and blue."

"One, no, two, just two." He discovered some velvety cockscomb the color of raspberry sherbet and took one. Yellow zinnias: two. Red zinnias: one. Always greedy for flowers myself, I marveled at his restraint. Still my friend moved slowly, deliberately like a ship through the waves, sometimes almost hidden by tall flowers.

We came to the end of the row and my friend was there, pointing, "What is it?"

"Red amaranth."

"I like it. I can take some?"

I nodded. My friend carried her armload of flowers like Miss America, back up the steep path. At the top, she asked her son, "Which you like better, video games or cutting flowers?"

"Flowers," he said without hesitation.

She flung out her free arm like she was embracing the sky, smiled up at the sun and said one word with each dusty footstep, "I am happy."

When we started our FWP Cafés in Fall 2010, the member who had picked flowers told other members about visiting Town Farm and trying out new vegetables from the farm share. Other caregivers talked about having diabetes and worrying about their children becoming diabetic. They complained about how hard it is to get children to try healthier foods. Hearing this, the children opened the back door of my classroom and led us out to the school garden. The children eagerly picked cherry tomatoes and brought them in for a snack, much to the surprise of their caregivers.

FARMERS MARKET OR FOOD MUSEUM

Years ago, when I first moved to Northampton, I lived in a small apartment, two blocks from the city's only farmers market. I barely made ends meet with minimum wage work to pay my rent and utilities. I purchased groceries with food stamps. Northampton has a beautiful downtown, but it is expensive. I used to take my son to a toy store on Main Street, where there were cool toys on display for children to play with. I told my son it was a "toy museum," not for buying, just for playing and looking.

The farmers market was also like that for me, a feast for the senses: bright bouquets of colorful flowers, freshly washed leafy greens sparkling with water droplets, richly colored heirloom tomatoes, energetic zucchini seedlings. There were whiffs of garlic and donuts frosted with maple cream. But you could not use food stamps at the farmers market in those days, so that market became a food museum for us, with beautiful things that we could look at and smell but never buy.

For our own food, I pushed my son in his stroller away from downtown, to the supermarket located on the commercial strip near the car dealerships. We bought boxes of macaroni and cheese, cans of beans, frozen spinach, and fish sticks with our food stamps. As I pushed the stroller home, we picked bouquets of Queen Anne's Lace from the weedy edges of parking lots and handfuls of blackberries along the railroad tracks. We knew our place, what we could look at and what we could have.

FOOD STAMPS X 2

Fifteen years later, the Tuesday Market was different. In 2010, FWP took a family field trip to visit Tuesday Market, the new farmers market in downtown Northampton. You could go with an electronic benefit transfer (EBT) card (otherwise known as food stamps, or SNAP, Supplemental Nutrition Assistance Program) to a table with a friendly worker and a machine, where you could get tokens to use with vendors at the market. Ben James and Oona Coy, the farmers who owned Town Farm, where I had a farm share, were the managers of the Tuesday Market. They were the first market in our area to accept EBT and debit cards. Better yet, they were piloting a new program called "Food Stamps × 2" to offset the more expensive price of buying local, organic produce from farmers who try to pay their workers a living wage. For example, if you ran your EBT card for $10, the market gave you $20 in tokens. This effectively halved the cost of local organic produce and actually made it cheaper than the supermarket's conventionally grown produce, much of which had been trucked thousands of miles. Our members took out their EBT cards, tried this, and liked it.

We invited farmers, public health officials, and market managers to our Cafés. We collaborated with them to open up access (both economic and social) to farm shares and markets; this included collaboration on educating

Figure 10.1. Families with Power made a family field trip to the Tuesday Market in Northampton to research how we would want our farmers market to be. (Front to back, left to right) Row 1: Joseury Rodriguez, Eliaz and Angela Robles. Row 2: Kim Gerould, Josefina and Reneury Rodriguez, A.J. Robles. Row 3: Ben James, Janet Namono, Mary Cowhey, and Elba Heredia (2010).

the community on why eating more fruits and vegetables (especially fresh, local, and organic) was healthier, and how to use food stamps to buy them. Ben Wood, Northampton's new director of public health, was providing equipment to accept food stamps at local markets and training market managers. He invited FWP members to participate in a weekend of public health training (and paid for their childcare) so they could participate in policy discussions with public health officials about access to healthy food.

Across our region, more farmers markets and CSA farm shares began to open up to low-income consumers using food stamps. Some farms began to offer discounted community supported agriculture (CSA) farm shares that could be paid for over time in food stamps. A credit union offered interest-free loans to pay for farm shares.

My son volunteered at Prospect Meadow Farm, a therapeutic farming community just started by the human services agency Servicenet. They hired him as a farm worker and job coach for people with developmental disabilities, autism, or mental health challenges learning vocational skills on the farm. Shawn Robinson, the director of Prospect Meadow Farm, began coming to the FWP Café. Prospect Meadow Farm also started a CSA with low-income shares that could be purchased with food stamps. They had distribution points across the city, accessible for those without transportation.

BRINGING THE FARMERS MARKET TO THE PEOPLE

While the Food Stamps × 2 program definitely increased *economic* access to fresh food, there was another barrier. Many low-income people of color didn't go downtown. The chic boutiques and cafés were expensive, and in our liberal New England city, racial profiling was alive and well. People of color were followed around suspiciously in some shops, making downtown less attractive than Walmart.

I had been aware of this dynamic, but it really hit home for me with my son's experience of racial profiling. The summer my son was 18 years old, he grew into a tall handsome Black man, and was twice stopped by the police. Once was while he was walking in our majority-White neighborhood. The other was while he was walking home from work along the side of a busy road. There was no 911 call for either; both stops were the personal decisions of officers who chose to "check out the situation" and stop my son for walking while Black. My son's experience of racial profiling in public space is certainly not unique to him or to Northampton, and it is just one example of the ways that racism restricts and discourages access to majority-White spaces, including Northampton's downtown.

Ben James (farmer) and Ben Wood (public health director) listened to our members and supported our efforts to fight racism in our community. They understood how the interplay of racism, economics, and transportation

Figure 10.2. Elba Heredia runs a cooking demonstration table to show how to make fresh salsa and sofrito, using ingredients from the farmers market in her neighborhood (2011).

make downtown farmers markets less accessible for low-income people of color. Together we brainstormed an idea: to pilot bringing a small farmers market to Hampshire Heights, an apartment complex in the Jackson Street School neighborhood where many FWP members lived. Ben James asked members what food they would like. Members wanted "basic foods," like fruits and salad items. They also requested specific ingredients that were hard to find in Northampton, like cilantro, *racao* (also called culantro or sawtooth coriander) and *ajies dulces* (small Puerto Rican sweet peppers), used together to make sofrito.

We planned monthly markets for July, August, and September, 2011. FWP members had ideas for more than just food. We thought about how to create a community event that would welcome whole families, where you knew you belonged and could hang out and see your friends and neighbors, and where you knew you could have fun. The housing authority gave us permission to have the market at Hampshire Heights, near Elba's apartment.

Josefina volunteered at the table to explain Food Stamps × 2 bilingually, to show how to use EBT cards and give people their tokens. Elba and Maribel ran cooking demonstration tables, using fresh foods from the market, providing recipes and free samples of salsa and sofrito.

The members wanted our youth to get some job training through the program, so older kids helped set up and take down the market and sell the produce.

Ben James mentioned that he had an ice shaver and asked our members what flavors they liked: *tamarindo* (tamarind), *guayaba* (guava), *china*

Figure 10.3. Ben James, Miguel Candelaria, Elba Cartagena and Elba's children talk while making *piraguas* at the Jackson Street Farmers Market (2011). FWP members asked farmers to bring popular culturally appropriate foods to our market, including *piraguas*, and cilantro for *sofrito*.

(orange), and *coco* (coconut). This generated excited conversation about our market having an iconic Puerto Rican summer treat, *piraguas* (paper cones of shaved ice, flavored with tropical syrups).

Barbara Black, the district's early childhood coordinator, helped set up a "story walk": a line of laminated picture book pages posted on pickets at the eye level of small children. We also brought boxes of used books that children could read and take for free. (See Figure 10.4.) There was hula hooping, drumming, and other music. The market was festive, distinctly and authentically local, organized by and for neighborhood families.

In 2018, Grow Food Northampton launched a Mobile Market Pilot to run a weekly pop-up farm stand for 10 weeks in the Hampshire Heights and Meadowbrook neighborhoods. Residents purchased subsidized farm shares, paying $3 a week for $11 worth of fresh, local produce from area farms. Customers who hadn't purchased a farm share could purchase produce at the wholesale price. Like our earlier farmers market at Hampshire Heights, it became a community gathering space. Residents started what they called "cooking classes," using products from the mobile market to cook a dinner from their culture in the community room, to share with neighbors. Sarah Bankert, a public health organizer, used grant money to buy ingredients for the dinners. After the mobile markets wrapped up in early November and the grant ended, the residents continued the dinners as potlucks.

Figure 10.4. Ben Wood, then Northampton Public Health Director, reads a book from the free book box to Angela Robles at the Jackson Street Farmers Market (2011).

OUR KIDS COUNT AT THE FARMERS MARKET

It is hard to describe all the ways this partnership flowed from school, through families, into the community and back again, but here is one example: Ben James was also a photographer. We decided to make our own FWP bilingual counting book, featuring our kids and the food at the farmers market. *OUR KIDS COUNT at the Farmers Market* was a spiral-bound book, about 4×4″, to fit the hands of small children, with laminated pages on which they could practice writing their numbers with dry-erase markers. We printed these professionally, distributed them at family math workshops, and used them at school. I always loved to see the spark of incredulous recognition when a student leaned in, looked closely at the picture and exclaimed, "I know her! That's Nani! She lives near me!" Imagine that, a book about kids like us! (See Figure 10.5.)

WHAT'S KALE? WHAT DO YOU DO WITH BROCCOLI?

When some FWP members purchased farm shares at Town Farm with their food stamps, they brought home lots of produce each week. But a lot of it was new to them, and they didn't know what to do with it, or even what it was. Elba and Josefina knew that one reason people didn't use fresh produce

Figure 10.5. Diana Soler reads *OUR KIDS COUNT at the Farmers Market* to her daughter, Melissa Lisboa Soler, at a book launch party at Hampshire Heights (2013).

was because they didn't know how to cook things like broccoli and kale. The cooking demonstrations were a small step to address that.

A local organization had a grant-funded program to offer a series of healthy cooking classes for families. They had nutritionists from the university and lots of food, but not many participants. In 2012, Elba, Josefina, and I attended a series of cooking classes at their office. We proposed a partnership: FWP could organize a convenient location in Northampton, recruit participants who wanted to learn to cook healthy food, and get them there. Elba and Josefina would help lead the cooking classes. The organization agreed.

FWP asked the school district for permission to use our school cafeteria and kitchen for this, but they wanted to charge us $800. This was a missed opportunity for the school district, but it didn't deter us. We kept looking and found a local church that donated the use of their large kitchen, the dining hall, and preschool classrooms for a childcare space.

Our collaboration with the partner organization didn't go so well because the university nutritionists who taught the cooking classes only wanted to use Josefina and Elba as interpreters. They did not respect them as peers or recognize their influence among the families we recruited to attend. They did not collaborate with Josefina and Elba as coleaders, interact much with the families, or make any effort to adapt their usual program and recipes to include more culturally appropriate foods.

The nutritionists had a different understanding of recruitment and appropriate numbers for the event. They asked us to recruit 24 people. At the

Figure 10.6. Elba Heredia at the Healthy Cooking Class (2012).

Figure 10.7. Anaisha Feliciano enjoys her dinner after helping to prepare it at the Healthy Cooking Class for families (2012).

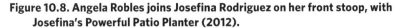

Figure 10.8. Angela Robles joins Josefina Rodriguez on her front stoop, with Josefina's Powerful Patio Planter (2012).

earlier series of classes, the three of us were the only community partici-pants there. The class cooked for 24 each week, and most of that prepared food went uneaten. So FWP recruited enthusiastically, stopping when we realized we had signed up 30. This didn't feel problematic to us. We orga-nized transportation with borrowed car seats and provided interpretation. We provided childcare for toddlers, while children 4 and up participated in the cooking classes. When everyone showed up every week, the nutritionists seemed nervous about the numbers, even though there was enough food. We considered the strong turnout a success, but they were peeved about it.

The nutritionists didn't respect FWP's vision of full family participa-tion in these healthy cooking classes, including our embrace of polychronic culture. Maybe the nutritionists felt it was too much, too chaotic, to have kids of all ages, caregivers and grandmothers, and multiple languages and cultures. Yet that's what FWP very intentionally organized and saw as beau-tiful. Perhaps it was that lack of shared vision that made our organizations so out of sync with each other.

GROWING OUR OWN

After that early Café in the fall of 2010, when the children led their care-givers out to the school garden to gather cherry tomatoes for snack, our conversations continued to probe the relationship between health issues (diabetes, obesity, high blood pressure and cholesterol) and access to healthy, affordable food, especially fresh vegetables. Some FWP members had been born and raised in cities, while others grew up in rural villages in the Caribbean, Central and South America, Africa, and southern states in the United States. There was a growing interest in the possibility of gardening, fueled by children's involvement with the school garden education program.

Our first small step toward gardening was an experiment that we called "Powerful Patio Planters." Farmers at the Tuesday Market donated seedlings. Maribel collected five-gallon buckets from the dining hall where she worked, and we drilled holes in the bottoms. The vocational high school donated soil and compost. One spring afternoon in 2012, families gathered to fill buckets with soil. The children transplanted cherry tomato and basil seedlings and planted cilantro seeds. The families took the buckets home to a sunny spot on their patio or stoop and nurtured them. For some families, these manageable buckets were their first gardens or their first opportunity to grow their own food since they'd come to our community.

In 2013, we began a partnership with Grow Food Northampton, which works toward food security and sustainable agriculture by providing access to land, food, and knowledge. Grow Food opened a large organic community garden in 2012 and approached FWP to ask for our help with outreach to the immigrant community. They wanted the garden to be a diverse and welcoming place, but they lacked contacts and relationships to get started. One of our members organized a house meeting at Florence Heights, an apartment complex near the new garden; several families signed up. The next year, Diana hosted a meeting in Hampshire Heights. The third year, the garden organizers asked if we could organize another meeting; they'd already arranged to use a room at the library. Many of the families we were inviting were unfamiliar with the library.

Santa offered to host the meeting at her home instead. A year earlier, she had attended a meeting like this at Diana's home in Hampshire Heights and became a first-time community gardener, sharing a plot with Diana. Santa had a successful growing season and wanted to recruit others. The night before the meeting, I saw an email from one of the garden organizers who had written an agenda, with one of the directors leading the welcome and introductions, and then their officers explaining various aspects of the program. I emailed back, saying that usually when we have a meeting, the person hosting the meeting welcomes everyone to her home and explains the purpose of the meeting, then facilitates introductions, which are important so everyone feels seen and heard. They graciously agreed.

Everyone who came to the meeting came because someone personally invited them. There were Ecuadoran, Dominican, Puerto Rican, Palestinian, Ugandan, and Chinese families. Our members invited immigrant and low-income families who would enjoy the physical and nutritional benefits of growing their own organic vegetables. The creation of this critical mass continued to diversify the community garden and made it more comfortable for other immigrants and gardeners of color.

Santa served *Chocolate Cortes*, a rich hot chocolate from Puerto Rico, with fruit, cheese, and crackers. Santa spoke in Spanish and her husband provided English translation. They warmly welcomed everyone to their home and shared their experience as new gardeners. The meeting unfolded, with garden organizers covering the details of how to register, the cost of the plot, the required number of volunteer hours.

Many of the FWP members, speaking softly when the leaflets with the registration date, time and place were handed out, were asking where this registration place (the vocational high school) was. They didn't know where the garden was either. One of the garden organizers said, "There is too much snow and mud to visit the garden today." Santa immediately read confusion and disappointment on participants' faces. Santa said that it would be a good idea for us to go to see the garden *today*, despite the weather. We could drive by the vocational high school on our way, so that everyone could see which building to enter for registration. Santa knew that for people to pay money to register, to make the commitment, they would want to see it first and know how to get there. Santa said, "I can take four in my car." It was settled. We piled into cars and drove in a caravan to the vocational school and then the community garden. FWP members and community gardeners, Roque and Santa, and our new gardeners walked in the freezing rain over the snow to see Roque's plot.

Hampshire Heights Community Garden

Late in 2018, Sarah Bankert, a public health organizer, was working with some Hampshire Heights tenant leaders interested in creating a community garden and playground. They asked if FWP could help with some outreach. FWP organized a series of reading parties, in the homes of members and also in the community room. A few 5th-graders were intrigued with the idea of having input to the creation of a neighborhood playground. They recruited other students and families to attend these meetings, posting hand drawn signs around the school. I overheard student conversations in the hallway, "You want a basketball court? You *gotta* come to this meeting."

At the first meeting, after introductions and reading together, we broke for snacks and discussions of residents' ideas for a community garden and playground. Sarah invited the kids to go to the childcare room upstairs. The students looked at her oddly, ignored that invitation, and started making suggestions. Joe, one of my 1st-grade students, began saying we should get some dwarf apple trees and cherry tomatoes. We should make labels for the plants in Spanish and English, as we did in our school garden. Sarah looked surprised for a moment, then quickly started writing the ideas on the chart paper. The Hamsphire Heights community garden began in the summer of 2019.

FARM SHARES COME TO SCHOOL

In the summer of 2018, Grow Food Northampton proposed a Community Supported Agriculture (CSA) program with Jackson Street School as a distribution point. Michael Skillicorn, a Grow Food organizer, and I brainstormed and sought input from families. Like the Mobile Market at Hamsphire Heights, it was a 10-week program, partially subsidized by grants that made produce more affordable, while supporting small, local farms. Anyone receiving food stamps (SNAP) was eligible.

The Jackson Street School PTO donated to add another subsidy, bringing the cost down to $2 a week. FWP shared that some immigrant families didn't apply for food stamps, either because they were undocumented or were documented but were afraid of Trump's "public charge rule" (that receiving any kind of public assistance would endanger their chance of becoming a U.S. citizen). In response, Grow Food broadened their criteria to "eligible for free or reduced lunch or SNAP."

I spoke to families of my students, in FWP and on the playground before and after school, to ask them to help me publicize the CSA program, explaining eligibility and how it would work. By simply inviting families to help me publicize the program, I wasn't making assumptions about anyone's socioeconomic or immigration status. In those conversations, some people asked generally about when and where to sign up. Others asked to sign up right away. Most of the sign-ups came from personal conversations. People who signed up often brought their friends and relatives to sign up the next week. Our registration window was 3 weeks (with fees pro-rated for later sign-ups), to accommodate peripheral recruitment.

On Wednesdays at dismissal time, families with farm shares came to the farm stand table set up in front of the school. A student could pick up their family's share and ride the bus home. A caregiver who worked later could pick up their farm share in the Hampshire Heights neighborhood where the Grow Food mobile market ran from 4:30 to 5:30 p.m. A Grow Food staff person and intern set up the farm stand table. As my teaching day ended, I joined them to help with outreach and registrations. As the contact person between the school and Grow Food, I handled logistics and publicity. With participant feedback, Grow Food improved the program each year. They created some unsubsidized farm shares, so that staff and other families could sign up. Later, it operated more as a mobile market, where anyone could buy whatever they wanted at the farm stand price, or pick up their CSA farm share. The shares became more flexible, with more customer choice.

WHAT WAS HAPPENING IN THE CLASSROOM?

In 2008, I read Barbara Kingsolver's *Animal, Vegetable, Miracle* (2007) and Michael Pollan's *Omnivore's Dilemma* (2007), which inspired a big shift toward local eating in my family and expanded our gardening efforts. Those books prompted me to take a summer graduate course with Mass Ag in the Classroom. My action research focused on the permaculture model of raising chickens with a chicken tractor (mobile chicken coop) as a way to fertilize the soil. I started raising chickens in my neighborhood community garden.

Gwen invited staff to have tea together near the end of that summer. I told my colleagues about the Mass Ag in the Classroom course I had taken. They got so fired up about it that we worked together the next day to weed and reclaim an overgrown and neglected butterfly garden behind the school library. We later transformed it into a thriving school garden.

As the school year began, the Mass Ag class provoked me to rethink the sustainability of our 2nd-grade science curriculum with my students. Our soil science kit required students to make compost in a Ziploc bag (very nasty). With the help of my student teacher, we instead built and tended an actual compost pile in the school garden. We constantly had to negotiate constraints; we could put weeds but not food waste in the school garden compost pile since we are located near a wildlife corridor with an active black bear population. A Green Team of families from the PTO organized composting in the school cafeteria and arranged for farmers to pick up food waste for composting.

My students noticed how much waste ended up in the trash can after snack. We soon started a "chicken scrap" bucket that a student with backyard chickens and I took turns taking home. We also started a worm bin and a compost bucket in our classroom. We set up a dichotomous key, like the ones you see in a plant guide, to sort our waste. My 2nd-graders peered into the shrinking contents of our trash can and kept asking questions: Could snacks be purchased in bulk and the container be replaced with something reusable, like a beeswax wrap or a Tupperware container? What if, instead of using paper napkins, everyone had a cloth napkin with their name on it? What if, instead of using disposable plastic or paper cups, we had a set of washable plastic cups with names on them?

The district's "life cycle" science kit provided each student with a painted lady butterfly larva. These were ordered from a laboratory, where they were genetically modified to eat a pasty food substance that could be shipped easily. After we learned that releasing those butterflies into the environment harms the genetic stock of our native butterflies, my students rejected the kit. (Ethically, you should euthanize all the butterflies hatched from laboratory larvae. At that point, it's not even a full life cycle.) Instead, we brought in just a few monarch caterpillars and some milkweed leaves from the school garden and observed them growing, transforming, and hatching in the classroom for quick release as butterflies. Each student mapped habitat where they could find milkweed in their neighborhood and then took home milkweed seeds to plant more.

We added the life cycle of chickens to our curriculum. We used an incubator to hatch eggs from Town Farm; we'd met their hens and rooster on a field trip. Students took responsibility for turning the eggs three times a day and then caring for the chicks. Students learned to wash their hands thoroughly. We investigated the questions that curious young minds want to know, such as:

- "If I put an egg from the grocery store in the incubator for 21 days, will it hatch?"
- "If I have four backyard hens and one keeps sitting on the eggs, will I get chicks?"
- "Is it gross to eat a fertilized egg?"
- "Doesn't the hen need a rooster to lay eggs?"

We read and wrote fiction and nonfiction stories and dozens of math problems about chickens and eggs. We noticed which picture books about chickens were inaccurate, like having chickens lay more than one egg a day. We made a physical graph in the hallway using the egg cartons students brought from home. We illustrated each mile the different cartons of eggs traveled from producer to consumer with an inch of yarn. Students asked their caregivers and grandparents to tell them how their families got eggs when they were children. Puerto Rican and immigrant children often had substantial funds of knowledge about chickens to share with the class.

My colleague Mary Bates took the lead on the school garden. She obtained funding for our school garden through our PTO. Later, she won a large grant from Northampton Education Foundation to establish school gardens at every elementary school in the district with garden educators and professional development. The grant paid teachers to develop garden lessons that integrated math, social studies, and language arts, as well as science curriculum frameworks. This was more equitable, so that every student received a developmentally appropriate and consistent garden education from kindergarten to 5th grade, whether or not their teacher in any given grade happened to be a passionate gardener or, conversely, hated getting dirt under their fingernails.

Building on the success of the school garden as an outdoor classroom, caregivers in the PTO provided the labor to develop the school garden, with raised beds and a mini-orchard. They created another outdoor classroom at the edge of the woods, with a sunshade sail and dozens of stumps for students to sit on. Over time, the development of curriculum and culture of our school shifted to normalize the use of these outdoor classroom spaces. All educators and students adopted routines for learning outdoors. Families saw how vital their volunteer efforts were to maintaining and developing these outdoor spaces. They signed up to weed and water the school garden over the summer, and to participate in volunteer work days and garden cleanups.

FACING THE PANDEMIC

On the evening of March 11, 2020, I was in the community room of Hampshire Heights, to meet with students and families to discuss issues about bullying. During our check-in, growing anxiety about COVID-19 came up. Several parents had asthma or children with asthma, and were considering keeping them home if schools didn't close. As we talked through the possibility of school closure, a parent with two kids said, "If schools close, there goes free lunch and breakfast. How can I come up with food for an extra 20 meals each week? I barely make it through the month on my food stamps right now." Families saw people on the news jamming grocery stores in panic, yet most of the families at our meeting didn't have extra cash or food stamps to stock up on anything.

The Northampton Survival Center increased its food distributions to families. Families with cars helped those without cars to pick up food. On March 13, our schools shut down. On March 14, a caregiver from that meeting called to tell me that her son had a fever, a cough, and difficulty breathing. Their pediatrician said she should not bring him to the office or the hospital, that he was presumed positive for COVID-19, that no tests were available. On March 15, all of Massachusetts locked down. We met on Zoom and families offered to share what they had, an extra roll of toilet paper or some canned food that they could leave outside their door. Some caregivers were laid off abruptly. Others had to continue working, without masks or protective equipment. Our PTO offered grocery gift cards to families in need. The Survival Center closed after their staff and volunteers became ill.

Grow Food Northampton stepped up to partner with Northampton Survival Center. The Grow Food network of mobile markets became the backbone of weekly emergency food distributions staffed with volunteers, including some FWP members. They restarted emergency food distributions, providing pickup and delivery in high-need neighborhoods across the city.

Years of cooperation between these community organizations and the schools built a strong foundation. Northampton Public Schools had closed because of the pandemic. The Jackson Street School cafeteria, with its refrigerators, freezers, and exterior doors, opened up as the location to receive massive deliveries of perishable and nonperishable food. A ramp was built over the steps to the cafeteria door, to make loading and unloading easier. Grow Food Northampton and Survival Center volunteers sorted food each morning to disperse to delivery sites around the city. Three afternoons each week, the Jackson Street School bus circle was used as a drive-through contact-free food distribution point.

Grow Food Northampton obtained a grant to purchase fresh produce from local farms, many of which lost their customer base when the pandemic closed all restaurants. Volunteers assembled food boxes consisting of fresh produce and nonperishable foods for pickup or contact-free doorstep delivery.

I volunteered at Hampshire Heights on Tuesdays with Grow Food Northampton's neighborhood food distributions. These were coordinated with the school district's twice weekly delivery of free breakfast, lunch, and milk. Families with children under 18 (whether or not they were students enrolled in the public schools, with no documentation required) could make a single outdoor stop. With masks and social distancing, they could pick up several days' worth of prepared meals and fresh milk from the school bus. Twenty feet away, they could pick up their boxes of nonperishables and fresh local produce.

Volunteers organized into small pods, so that if any one volunteer got COVID-19, the whole pod could drop back and let another pod take over while the first pod quarantined. We wore masks, face shields, and gloves. We worked outdoors with social distance to keep the community and each other safe. We distributed cloth masks sewn by volunteers to families as they came to pick up food.

Every Tuesday, Joan Cameron, a 3rd-grade teacher at Jackson Street School, came to the distribution at Hampshire Heights, with books, paper packets, and other materials for her students. One of them walked with his younger siblings and mother from a nearby neighborhood. They had recently arrived as refugees, and the mother spoke very little English. They lacked access to the Internet, which made it impossible to participate in remote learning. But they reliably arrived every Tuesday morning at the neighborhood food distribution, where Ms. Cameron greeted them warmly. She asked how they were doing and provided learning materials.

Ms. Cameron carried heavy food boxes to the porches of residents. At the homes of her students, she would knock and step back, give a wave, answer questions and provide teaching materials from a safe distance. Another JSS teacher, Brian Rodrigues, and his wife, Millie Lopez, a paraprofessional, came every week to help with the school's breakfast and lunch distribution

at Hampshire Heights, greeting students and their families. The district social worker was another regular at the Tuesday food distribution, picking
up food boxes to deliver to families outside of the neighborhood. She also
helped families obtain Internet hotspots and laptops for the transition to
remote learning. These educators provided a strong thread of continuity
between school and families during a scary and difficult time.

WHAT WE LEARNED

FWP's ideas and programs about healthier eating evolved over the years
through dialogue during the informal culture circles of our Cafés. As FWP
members developed authentic relationships with farmers, community garden organizers, CSA and farmers market managers, public health workers,
and school staff, a mutually beneficial interdependence grew among them.
These experts and professionals valued the wisdom and expertise of FWP
members and sought their advice.

In the more successful collaborations, these professionals had the humility to step back and promote the leadership development of FWP members. They took their advice and tried members' suggestions, even if they
seemed outside the box, such as hula hooping, drumming, a story walk, free
book exchange, or kids making change for customers at a farmers market.
These professionals made it possible for FWP members to attend public
health conferences and access opportunities for job training.

FWP had a process for analyzing concerns that affected the community. FWP also had authentic relationships cultivated through the creation
of community spaces, including the Cafés and our neighborhood farmers
markets, which brought people together to create solutions.

Some of FWP's programs were short-term, like bringing three monthly
farmers markets to a high-need neighborhood as a pilot one summer. The
short-term projects helped pave the way for longer-term programs like the
school- and neighborhood-based mobile markets that now operate across
our city, accepting SNAP, and more diverse and accessible community gardens. And all these programs had long-term impact in changing the health
habits of FWP caregivers and children.

CHAPTER 11

Cultural Organizing

"ABRE LA PUERTA!"

Javier invited me to my first *parranda* in Trenton, New Jersey, in 1983. My Spanish was weak. It was in December, and I understood it involved singing. I asked Javier if it was like Christmas caroling. He laughed. He described it in Spanish. It sounded kind of like a party, but it involved pounding on doors and yelling, "Abre la Puerta!" ("Open the door!") The singers woke people up and barged into their houses with instruments and song, then demanded food and drink. There was something about going from one home to another, late into the night. Perhaps I misunderstood. I said it sounded illegal. Javier laughed and said, "No, it's fun!" And it was.

At the Highlander Homecoming in September 2007, Doña Lucas and Eneida attended a workshop about "cultural organizing," which Highlander defines as "the strategic use of art and culture to move progressive policies and practices with marginalized communities" (https://highlandercenter .org/programs/methodologies/cultural-organizing/zilphia-horton-cultural -organizing-project/cultural-organizer/). Myles Horton described how music and storytelling enriched Highlander:

> The cultural aspects of Highlander have always played a very important role because we were trying to deal with the whole person and not just a segment of a person. In fact, the history of Highlander could in many important ways be told by the music—traditional songs and songs of struggle—that was brought here by the people. (Horton, 1998, p. 133)

A few months later, inspired by the workshop at Highlander, Eneida initiated our first cultural organizing program. Families with Power, in cooperation with Casa Latina, organized a *parranda*, a traditional Puerto Rican celebration of music and food in the season from the start of Advent in early December through Three Kings Day on January 6. Eneida rounded up musicians and instruments and planned the route we would take in her Hampton Gardens neighborhood. It is always warm in Puerto Rico in December, but in western Massachusetts, it's cold. After practicing a

Figure 11.1. On a cold night in western Massachusetts, the *parranda* approaches the first home on its route (2010).

Figure 11.2. FWP member Candy Candelaria sings and plays *maracas* at a parranda (2013). A *pandero* (hand drum) is visible on the right. Grandparents like Candy pass on vital Puerto Rican traditions to younger generations by leading cultural organizing activities, like the *parrandas*.

few songs at Eneida's apartment, we went with our guitars, *panderetas* (tambourines), *palitos* (thick wooden sticks), *maracas* and *güiros* (notched gourds scraped with a comb) through the snowy night. Eneida pushed her son, Freddy, in his wheelchair. Caoma's house was our first stop. A Taino elder, Caoma* was the grandmother of some of my students. We sang, banged on the door, shouted, *"Abre la Puerta!"* and tumbled into Caoma's living room, where we kept singing. After singing and eating, Caoma and her family joined us as we walked to the home of another of my students, Sebastian.* There was more singing and dancing. We ate *sancocho*, a traditional soup.

The *parranda* songs are not just songs for the Christmas season. This is Puerto Rican *música jíbara*, which has its roots in Taino and Spanish culture in the interior mountain villages. The *parranda* celebrates *jíbaro* culture with pride in families' rural roots. In Lourdes's home, for example, where others might put a star or an angel at the top of their Christmas tree, she had placed a traditional *jíbaro* straw hat. There is a whole collection of *parranda* songs that Puerto Rican adults know by heart. *Parrandas* are an important way to pass this oral tradition on to the next generation.

It was through *parrandas* that I learned of the Puerto Rican tradition of *bomba*, a funny and fabulous kind of rhythmic word play. Eneida's sister, Santa Garcia, and her friend were particularly gifted at this. The *parranda* musicians play music to introduce a *bomba* song, which everyone sings together. Then the group stops singing and one person, like Santa, delivers a kind of rhythmic playful taunt and another responds, ending with a *bomba*, a well-crafted punchline. Everyone leans in to wait for it, then yells,

Figure 11.3. Angela Robles plays the *pandereta* at a *parranda*, where children learn everything from singing the traditional lyrics to playing the instruments in a multi-age community setting (2010). *Maracas* and *güiros* are traditional Taino instruments. Children learn in the polychronic environment of the *parranda*, where everyone is singing, dancing, playing different instruments, eating, talking, joking, and laughing at the same time.

"Bomba!" when it's dropped, falling back in laughter. *Bombas* are usually funny, witty, and often bawdy. If the *bomba* isn't funny or rhythmic, or doesn't rhyme well, the *parranda* participants sing back their criticism: *"No sabe na, no sabe na. No sabe na de bomba, no sabe na"* (You don't know anything about *bomba*). *Bomba* is also an Afro-Puerto Rican dance of resistance, with African and Taino roots, in which the dancer and drummers are in conversation with each other.

Eneida also proposed an educational project featuring *plena*, a traditional style of Puerto Rican drumming, singing, and dancing. She explained that long before television or newspapers on the island, *plena* singers and drummers were the earliest reporters, sharing news between villages. *Plena* lyrics are narrative, often about current events, protests, and political movements. The first *plena* song I ever heard was about HIV protection. *Plena* uses *panderos* of different sizes and *güiros*. *Panderos* are handheld frame drums in three sizes, with different tones. We used a small grant from Northampton Education Foundation to start an after-school *plena* program for students; the young FWP *pleneros* later performed for the whole school community with a professional *plena* group. The grant provided an honorarium to the *plena* musicians and purchased *panderos*.

LOVE YOUR FAMILY DINNER

Elba began the tradition of organizing our annual "Love Your Family" dinner each February, featuring a traditional Puerto Rican menu. The dinner was a community celebration of culture, family, joy, and abundance, where all were welcome. Unlike many other FWP events that were small and held in the community, the dinner was large and held in the school cafeteria. FWP invited educators, administrators, and elected officials to join us. Sometimes these guests felt awkward. They were in a familiar, typically White-dominated space, but the people in charge were people of color, many of whom district administrators had never met or seen before. Added to this, the music, the language, and the food were unfamiliar. If the guests looked disconnected, we asked them if they'd like to help out. We usually got a relieved, "Yes! What can I do?" We then introduced them to an FWP caregiver or student to give them a task, allowing a previously awkward guest to play on the home team and get to know FWP.

Part of the beauty of cultural organizing is that when families who are not in the culturally dominant group plan it, they take over the space and transform it. Two things happen: Students and families see themselves as leaders and experts; educators experience cultural immersion and can embrace and enjoy how a Puerto Rican or other cultural event feels. When school administrators run something like a "multicultural potluck" with families bringing ethnic food, it can still feel like a typical event that a school

Figure 11.4. Elba Heredia Cartagena speaks at an FWP Love Your Family Dinner (2015). When Elba spoke at the first Love Your Family Dinner she organized (2012), it was her first public speaking experience in front of a crowd.

Meet Elba

Elba Heredia Cartagena was born in Holyoke, MA. As a child she moved to Chicago, then returned to Holyoke, where she was raised by her paternal grandmother. At different times, she also lived with her mom in Northampton; she attended Jackson St. School for a time and Smith Vocational High School, where she studied cosmetology. She later studied culinary arts with Job Corps in Worcester. As a teenager, Elba lived at Hampton Gardens and babysat for Eneida. Elba moved back to Northampton as an adult with her three young children in 2009, settling with her children in Hampshire Heights. Her oldest child, A.J., enrolled at Jackson Street School.

Eneida invited Elba to come to a Family Reading Party and then to participate in the Family Writing Project. At first, Elba was very shy, but she quickly got more involved and emerged as a leader. In addition to participating in all FWP projects, Elba initiated many, including Family Dances, Healthy Cooking Classes (with Josefina), and Morning Math Club (with Edwin and others). An excellent cook, Elba organized the annual FWP Love Your Family Dinner. Along with Josefina, Eneida, Irma and others, Elba planned and facilitated the FWP annual retreats (residential workshops). Elba also served as copresident of the JSS Parent-Teacher Organization for 2 years.

In 2014, Elba married Carlos Cartagena, who worked as a custodian at Jackson Street School. In 2015, Elba, Carlos, and their family moved to Florida, but they continue to visit Northampton and Holyoke regularly.

puts on for families, with the same people in charge. It is distinctly different when families organize their own cultural events.

CELEBRATING EDUCATORS OF COLOR

For years, our civil rights committee was telling district administrators about the importance of hiring more diverse educators. District administrators kept saying they really wanted to hire more diverse educators, but they just didn't get diverse applicants. When we discussed this within FWP, there was enthusiastic agreement that we needed more diverse hiring, but there was a lot of skepticism in response to the administrative assertion that there just weren't any candidates. Rather than argue the point, FWP leaned into our principle of starting with what you have. In 2007, FWP organized a reception for educators of color, personally inviting staff of color from clerical and janitorial to instructional assistants, faculty, and student teachers from schools across the district, as well as the superintendent and other administrators, so they could meet each other.

Families with Power collaborated with the Student of Color Association (SOCA) at Northampton High School to organize the event. Maribel organized refreshments. We arranged lots of fresh flowers and seated all the educators of color as guests of honor. FWP and SOCA members (including Veronika Hean, once a member of my 1st-grade class) talked about how powerful it was to see educators of color in our schools. Eneida made a personal appeal to student teachers of color to apply to work in Northampton. Janet, who worked as an instructional aide in the preschool, made a special acknowledgment of teachers who started out as instructional aides. Doña Lucas sang a musical offering in Spanish, particularly moving to the Latinx staff. Many staff of color were moved by the tribute, saying they had never been honored before.

The FWP reception didn't diversify hiring in the district overnight. Most of the student teachers we invited had already been hired by other districts by then (our event was in May, a few weeks after our first FWP retreat), but the reception made it clear to administrators that there were in fact some student teachers of color that they could make a point of getting to know (and potentially recruit) at the start of each semester. It shined a light on the importance of the pipeline of instructional aides who could, with more district support, become teachers and counselors. Students and families of color voiced demands about the issue of hiring and opened the door to diversifying participation on hiring committees.

THE ROLE OF CULTURAL ORGANIZING

Families with Power's cultural organizing:

- Affirmed the rich and vibrant presence of all-too-often unacknowledged communities in our schools
- Celebrated these communities in culturally appropriate ways
- Cultivated leadership among caregivers and youths
- Uplifted cultural traditions of liberation and connection

Cultural organizing has always been a small but mighty part of FWP's work. Elements of cultural organizing found their way into other FWP events, from the annual FWP retreat to the Farmers Market. At these events, you could always find Latinx music and food, as well as dancing and drumming. At our retreats, we welcomed all the different languages spoken by people in the room. We broke up our workshop schedule with cooking and eating together, and *café con leche* breaks. Dancing and bonfires enlivened the evenings.

Figure 11.5. Roque Sanchez teaches Melissa Lisboa Soler how to coax a note out of the trumpet at the FWP Retreat in Hawley (2013). Participants brought instruments to FWP retreats for both planned and informal musical activities.

Figure 11.6. Elba Heredia and Eneida Garcia dance during a *dynamica* activity at the FWP Retreat in Hawley (2012).

Talking about literacy in Chapter 5, Eneida said, "This 'read aloud' is not part of my culture." What I learned through cultural organizing was that while Eneida did not grow up with public libraries and parents reading bedtime stories, she was steeped in culturally and linguistically rich oral traditions like the *parranda, bomba* and *plena* that had previously been unrecognized and unvalued by most of our faculty and school. FWP's cultural organizing illuminated these huge "funds of knowledge." When a cultural group is essentialized by White-dominant school culture to a "costume," flag, greeting, or ethnic dish, we all lose.

CHAPTER 12

Immigration: How Schools Work

"WHAT IS MY SON'S NUMBER?"

In 2010, I had a student, Hakim, who had just come from Pakistan with his mother and siblings. His mother, Ishqa, was an Urdu speaker who had learned some written English in school. Her husband had arrived a few years earlier. After I sent home Hakim's report card, Ishqa came to the classroom very upset, demanding, "What is my son's number?" Our district has a student identification number for keeping track of data on each student, but most parents aren't aware of those. It seemed unlikely that was the number wanted.

I noticed Ishqa had the report card, so I asked her if she wanted to talk about it. As we talked through it, I realized how incomprehensible the report was. There were hundreds of words, four pages in tiny print. Each section had a different key of letter codes: M for mastery, N for needs improvement in one section. Another section used a different code: C for consistently, I for inconsistently and O for Occasionally, and so forth. There were no numbers on the entire report card, except for absences. Ishqa listened politely. When I finished, she asked again, "What is my son's number?" I still had no idea what she wanted, and we were both frustrated. I think Ishqa felt I was withholding information. I felt clueless and terrible.

I scheduled a meeting with an Urdu interpreter and finally learned what Ishqa wanted. In Pakistan, all children in the grade are given a number that reflects their rank in the grade. If there are 72 children in second grade and a child has a rank of 12, they are near the top; a rank of 68 would be near the bottom. Later, an Iranian math professor at UMass mentioned they have the same system in Iran. It is visible in the classroom, because the children with the highest numbers (lowest rank) are seated in the very front, closest to the teacher. Those with the lowest numbers (highest rank) are seated in the back, because it is assumed they have better behavior and can work more independently. I thought I was accommodating an English language learner by giving what in the United States we call "preferential seating" up front. Ishqa noticed Hakim's seat up front and interpreted his seating assignment as my perception of low achievement, lack of effort, or misbehavior on his part. No wonder she was upset!

HOW SCHOOLS WORK

Many of my students were English language learners (ELLs) with families new to schools in the (mainland) United States. At every school event, I always asked myself, "Who is here? Who is missing?" I often heard teachers say, "A lot of the parents came, except X and Y; they don't speak English." I heard a few teachers sound judgmental about caregivers who didn't come to Open House or parent–teacher conferences, or who kept their children home from school in bad weather when there was a delayed opening. I wondered how often these were the result of inadequate communication from the school, cultural misunderstandings, or limited English or literacy.

My experience with Ishqa made me realize that my undergraduate and graduate teacher preparation programs (and those of my colleagues) didn't include international education. I needed to learn how schools worked around the world. I haven't traveled much, but when I did (to South Africa, France, the United Kingdom), I made a point of connecting with teachers and visiting schools. I am fascinated by how our schools are similar and different.

In June 2011, FWP took a family field trip downtown to visit three places: the Tuesday Market for some action research about farmers markets, and two nonprofit adult education resources, the Center for New Americans (CNA) and the Literacy Project. CNA serves the immigrant, migrant, refugee, and asylum-seeker community with resources to learn English and

Figure 12.1. Kids wearing their FWP tee shirts on a family field trip to Center for New Americans try out the whiteboard in the classroom of Maureen McMahon, who taught many of their parents (2011).

develop skills to become involved community members. The Literacy Project provides instruction in basic academic skills, high school equivalency and college readiness. Both programs are free and had recently opened an on-site childcare program for caregivers during classes. Some FWP members were attending these classes or had done so in the past.

In July 2011, after many ideas from Mariana Souto-Manning's book, *Freire, Teaching, and Learning* (2010), had been percolating in my head, I got the idea to work with FWP members who were English language learners, in collaboration with Casa Latina, Center for New Americans (CNA), our English Language Learner (ELL) department, and our Early Childhood Education program to organize a series of workshops about how schools work locally and globally. Casa Latina was the only Latinx-led and Latinx-focused community organization in our county at that time; its mission was to promote self-sufficiency and a sense of community among local Latinos. FWP cofounder, Eneida Garcia, was codirector. From the start, Eneida and I thought of How Schools Work as a kind of reciprocal education: Immigrant caregivers learning from each other, and educators listening to and learning from caregivers.

A Note on the Status of Puerto Rico, Also Known as Borikén

Taíno was the Arawakan language spoken by Taíno people throughout the Caribbean. It was the first indigenous language Europeans encountered, which is why Taíno is the source of many words used in English and Spanish today. These include Boricua/Borikén, barbecue, canoe, hammock, iguana, papaya, and tobacco. Taíno is not spoken as a first language today, but it is being taught in language revival programs. For Puerto Ricans born on the island, Spanish, imposed by colonizers for more than 400 years, is their first language. English is their second.

The United States invaded Puerto Rico in 1898, during the Spanish-American War. Puerto Ricans have been U.S. citizens since 1917 (though without Congressional representation). Therefore, Puerto Ricans who move to the mainland U.S. are technically internal migrants, but many self-identify as immigrants. The Puerto Rican Self-Determination Act of 2021 proposes a convention on Puerto Rico's status with elected delegates and eventually, Puerto Ricans voting in a binding referendum on the status of the island.

Migration surged after World War 2, with more than a million Puerto Ricans arriving on the mainland by the mid-1960s. According to the Boricua Solidarity Movement, Massachusetts now has more than 300,000 Puerto Rican residents. Holyoke, just south of Northampton, has one of the highest Puerto Rican populations per capita on the U.S. mainland. According to the 2008 American Community Survey, there were 4.2 million Puerto Ricans in the mainland United States, more than the 3.8 million remaining on the island of Puerto Rico. Puerto Ricans represent the second largest Latinx population in the United States, after Mexican Americans.

When families first arrive from Puerto Rico, they may have relatives here who help them settle and serve as guides. Many Puerto Ricans maintain close ties to the island and some visit often. Migration continues in both directions. Other than issues of documentation and citizenship, many issues of immigration are familiar to Puerto Ricans, who most often migrate for economic and family reasons. Many leaders and members of FWP are Puerto Rican, including Eneida, Doña Lucas, Elba, Nydia, Irma, Carmelo, Lourdes, and Edwin.

Immigrant and Puerto Rican caregivers from FWP and Casa Latina brainstormed with educators to help to plan and organize How Schools Work. We were guided by immigrant caregivers like Josefina Rodriguez, who described how she felt in a typical school meeting for parents: "You feel like you don't fit in, like I didn't understand the language they were talking about because it was so sophisticated and the way how they act different, just listen to the person who is in charge of the meeting. I feel like it is not equal. Everybody's voice is valuable. . . . I can't be there just sitting without saying what I think, because I think that my voice has power. I might have to say something really interesting. It felt really weird to be in that position, and I didn't come back."

Figure 12.2. Josefina Rodriguez greets participants at the first How Schools Work meeting (2011).

In our planning sessions we debated whether or not we should have Spanish interpretation. We initially thought we would, as FWP events were usually bilingual. Maureen McMahon, who has taught adult ELLs at Center for New Americans for decades, pointed out that this would not be equitable for ELLs who spoke other native languages. She also said that many of her students were looking for opportunities to practice using their English. Our solution: The majority of facilitators would be caregivers who spoke English as a second language. They would address the group in English, speaking more slowly than native speakers of English, with less academic vocabulary and educational jargon than educators. Newcomers who didn't have any English yet were able to partner with a bilingual speaker of their native language in their small group.

SOME PRINCIPLES WE DEVELOPED FOR HOW SCHOOLS WORK

Our target group consisted of families new to schools in the mainland United States. Some had arrived recently; those who had been here longer could relate to and support the experiences of newcomers. Caregivers were always the majority of the participants.

K–12 educators came to listen, learn, and build relationships with families. They also came to help make institutional changes to create more welcoming schools and provide logistical help as needed. Educators were not there to teach, make presentations, or give speeches. If we invited an administrator to listen to concerns or answer questions on a topic, it was our responsibility to brief the visitor on this approach.

Meetings were active and participatory, with everyone at the meeting getting a chance to speak, because, as Josefina said, "Everybody's voice is valuable." We spent 20 or 30 minutes on introductions. Immediately, everyone was talking with an interested partner about themselves, their families, and their experiences with school. Each person present was seen and heard. Everyone became accustomed to silence, as we used longer wait times for people to formulate their questions and ideas. The majority of facilitators were caregivers who spoke English as a second language. Most of the partner and small group work was spoken in slow, comprehensible English. As in all FWP activities, caregivers were up front, running the event. If educators were present, we were there as participants and sometimes for logistical support.

INSIDE A HOW SCHOOLS WORK MEETING

The first meeting of How Schools Work was in October 2011 in the Math Club room at Jackson St. School, where FWP activities like Cafés and

Family Dances were held. Volunteer drivers picked up families. FWP members and educators, several of whom were ELL teachers from a variety of district schools, started arriving at 6 p.m. to set up childcare, refreshments, and a welcome table.

As participants arrived, an FWP member greeted them and invited them to sign in, fill out a name tag, and help themselves to refreshments. Older FWP students helped bring children to the childcare room, take snacks, and settle in there. At 6:40, with participants seated in a circle, FWP member Josefina welcomed everyone, after which Janet explained that How Schools Work is a reciprocal education project, with immigrant caregivers learning from each other, and educators listening to and learning from caregivers. Next, Elba facilitated introductions. She divided the total number of participants (for example, 24) in half and then asked people to go around the circle, counting off from 1 to 12, with the remaining participants also counting off from 1 to 12. Then participants found their partner with the same number, introduced themselves and discussed: What is a difference between schools where you grew up and those in the United States?

Note that immigrant caregivers attending this meeting were greeted by other immigrant caregivers, and that the first three speakers were FWP members who were parents of color from the Dominican Republic, Uganda, and Puerto Rico, all of whom spoke English as their second language.

Figure 12.3 Josefina Rodriguez speaks in her small group at a How Schools Work meeting (2013).

More Prompts for Pair and Share Introductions

For variety, we occasionally started with 5-10 minutes for caregivers to draw in response to a prompt before sharing with their partner. Making a sketch allowed participants with less English or partners who didn't share a common language to express more. Sharing and discussing the drawings was a good way to notice similarities and differences, with repeated and powerful images pointing to generative themes. We only used one prompt per meeting:

- What are your hopes and dreams for your children?
- How were you taught math as a child, and how is that different than how your child is learning math now?
- Where you grew up . . .
    - » how did schools respond to differences or disabilities?
    - » what was school like for you?
    - » what did schools expect of your family?
    - » how did schools report to families about a student's progress?

Maureen, a well-loved English teacher from Center for New Americans, facilitated the introduction sharing. In pairs, partners introduced each other to the group, telling what they had learned about schools in their partner's country. After that, Eneida, who was familiar to many because of her work with Casa Latina, introduced Culture Circles. Participants counted off to create small groups, chose a photo or drawing representing a generative theme, and discussed it, making sure each person had the opportunity to talk. These simple line drawings or photos illustrated topics suggested by caregivers, including homework, Open House, and standardized tests.

The next facilitator was Barbara Black, Early Childhood Coordinator for Northampton; Barbara was often the first point of school contact for immigrant families with young children and served as both resource and advocate. Barbara invited each circle to share their discoveries with the group. On large chart paper, we took note of topics that arose from these discussions for future meetings, with a show of hands for interest.

Josefina closed the agenda, asking everyone to come to the next meeting with friends and relatives. She invited everyone to the upcoming FWP Café and Family Dance and connected people with rides. Participants socialized and exchanged contact information as they helped clean up. Through this informal networking, recently arrived caregivers found referrals to doctors, job leads, or someone willing to orient them to riding the public bus. Many friendships arose from these introductions, within and across ethnic groups. In our first FWP retreat, every immigrant caregiver spoke about how isolating their early experience in our community was. The relationships that grew from How Schools Work were an effective antidote to that isolation.

At our first meeting of How Schools Work, there was a lot of interest in upcoming parent–teacher conferences, which became the topic of our second meeting. We encouraged teachers to invite immigrant families from their classes, and to come themselves if they wanted to participate in role-plays with caregivers. Opportunities like this, which were specific about how to invite families, as well as the ways educators could participate, opened the door for more colleagues to take part. This kind of grassroots professional development immersed educators in family engagement and international education.

We invited educators, starting with ELL teachers from other schools, and they in turn brought their students and families, who often had children of many different ages. From the beginning, our focus was larger than just elementary school, with concerns ranging from preschool through high school. While these meetings started at Jackson Street School, they eventually alternated locations with another elementary school in our district. How Schools Work started meeting monthly in October 2011 and continued until March 2016.

We asked questions such as these at every meeting:

- What kinds of activities would you and your children like to find at school?
- What do you want educators to know about organizing events?
- What are culturally appropriate ways to invite families?
- What days/times are good for you to attend activities?
- What would you like to learn more about?
- What community activities should educators attend?
- What community leaders should educators get to know?
- What seems weird to you about the way our school does things?

GENERATIVE THEMES

The generative themes that sparked a lot of discussion in the Culture Circle process became topics of future workshops, for more problem posing, dialogue, problem solving, and action. This is a sampling of topics we explored:

- Report cards: how to understand and respond to them, how they make caregivers feel, how to learn about curriculum and grade level goals.
- Getting help for your child; learning what resources exist in the school and community for children (toddler through teenage years). We discussed how to obtain early interventions like speech, physical, and occupational therapy; what ELL services are "automatic"; and how to request a native language interpreter for a newcomer. We

discussed how to find bilingual therapists in the community, as well as how to advocate for academic support for your child.

- Homework: reasonable expectations, how to help with study, how caregivers handle arguments from students or not handle understanding the material.
- Language and culture: how to maintain and develop native language and literacy and affirm culture in the face of English dominance and assimilation pressure.
- Open House: what it looks like in elementary, middle, and high school; why it is worth going; and role-playing Open House interactions with teachers.
- Concerning standardized state tests: who is exempt (newcomers only in their first year) and how to understand the results; the "screener" assessments the district used to determine if elementary students were eligible for Title I support; the state tests used to show the progress of English language learners.
- Communication: the school newsletter and how to get it interpreted; how to communicate with the office, and with your child's teacher.
- Parent–teacher conferences: how to schedule one; what to expect in one; role-playing how to ask a question or raise a concern with a teacher.

One Immigrant Family's Experience

Interview with Rania Al-Qudsi, participant in How Schools Work

What was your experience before coming to Jackson Street School?

When my daughter, Rasha, started at the other school, we were fine. As the time goes on, she doesn't want to get up when I wake her, she cries. She used to be excited to go to school. I start getting worried, that there's something at the school that changed her mood so fast. When I asked her about her day every day, she was upset, told me "I hate my teacher because she doesn't let me go to recess or give me stickers like other kids." I knew there was something going on with the teacher. So, I went to the school, decided to talk with the teacher, why Rasha doesn't want to go to school anymore, every day comes home upset and crying. I talk to the office. They told me I have to make appointment but didn't give me any specific time. Every day after school I tried, but it didn't happen. After two weeks trying to meet with the teacher, I got so mad because my daughter was getting emotionally worse about the school. Finally, I got mad and said, "If I don't see the teacher right now, I have to go find an attorney." Two minutes later, everyone was in the meeting room with me, the principal, teacher, another two staff. I told the teacher and staff Rasha isn't happy. I explained she isn't going to recess with other kids, never got stickers or anything. The teacher complain that Rasha never finished the classwork, had to stay in the classroom. I didn't agree, because when Rasha is home, I do the work with her and she does it on time. It wasn't true what the teacher said. I told the teacher, "Even if she didn't finish the work, she's a child, 6 years old, and she needs to be treated equal with other children. You punish her for something she doesn't understand." The staff was supporting the teacher, backing her up, trying to cover her, because they were worried when I said attorney. After that, the teacher start to slow down her behavior with Rasha, but she was never happy with her.

This teacher, I could touch her hate toward Rasha. Kids know when the adult doesn't like them. If you show them love, they will love you back. One day when I went to pick up Rasha, the teacher looked mad and started to complain about Rasha's behavior. "Your daughter was rude, didn't listen."

I didn't understand why the teacher was so mad. I talked to Rasha at home in Arabic. She said, "The teacher drew a "happy pinky" (happy face on the finger) to all the other kids but not me, so I took the pen and put the happy pinky on myself." That made the teacher so mad.

After a while we had to move to different school. We were so happy we don't have to deal with that teacher any more.

What can teachers do to make students and families from other countries feel welcome in their schools?

The teachers can be more close with the children, especially if the children come from other countries. If they start to show some interest in their language, even if they know just a couple of words, it will make the children feel more comfortable. They feel they are at their home. I think they will feel happy. Also, the teacher makes the idea to meet with their families. Even if they don't speak English, start to communicate with them. Start with a small meeting, and that will make parents more comfortable with the school. They don't feel, "I'm lost. I don't know what to do." If the teachers start doing that, it will be so helpful for the people to communicate with the school in a better way.

ENGAGING CAREGIVERS IN EDUCATIONAL DECISION-MAKING

Parents of all backgrounds are concerned about how their children are doing in school. For immigrant parents, this may be complicated by vastly different curricula and pedagogy, as well as by age level expectations and interrupted schooling. If a child is not meeting a teacher's expectations, parents may wonder how much of this is related to English being a new language, as well as to the lack of instructional support in their native language. There is, of course, the added fear of a possible learning disability. This can cut both ways. Sometimes a parent suspects there may be a disability and a teacher dismisses that anxiety, chalking it up to learning English. At other times, caregivers may feel a teacher is too quick to refer an English language learner to be evaluated for a learning disability, feeling the child just needs more time to adjust to a new language and culture or to mature. There is well-documented overrepresentation of English language learners in special education.

One immigrant father of a 1st-grade student who was a newcomer to English learned from the end-of-year report card that his son had not yet learned to read. The father was angry, saying, "Every day, every day I pick my son up from school, find his teacher and ask how he doing. And every day, every day the teacher tell me fine. Now I see he cannot read. This is not fine!" This was an instance where the teacher was giving the student the benefit of the doubt, wanting to give him more time to acquire English, saying "Fine," to mean that the student was well behaved and tried hard. The teacher hadn't had a clear conversation with the parents about his progress or challenges, nor had the teacher heard their concerns or given them options.

As educators, we know these are complicated questions and that there is no one-size-fits-all solution. In my experience, I have observed that White, educated, professional parents are more likely to demand and receive extra meetings and have their requests granted than low-income and immigrant parents with less education, who are more likely to be intimidated or overruled by the authority and expertise of educators. Effectively, more of the latter's requests are denied, and their role in making educational decisions for their children is reduced.

Our Title I programs in reading and math are considered regular education programs; they give struggling students expert, targeted, small group instruction to bring them up to grade level. I was a Title I math teacher, but I was also certified in teaching English as a second language, as was Linda Barca, our Title I reading teacher. While this isn't the case in all schools, our Title I math and reading students received an extra helping of ELL support. As a result, we were able to provide Title I academic support for newcomer ELLs sooner. This helped to bring them up to grade level more quickly.

In response to what we were hearing from immigrant parents in How Schools Work, Linda and I worked to make the "parent engagement" aspect of Title I real, not just an exercise in required paperwork. We invited immigrant parents from How Schools Work and other caregivers of Title I students, especially low-income and people of color, to participate in the process of drafting the family involvement policy. Together we wrote the "Partners in Learning Agreement" which included commitments from the caregiver, student, and teacher. Writing these documents with caregivers and getting them translated into English, Spanish, and Arabic was an important step, but they are only pieces of paper if all we do is ask people to sign them.

When I first thought about caregivers making educational decisions, I tended to think about *personal* decisions regarding their own children, such as receiving a native language tutor, Title I reading or math support, when or whether to request an evaluation for special education. It was only later that I began to think about caregivers, especially those who were historically underrepresented, making *institutional* educational decisions about things like hiring, policy, budget, and programs.

Caregivers need accurate information about how their child is doing in reading and math. They need to feel comfortable talking with the educator about their "whole child": their level of English acquisition, access to the curriculum, and social and emotional development. This may include discussion of family stressors, such as missing an absent parent. The caregiver needs information about the curriculum, grade level expectations, and pedagogy, which may be unfamiliar, as well as ways to support their child. For example, in many countries, children learn to write in cursive in kindergarten or 1st grade or start to memorize multiplication facts in 2nd grade. The caregiver needs to feel comfortable understanding, asking questions, and making decisions about what services they would like for their child. They need information about their rights, and about how to advocate effectively. To get all of this information at once, for instance, in a booklet or single meeting, can be overwhelming, especially if it requires listening to or reading a lot of educational jargon.

Rather, the most important element is the reciprocal relationship between caregiver and educator. We need to establish effective two-way communication in each unique relationship. In this way the caregiver will have authentic and ongoing access to critical information and will be able to use it to make decisions about their child's education. This is not easy to accomplish, but it is essential for effective partnerships with families. Some schools never get there. They check an obligatory box after doing some superficial, one-way communication: a meeting leaflet, a signed permission slip, or attendance at a lecture-style meeting. I know from experience that those do not yield equivalent results.

The other kind of educational decision-making is broader and carries more institutional impact. At first, Linda and I hadn't read the law, so we didn't know the requirements, or even that there *was* a district budget for family engagement, let alone how much it was, or how we could spend it. If *we* didn't know, surely the caregivers didn't know. We partnered with a willing administrator to educate ourselves and share the information with other Title I teachers in the district, turning that knowledge into power. But it wasn't sufficient to empower educators. That was just a step toward the goal of caregivers making educational decisions at the school and district level.

It is good to offer families workshops about math and reading, but it is better to enable families to make these decisions. I offered a variety of programs, developed with caregivers: Morning Math Club, Family Math

Parties, and How Children Learn Math family workshops, but I needed, always, to stay open to new ideas. I had to remember: It's not *my* party. Real family engagement is not just what I am willing to offer. It needs to be what families want.

Immigrant parents who became active through How Schools Work became the backbone of our Title I family engagement program. At first, they seemed unsure about why Linda and I were asking for their ideas and opinions. As they grew to understand the importance of their role as decision-makers, they rose to the occasion with enthusiasm and innovation, to create programs and activities they felt their children needed.

FWP programs like Morning Math Club and Healthy Cooking Classes were entry points for immigrant families to participate at school. They fed naturally into How Schools Work, where families were confident they would not be "the only one." In fact, they were often walking or driving to How Schools Work meetings with other immigrant caregivers they'd met at Math Club or cooking classes. The development of immigrant caregiver leadership through How Schools Work intertwined with authentic family involvement in Title I. How Schools Work and the language and culture clubs it generated strengthened and deepened authentic relationships between immigrant caregivers and educators. We did not know it back in 2011, but the years to come would test the strength of that foundation.

CHAPTER 13

Immigration: Language and Culture Clubs

"Rasha, your mother and aunt invited me to the masjid [mosque] this afternoon. This will be my first time going. Do you have any advice for me?"

Rasha, a 5th-grader, looked at me thoughtfully. "Before you go in the prayer room, you will see where to leave your shoes. Ms. Cowhey, just after you go in the first door, before you go in the second door, say a little prayer in your heart."

Rasha's mother and aunt, Rania and Reem, had invited me to attend a meeting about resettling Syrian refugees in our area. My daughter and her friend, Laura, both high school juniors who were studying Arabic, had asked if they could attend. Our early childhood coordinator, Barbara Black, asked to come too.

During her sophomore year, Laura had been an exchange student in Oman, where she wore a head scarf when visiting a mosque. Barbara said that when she visited Israel, she would always bring a shawl to cover her head. Laura brought some scarves and offered to fix one for each of us in our little car. We followed others to the front door of the mosque. I didn't see a place to leave shoes. We followed others through the second door.

We found seats on the right side, where other women were sitting. More people arrived; all kept their shoes on. I saw a couple of women I knew; neither wore a scarf. Eventually the meeting started, with an overview of the Syrian refugee crisis and the work of the three largest refugee resettlement agencies in our region. The president of the Islamic Society of Western Mass proposed that they should step up their support for refugees. During the discussion, a member said that he did not know how useful he and other members who did not speak Arabic would be in supporting Arabic-speaking Syrian refugees. This reminded me that not all Muslims are Arabs, and not all Arabs are Muslims. Rania and Reem spoke Arabic as their native language. But I remembered that I knew Albanian and Pakistani families who belonged to this mosque; they spoke Albanian and Urdu, not Arabic. I reminded myself that being able to recite prayers or read the Qur'an in Arabic was different from being able to have a conversation in Arabic. Of course, the mosque had many members who were not fluent Arabic speakers.

I focused on the conversation that was now about how schools could best support Syrian refugee children. I heard a soft giggle and looked across the room, to a second row of chairs that had filled in with latecomers. I saw Rania and Reem;

apparently, they had just recognized us. Rania took out her phone and snapped a photo. That's when I remembered to say a little prayer in my heart.

After the meeting, Rania and Reem came over, hugged us, thanked us for coming, and Rania giggled again. She took out her phone and showed us the photo she had taken of us, with our drooping scarves. I laughed along with her at the comical sight. (November 2015)

On my first visit to Rania and Reem's mosque, I learned many things. These were baby steps in my cultural education. Masjid is the Arabic word for mosque. Many Arabic speakers in our community use the word masjid when speaking English. The mosque has a large community hall, which I returned to many times over the years, for interfaith vigils, Iftar meals during Ramadan and other community meetings. In that space, there was no expectation that non-Muslim women would cover their heads. Some Muslim women wore the hijab and others did not. After the meeting, there was a community meal with one buffet line for women and another for men.

I next visited the mosque for an interfaith gathering. When the call to prayer came, Rania invited me to join the women for prayer. I followed her down a corridor from the community hall, out one side door and back into another, where there were benches to sit down and shelves to leave one's shoes. I recognized this as the space that Rasha described before my first visit. I pulled a shawl over my head and said a little prayer in my heart. As we entered the prayer room, other women smiled at me. I said, "Al salaam alaikum." They smiled even more warmly and replied, "Waa alaikum salaam."

STEPPING OUT OF OUR CULTURAL COMFORT ZONE

Student teachers have often expressed anxiety about making home visits, usually—though seldom explicitly stated—to the homes of families who are culturally different from themselves. In our conversations, I try to gently probe that anxiety, to ask what frightens them. After some hesitation, they offer, "What if it's awkward? What if I make a mistake? What if they laugh at me?" To be honest, these are all distinct possibilities when entering a culturally different space, as this story of my first visit to the mosque illustrates. And yes, that could feel scary, so I would like to share a story with you about when scary things happen.

When my son was 12 and my daughter was 5, my husband and I brought them on a 10-day wilderness portage canoe trip in the Adirondacks. Back then, my son was afraid of thunder and lightning, spiders, bears, and getting lost. We had daily and nightly thunderstorms. When we got out of the canoe to portage, the boggy ground slowly sank beneath us, and my daughter yelled, "The water is coming over the top of my boots!" Packing lightly, we each had only two pairs of socks. We saw large piles of bear scat on the portage trails. On the third day of the trip, in a downpour, my son got lost. We were 3 days away from reaching a ranger to ask for help, and my son was carrying our food pack. We searched and found him within an hour. On the tenth day, a spider bit him. I had been upset with my husband that the trip was harder and more dangerous than I anticipated and was afraid that my kids would be traumatized by it. A wise family friend said, "Why? They learned that all of the scariest things could happen, and they could still be okay."

Remember this when you step out of your cultural comfort zone: *All of the scariest things could happen, and you could still be okay.* As a White person, I am acutely aware that I am *choosing* to make myself vulnerable when I leave the White-dominated spaces I often occupy. For many immigrants and people of color living in the United States, stepping out of one's cultural comfort zone isn't a choice; it's a daily necessity. It is when I am outside my usual cultural comfort zone that I gain the most insight into the importance of having nondominant cultural comfort zones within our school.

This chapter will focus on the language and culture clubs that grew from How Schools Work and how the clubs created other cultural comfort zones in our school. We had three clubs: French, Spanish, and Arabic. I will begin with telling you how the francophone club began, and then focus on the Arabic Community Club, which had the greatest impact.

CLUB DES FAMILLES ET DES AMIS FRANCOPHONES

At a How Schools Work meeting in 2014, francophone parents from France, Haiti, and Côte D'Ivoire, most of whom had just met, were talking together about how frustrating it is to see their children stop speaking French after moving to the United States. Other immigrant parents echoed this concern. Eneida Garcia, one of the FWP founders, said that she had a strict rule that her children could only speak Spanish in her home. In fact, she charged them a quarter if they spoke English.

While the FWP reading parties were often bilingual (Spanish and English), Eneida wanted those to be welcoming to people who spoke any language, so they were never only in Spanish. Yet she said she wished there was some kind of club that was all Spanish-speaking, to encourage kids to speak Spanish more and realize how important, valuable, and cool it is to be fluent in two languages. Mathilde, Rose, and Alfred were intrigued by Eneida's language club idea.

In November 2014, Mathilde, Rose, and Alfred started a small club. Mathilde said she'd bring pizza, some French picture books and games we could play in French. They all contacted French-speaking families they knew, and I asked the ELL teachers to invite French-speaking families in our school. We met in my room one evening. Several families and a teacher who had attended a French bilingual school came.

Alfred came with his children, Brian and Chloé. Brian was fluently reading and writing in French when he arrived in 1st grade. Now in 4th grade, he could switch effortlessly between English and French. Chloé, a 1st-grader, had arrived as a preschooler and was now English dominant. Mathilde's daughter, Charlotte, and Chloé liked the pizza but balked at the idea of speaking French. Mathilde, Alfred, Brian, and my daughter, Mairead, spoke in French. After a short while, Charlotte gave up begging them to speak English. She liked to play teacher and realized that if she spoke French, she could hold the marker and stand at the easel, which made it worthwhile.

Chloé was frustrated and said to me, "I hate this! I don't speak French. This is stupid. Why should I speak French?"

I answered her very slowly, "*Chloé, tu née francophone en Côte D'Ivoire. Parler français et anglais est très cool, plus cool de parler anglais solamente.*" (I was trying to say, "You were born a francophone in Ivory Coast. To speak French and English is very cool, cooler than speaking only English.) When she smiled, I realized I'd accidentally thrown in a little Spanish (*solamente*), as I often do when searching for a French word, but more importantly, she'd recognized it was out of place. I pressed on, "*Je parle un peu de français, comme un bébé, mais je comprends un peu plus.*" (I speak a little French, like a baby, but I understand a little more.) Chloé stifled laughter. "*Ici ce soir, j'écoute et je parle un peu en français. C'est difficile et je fais mucho mistakes, mais j'ai un growth mindset, comme el Club de Mathématiques de Matin.*" Chloé giggled. "*N'est-ce que pas?*" (Tonight, I listen and speak a little French. It's difficult, and I make a lot of mistakes, but I have a growth mindset, like in Morning Math Club, right?) She shrugged. Her father said something to her in French. Chloé made a face at me and sighed, then answered in French. Her French was better than mine.

Mathilde had chosen a theme of animals for the first meeting, so we sat in a circle, introduced ourselves in French and named our favorite animal. Mathilde had written sentence stems on the board, to support the less fluent. She read a picture book about a bear. We played games like Twenty Questions about animals, animal bingo, and *Jeu de L'oie* (Game of the Goose), a classic French board game, all in French. At each table there was an adult who spoke French fluently leading an activity, so that less fluent children (or adults, like me) could get support and encouragement in speaking French.

At the end of the first meeting, a consensus developed to meet monthly, and to give families more notice about the meetings. We discussed naming the group. Mathilde suggested, "How about French Club?" Alfred objected. Mathilde looked at him, surprised.

Alfred said, "You are French, but I am not French. Not every French speaker is French. I am from a former French colony. I am a francophone.

How about Francophone Family Club?" Mathilde agreed, and in the end, they amended it to *Club des familles et des amis francophones* (Francophone Family and Friends Club) or "Le Club" for short. Le Club continued to meet monthly. Haitians, French Canadians, Swiss, and other francophones joined us.

One of the cool things about having a club is being part of it. When I saw children or adults from *Club des familles et des amis francophones* in the hallway they would always say, *"Bonjour! Comment ça va?"* Other students looked with curiosity and admiration at their classmates who could speak two languages.

ARABIC COMMUNITY CLUB

At the December 2014 How Schools Work meeting, Alfred and Mathilde reported on *Club des familles et des amis francophones*. Rania said she would like to start a class to teach Arabic to children. She thought her sister, Reem, would help. Reem was an engineer on maternity leave from her job, running a small Arabic-speaking daycare in her home with her children in a nearby city. I explained that our school had an afterschool program and that they could submit a proposal to lead a class. I didn't know all the details about the program, but Pallavi, who was active in both How Schools Work and Morning Math Club, had just submitted a proposal to start a computer coding club. She offered to help Rania fill out the paperwork after Math Club the next day. A few children signed up, but not the minimum of six needed for an after-school class.

I felt bad breaking the news to Rania. She was quiet a moment, then said, "We have to find another way." While an afterschool class needed a minimum of six students to sign up, there were no rules about family clubs.

In January 2015 we scheduled our first Arabic Club meeting at 5 p.m. on a Friday. I realized my daughter had a track meet at 4:00 that day and told Rania I'd be a little late. When I arrived at 5:15 the room was already crowded with adults and children sitting in a circle. Arabic-speaking students attended with their parents and some of their teachers. Rasha's 3rd-grade teacher, Kim Gerould, and her daughter, Yamila Irizarry-Gerould, were there. Yamila had recently moved home from Jordan after living in the Middle East for 4 years. Rasha's ELL teacher was there too. There were many other people I did not know. I greeted the group, *"Al salaam alaikum"* (using my entire Arabic vocabulary), and sat down to listen. There was Arabic writing on the easel. It sounded like people were saying, *"Anna iss me"* and then their names. When it was my turn, I said, *"Anna iss me Mary Cowhey,"* and everyone nodded. Arabic speakers said more, like names of their children or countries.

Next, Rasheed, a 5th-grader, chose a picture book to read aloud in Arabic. The Arabic speaking children enjoyed this, but I noticed he was also reading to his teachers, showing us that he could do this very well. He touched certain pictures, repeating the vocabulary words for those who were new to Arabic. We leaned in and repeated after him. I whispered what the pictures were to Barbara Black, who is blind, and she said them softly in Arabic.

Later, Reem gave a signal, and it was time to eat. First, Amena offered everyone a date. Then Rasheed came around with a carafe of Saudi coffee, while his little sister, Safiya, carried small cups. Everyone seemed excited about the Saudi coffee, and several people whispered to me that Saudi coffee is *very* good. When I asked if it was decaf, they laughed at my ridiculous question and shook their heads no. I was surprised when Rasheed poured my coffee, and it was yellow. No one put milk or sugar in the coffee. Rasha offered squares of *namoura*, a cake soaked in sweet syrup, with a whole almond pressed into the top of each piece. Over coffee, the group decided to meet monthly and call itself Arabic Community Club.

For the next meeting, Rania invited her friend, Luisa, and her husband, Angel, who worked at a Moroccan restaurant and wanted to understand more Arabic. Angel took as many notes as I did. After everyone left, I found Angel's notes and realized he was doing what I was doing but with Spanish definitions and phonetic spelling for the Arabic. Other non-Arabic speakers from the school and community began to come regularly too.

From First Impessions to Challenging My Own Stereotypes

When I first started teaching Arabic-speaking students, their fathers came to school, introduced themselves and took care of school business. They tended to be highly educated graduate students at nearby UMass and spoke English fluently. These fathers said their wives didn't speak English and that I should contact them (the fathers) about school matters. My students told me that their mothers were in fact the ones who supervised their homework because their fathers spent long hours as residents at the hospital or at the university as graduate students. (In nearby Springfield and West Springfield, there are more Middle Eastern refugees and immigrants with more diverse levels of education and English fluency.) Sometimes I saw the mothers, wearing hijabs and long coats, walking their children to school, often kissing them goodbye at the crosswalk. I rarely interacted with the mothers at first, so my impression was that they seemed shy.

That first impression of shyness changed as I got to know the mothers through Arabic Community Club, and then through Morning Math Club and How Schools Work. In these other contexts where there was a critical mass of Arabic-speaking, Muslim, and other immigrant women, I learned how friendly, helpful, curious, and opinionated these women were. Further, Arabic Community Club had members from Jordan, Palestine, Morocco, Syria, Saudi Arabia, and Egypt. The more Arab families I met, the more variation I found, as is the case in every culture.

Meet Rania and Reem

Rania and Reem are Jordanian-born Palestinian sisters. Their parents were among the 700,000 Palestinians forced to leave their homeland in 1948 in the Israeli invasion that Palestinians call the *Nakba* (Catastrophe).

Rania moved to the United States in 2011 and lived in several different towns before settling in Northampton in 2014. She was divorced and lived with her daughter, Rasha, in public housing near Jackson St. School. They were the only Arab family who lived there. Most other Arab families lived in the apartment complex next to it. Rania is soft-spoken, with a high voice. She is funny, with an easy, beautiful smile and a delightful laugh.

Rania is a model for growth mindset. She is eternally curious and constantly learning, always asking the meaning of a word or idiom, or how to put together a phrase, or about cultural ways of doing things. Rania strikes me as an informal diplomat, always looking to develop relationships, to communicate across cultures. When we met in 2014, she was learning English and preparing for her high school equivalency exam at the Literacy Project. Her dream then was to attend community college to become a phlebotomist or ultrasound technician. She later became a citizen and went on to graduate from community college; she recently transferred to Smith College to complete her bachelor's degree. Rania is persistent in her soft-spoken way. When she has something to say, she will say it. She does not let anyone silence her.

Reem is more serious, but her humor is witty and a bit sarcastic. She is confident in her intellect, English fluency, and professional ability as an engineer. She is married and shares childcare with her husband. Reem is more reserved than Rania, but she is forceful when she speaks.

For me, one of the most powerful things I gained from Arabic Community Club was breaking my stereotypes about Arab culture. Of course, I would have been offended by an obvious stereotype, like someone saying that all Arabs are terrorists. However, it was only as I got to know more Muslim women through Arabic Community Club that I began to think critically about stereotypical media portrayals of Muslim women that I had internalized. In her book, *Do Muslim Women Need Saving?*, Lila Abu-Lughod (2013) explores the impulse to blame gendered violence on (Muslim) culture. "After the attacks of September 11, 2001, the images of oppressed Muslim women became connected to a mission to rescue them from their cultures" (pp. 6–7). That media narrative promoted the stereotype that Muslim women were passive, oppressed, and in need of "saving." That narrative also served the larger purpose of rationalizing the U.S. occupation of Afghanistan. While getting to know one or two Arab individuals didn't dispel all my stereotypes or give me a complex understanding of Arab culture, getting to know more Muslim women did challenge stereotypes I hadn't recognized before. As a non-Muslim, I cannot do justice to understanding or explaining the complexity and depth of Islam or Arab culture, but I encourage you to learn more, as I continue to learn.

Alif, Baa

Amena, who had been a science teacher in Saudi Arabia, was trying very hard to teach the adult Arabic learners the letters, starting with *alif* and *baa*. After several lessons (and little or no practice) I still could not write or recognize them. I could relate to how hard it must be to learn English, with different letters and very different sounds that are difficult even to record phonetically with English letters. Yamila helped with calling certain sounds "Papa H" or saying, "It's like a Darth Vader sound." I had to repeat many words four or five times, often sounding like a cat bringing up a hairball, to even approximate the pronunciation. I said that I thought maybe I'd do better with just conversation for now and work up to the reading and writing later.

In the June 2015 meeting of Arabic Community Club, we gathered to discuss ideas for the coming year. I asked if the group planned to continue meeting monthly in the fall. Reem's husband, Abdul, looked at me kindly and said, "Ms. Cowhey, at this pace, you will never learn to speak Arabic. Once a month is just not enough. It must be weekly." I knew my progress had been pathetic, but . . . I looked around the circle. Everyone else was nodding in agreement.

For the previous 6 months, I had been thinking that the primary purpose of the Arabic Community Club, like *Club des familles et des amis francophone*, was to encourage the children to maintain and take pride in their native language. In Arabic Community Club, that specifically included teaching the children to read and write Arabic. Reem, Rania, and Amena were also teaching the other educators and me Arabic. I started trying to learn Arabic to be polite, so that maybe I could say something besides "*Al Salaam alaikum.*" Of course, if I could say only one thing in any language, "May peace be upon you" is a good place to start. I enjoyed learning a handful of high-frequency expressions, like *in sha Allah* (God willing), *al-hamdulillah* (thank God), and *yallah* (let's go, useful for herding young children). I had low expectations for myself and honestly hadn't invested additional time to study; indeed, I hadn't even truly considered myself a learner.

As the months passed, I felt that perhaps my presence had hijacked the purpose of the Arabic Community Club, that the members were wasting their time trying to teach me. Suddenly, with Abdul's honest assessment of my progress, I understood. I had felt that Arabic Community Club wasn't quite successful because members had not identified problems or issues they wanted to pursue in the way that FWP usually did. I asked if there were community issues or other concerns members might want to discuss, but Reem sternly said, "We should not discuss politics here. It is divisive." Suddenly I could see what had been there all along: that teaching American educators Arabic empowered the Arabic-speaking students, parents, and community members because it gave them an opportunity to demonstrate their expertise and competence in doing this and built a bridge between us. Maybe it was also good to practice their English and hang out with some friendly Americans, to have a safe space to ask cultural questions. I was embarrassed that it took me 6 months to understand what everyone else seemed to know from the start.

The Arabic Community Club is patient, and like Rania, persistent. I vowed to study and practice Arabic more. It did not matter that I did not learn Arabic rapidly. What mattered was that we spent a lot of quality time together as the families taught me, and I tried to learn.

"Break the Scare Between Us"

Interview with Rania Al Qudsi, founder of Arabic Community Club

What is the role of culture clubs in breaking down stereotypes?

Americans grow up in the different country. They never see our culture before. The culture clubs will break the scare between us. Before we start these activities, I was really close to myself, my family, and my culture, but after starting Arabic Community Club, I start to join other people. It really helps us to understand other people to join with their life.

Why did you start the Arabic Community Club and how?

The first or second week that Rasha was at Jackson Street School in second grade, her teacher came out to talk to me after school. He said, "I want to tell you something! I can count to ten in Arabic!"

I said, "What? Who teach you?" He said Rasha.

I asked Rasha why she did that. She said, "He wants me to learn English numbers. I said, 'Do you know Arabic? I can teach you Arabic numbers.'

From there, I start thinking *Why not teach Arabic to the teachers and whoever wants to learn?*

My sister and I start this club. Why don't we meet once a month for community, for everybody who speaks Arabic to come and the teachers in Jackson Street School and anyone who would like to learn some Arabic? It was a really good idea. Many people start to join. We have fun in Arabic Community Club. Then we decided to make the club every week.

I really want Rasha to know there are some [non-Arab] people who speak Arabic and your teachers also, they can learn Arabic. The Arabic is not like something weird, because we live in the U.S. This idea was very helpful for us and for the families who joined us. Rasha taught her teachers some Arabic words and numbers. They are really interested about Rasha's language because they want to be more close with her.

In this school they mix like international school. It is open for any other community so it's not like they're from another planet. It's Middle East. It's part of the Earth. It makes people open, like there's some people speak Arabic, Spanish, French. This really good idea in this school because it makes the children understand the whole world, not just stay in their classroom, do their homework, and go. No, it feels like college, not school for children. I love in this school, any idea the parents have, Jackson Street School embraces the idea. They never say, "That sounds weird. We never had that before. Who's going to come if we make Arabic Community Club?" They just do it [gestures a flinging motion]. This is a really beautiful idea for our school, and I love it.

I noticed at Families with Power reading parties that you speak some Spanish.

Yes, I love learning Spanish, and Rasha love it too, because many people around here speak Spanish. Sometimes it's really difficult for us to communicate because my English is so-so and their English is so-so. I love to talk to them in their language, because when you talk to people in their language, you talk to the heart.

This is a very important idea because we teach our children there is another people like us but they speak another language, have a different culture, sometimes different food, but at the end of the day, they are human like us. We have to respect their culture. We have to understand their rules and their life. If we keep our children close only in their culture, they will have a difficult time to communicate with others. They would think, "These people are different. These people don't understand me." No, our children will understand everything when we make different cultures in the school. This is really important for our children, to teach them every different culture, to grow up in a healthy way.

CHALLENGING ENGLISH HEGEMONY

In the spring of 2015, Courtney Vargas, a student at Marlboro College in Vermont, asked me to be an outside expert to help evaluate her final project, *Incorporating Social Justice Ideology into English Language Teaching*. In her project, she referred to the work of Joseph and Ramani (2006) on multilingualism and English hegemony. Vargas wrote, "The hegemony of English needs to be challenged. Having a bilingual or multilingual program set in the multilingual context of global English would make this possible. The problem is that people are not only desiring English but also believing it is natural to treat English as the dominant language."

As I read Vargas's paper, I thought about Arabic Community Club and my conversation with Rania. Every member of that club studies English seriously. They desire English, but their participation in the club demonstrates that they do not treat English as the dominant language. They celebrate Arab culture and Arabic language, which is spoken by more than 400 million people around the world.

Vargas also cited the work of Jasone Cenoz (2009), who wrote that a shift from English language teaching to multilingual education will help create a "transformed multilingual identity" that will challenge a monolithic view of culture.

I reflected on the story of Rasha's creative resistance as a tiny 1st-grader standing up to a powerful teacher's discrimination. That teacher's authority rested on a monolithic view of culture that her colleagues and administrators reinforced. When the teacher refused to give Rasha the "happy pinky" she had given every other student in the class, Rasha took the teacher's pen and drew the happy face on her finger herself. Her teacher saw disobedience; I saw agency and a child's challenge to her school's monolithic view of culture.

"English-Only instruction"

In 2001, I earned my master's degree in multicultural education and in teaching English as a Second Language. But by 2015, a discussion of multilingualism was not flourishing in public schools in Massachusetts. Massachusetts had been the first state in the nation to pass a law mandating "transitional bilingual education" in 1971, but bilingual education was outlawed in Massachusetts in 2002 with the passage of an "English-only instruction" ballot measure. According to the Massachusetts attorney general's summary of the ballot initiative, the law required "public schools to educate English learners . . . through a sheltered English immersion program, normally not lasting more than one year. In the program, all books and nearly all teaching would be in English, with the curriculum designed for children learning English. . . . All English learners in grades 2 and up would take annual written standardized tests, in English, of academic subjects" (Galvin 2002).

The English Language Education in Public Schools Initiative was punitive toward educators, allowing parents and guardians to sue educators to enforce it. A teacher who used a language other than English for instruction in violation of the law could be personally sued and would have to pay legal fees and damages personally (rather than be covered by liability insurance through the union). They might also lose their right to teach in public schools for five years. To say that it had a "chilling effect" would be an understatement.

In 2014, I became active in the Massachusetts Teachers Association, as a member of Educators for a Democratic Union (EDU), a caucus of rank-and-file unionists in the MTA working to build a participatory, democratic, social justice movement in our union and communities. EDU's vision of solidarity with educators, students, families, and activists in our communities taking action to improve our public schools appealed to me. EDU dramatically increased democratic rank-and-file participation in the union, encouraging members to bring new business items to the annual statewide meeting. In relation to "English-only instruction," members proposed the creation of a committee on bilingual education and voiced support for legislation to repeal the English Language Education in Public Schools Initiative. This policy work of MTA at the legislative level was vital in changing existing laws that fail students and constrain teachers from engaging in research-based best practice. Those union efforts are strengthened by family partnership in the legislative process.

In 2017, after years of MTA advocacy, the Massachusetts legislature finally repealed the English-only law and allowed schools and families more flexibility to choose programs to best meet students' needs. Students who attain high proficiency in English and an additional language can earn a "seal of biliteracy," a special recognition now offered in almost 30 states.

The English-only law in Massachusetts created an extreme version of a subtractive model of language education. Parents were justifiably upset about children losing their native languages. Many viewed it as a failure. According to the Massachusetts Department of Elementary and Secondary Education website report of 4-year graduation rates for the 2014 cohort, 63.9% of ELLs graduated, compared to 86.1% of all students. The English-only law was a manifestation of a "monolithic view of culture." The language and culture clubs challenged that view and demonstrated an alternative.

I was interested in the connection between the ideas that Vargas raised in her project and my developing understanding of caregivers' perspectives about the language and culture clubs growing at Jackson Street School. For me, Rania embodies this ideal of a "transformed multilingual identity." Not only did Rania start the Arabic Community Club, but she regularly attended our Spanish bilingual reading parties. I savored how participants enjoyed themselves in multilingual settings. At one reading party, in the living room of her Colombian neighbor, she and Diana sat side by side, reading the English and Spanish versions of the same picture book, and then Rania read a poem in English and Arabic.

CULTURALLY SUSTAINING PEDAGOGY

In the spring of 2015, I also spoke to Professor Alison Schmitke and her students in the Department of Education Studies at the University of Oregon. I described the growth of these language and culture clubs at Jackson Street School. Alison said she used this as an example of "culturally sustaining pedagogy" and introduced me to the work of Django Paris. Much of my teaching practice is grounded in culturally relevant pedagogy, in contrast to deficit approaches. In *The Dreamkeepers: Successful Teaching for African-American Students*, Gloria Ladson-Billings describes culturally relevant pedagogy as "a pedagogy that empowers students intellectually, socially, emotionally, and politically by using cultural referents to impart knowledge, skills, and attitudes" (1994, pp. 17–18).

Paris writes that the purpose of deficit approaches "was to eradicate the linguistic, literate, and cultural practices many students of color brought . . . and to replace them with what were viewed as superior practices" (Paris, 2012, p. 93). Paris wrote that culturally relevant pedagogy and related resource pedagogies "repositioned the linguistic, cultural and literate practices of poor communities—particularly poor communities of color—as resources to honor, explore and extend in accessing Dominant American English language and literacy skills and other White, middle-class dominant cultural norms of acting and being that are demanded in schools" (Paris, 2012, p. 94).

Culturally sustaining pedagogy would not only respond to "the cultural experiences and practices" of students, but actually support students in "sustaining the cultural and linguistic competence of their communities" (Paris, 2012, p. 95). Our language and culture clubs did exactly this, especially when other educators and I participated as learners and let the community members drive the agenda. The clubs were a vehicle to "perpetuate and foster—to sustain—linguistic, literate, and cultural pluralism as part of the democratic project of schooling" (Paris, 2012, p. 95).

As a teacher in an "English only" state for most of my career, I agree with Paris that the monolingual and monocultural climate reinforced by English-only laws created the need for "equally explicit resistances that embrace cultural pluralism and cultural equality" (Paris, 2012, p. 93). I agree with Schmitke that the language and culture clubs that grew out of How Schools Work are an example of that kind of resistance.

We were unaware of Paris's theoretical framework of culturally sustaining pedagogy when caregivers created these clubs to solve a problem articulated by immigrant families who felt unseen and unheard in traditional school settings. These families were unwilling to watch the gradual erasure of their native language and culture; they resisted by creating space to preserve and promote it. I share this story of our experience with growing language and culture clubs as one example of what "explicit resistance that embraces cultural pluralism and cultural equality" can look like in a school community.

Figure 13.1. On a trilingual sign welcoming families to a Morning Math Club engineering exhibition, a student proudly annotated, "This is in Arabic" (2015).

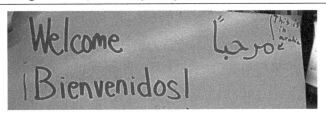

At the previous school her daughter attended, Rania was invisible and ignored, brushed aside until she finally got angry, and then she was probably considered a problem or a threat, certainly not an asset. At Jackson Street School, she was visible and heard. She was, without question, a valuable leader. Rasha's 1st-grade teacher had used the banking model of education, treating her like an empty glass, trying to force her to learn. Her teacher's deficit view of Rasha's language made her not even want to go to school, let alone to learn English. So Rasha resisted. In contrast, Mr. Adams, her teacher at Jackson Street School, celebrated her multilingual identity and humbly admitted his ignorance of Arabic, accepting his role as learner and Rasha's role as teacher. When he treated Rasha with kindness and respect, she felt brave enough to teach him. His eagerness to learn Arabic from Rasha opened the door to her willingness to learn as well.

Learners and producers of knowledge

In the late winter and spring of 2015, Arabic Community Club grew quietly at Jackson Street School. Members brought coffee, chicken, salads, and sweets to Arabic Community Club. Certain routines developed: Putting the food on a certain table, setting out utensils and plates, sharing out the leftovers and washing dishes at the end of the event. Everyone knew where to find things and put things away. Often, Reem would sit at one table with the children, leading them in activities that involved reading and writing in Arabic, while adults sat at another table with the others, playing a game or engaging in supported Arabic conversation.

Eventually my students proposed using some of our math games to teach Arabic, such as bingo games and a favorite involving fly swatters. It was beautiful to see my students stepping up alongside their mothers in the teacher role, erasing the earlier child/adult distinction. The children were callers and checkers in vocabulary bingo games as well as our partners in conversational role-plays. They enjoyed speaking Arabic to direct the adult learners (their educators and some community members), who held posters with Arabic numerals and mathematical operation symbols as we struggled to arrange ourselves in equations. I cherished those moments. Farida, a shy 2nd-grader, shone with confidence in her teaching role as she patiently and kindly taught me numeral names and symbols in Arabic, as I had once taught her in English. She was far more bilingual than I was, but she helped me make progress.

I thought of Freire's writing about humility as I was humbled by this challenging learning task. Learning to read, write, and say numbers forward and backward to 10 in Arabic was harder for me than learning to do it in Spanish or French. As a math specialist teaching lots of ELLs, it was healthy for me to struggle with it. I think about how Freire says that students must play an active role in the learning process, and how teachers and students are simultaneously learners and producers of knowledge. As Arabic Community Club evolved over time, young students developed their own transformed multilingual identities as they emerged alongside their mothers as teachers of their teachers.

"EEJIRI, AZRAQ! EEJIRI!" (RUN, BLUE! RUN!)

Over the summer of 2015, relationships continued to grow and deepen. Sometimes Arabic Community Club gathered at different homes for *shai* (tea) and picnics in the park. As that school year started, my daughter, Mairead, a junior in high school, started the first of what would become four semesters of studying Arabic at Smith College. Mairead's choice pleased members of the Arabic Community Club, who took particular pride and interest in her studies. Mairead was also a serious runner throughout high school and helped coach elementary and middle school students in the local youth track league. She invited families from the Arabic Community Club to her cross-country team's home meet. We carpooled over to the trail and gathered at a picnic table, where members made posters in support of Mairead and her team. As the meet time approached, we moved to the starting line.

The excitement was palpable, among the children, the mothers, and even the visiting grandmother. We stood along the sidelines with other spectators, children in front and the women behind them, all waving posters that said things like, "Run fast!" and "Go Blue!" (for the team's blue uniforms) in flowing Arabic calligraphy, as they strained to spot Mairead in the throng of runners at the starting line. The starter pistol fired in the air, the runners pounded forward, and I was suddenly surrounded by a spontaneous wave

Figure 13.2. Families from Arabic Community Club hold their signs supporting the Northampton cross-country team at a meet.

of celebratory ululation, a loud high-pitched warble, kind of a cross between trilling and howling, that expresses and evokes strong emotion. Startled spectators' heads turned in our direction, but the women and children were so exultant in the moment, they seemed not to notice.

Mairead had explained to the club members beforehand that after the start of the meet, we should follow the other spectators who would take off (doing what Mairead fondly called "the Mom Jog") along another trail across a small field and then into the woods, so that we could see the runners pass over there. We started our Mom Jog, holding the hands of the smaller children, long skirts and coats, hijabs and posters blowing in the wind. Breathlessly, we arrived at the intersection of the trails in the woods and waited for the first runners to round the bend and climb the hill. The parent of one of Mairead's teammates walked over and struck up conversation with me. Nodding to the families from the Arabic Community Club, she asked quietly, "Where are they *from*?" I knew she meant "what countries," but I smiled and said, "Northampton." She looked puzzled, maybe peeved. I added, "Mairead is part of Arabic Community Club at Jackson Street School, and these are her friends." As the runners climbed the hill, the kids yelled, "*Eejiri, azraq! Eejiri!*" (Run, Blue! Run!), and the ululation rose again.

How many times over the years have White people in school and the community asked variations on this question? On the surface, it seems harmless, like friendly curiosity. There is a natural tendency to notice what seems unusual or "out of place," but that observation can rapidly turn to unwarranted fear, surveillance, or violence when the one deemed "out of place" is Black or Muslim, especially amidst strong currents of White supremacy and Islamophobia.

WHAT CHANGE LOOKS LIKE

Pallavi, another parent, said, "As a Hindu in India, I was raised to fear Muslims. I never asked why, I just did. I never got to know any Muslims there, because I was afraid. I am ashamed to say that it is only now that I have gotten to know Muslim parents through How Schools Work and Math Club, I see how wrong that was. I have to raise my children differently." Pallavi began to coordinate our school's annual Science Night and asked Rania to invite the entire Arabic Community Club to attend. In a beautiful demonstration of the principle of "critical mass," many Arab families came, with toddlers in strollers and soft waves of Arabic rippling through our hallways.

This is how schools change. The first time it happens, some people who are used to being around a lot of people who look like themselves may ask, "Where are *they from*?" and learn "they" are "from" our community. The next time it happens, those people start to realize "they" are part of "us." *This* is how our beautiful community looks.

CHAPTER 14

Immigration: Solidarity in the Streets

"NO CHOICE NOW BUT TO BE POLITICAL"

The community that grew from How Schools Work and Arabic Community Club took on new importance as the political climate in the country shifted in 2015. Increasingly, anti-immigrant and anti-Muslim rhetoric flooded the media.

September 2015 started with the controversial photograph of a drowned Syrian toddler on a Turkish beach. The photo smacked passive onlookers in the face with the reality of the Syrian refugee crisis. That same month ended with then-presidential primary candidate Donald Trump threatening to kick all Syrian refugees out of the United States, claiming, "They could be ISIS, I don't know. . . . A 200,000 man army, maybe" (Johnson, 2015). The next month, he said he would "certainly look at" the possibility of closing mosques in the United States (Basu, 2015). Reem, one of the founders of Arabic Community Club, who not long before had insisted that the Club should not discuss politics, now said, "We have no choice now but to be political."

On the night of November 13, 2015, I was attending a family science event at school with many families from the Arabic Community Club. Many were suddenly shaken by the news that started to reach them on their smartphones about the Paris attacks, a coordinated set of actions by people associated with Islamic State in the Levant (ISIL, also known as ISIS) that killed 130 people and injured hundreds more.

Reem said that ISIS hurt Muslims more than anyone else. Most Americans ignored months of ISIS violence against Muslims in Syria, but suddenly paid attention when Europeans became the victims. Reem was devastatingly correct. I, in my White liberal way, was quick to object to stereotypes of Muslims as terrorists, but had somehow overlooked this reality. According to the 2019 Global Terrorism Index, "ISIL emerged in 2014 . . . Since then, ISIL has been responsible for 27,947 terrorist deaths. Of these, 80 per cent were in Iraq and 17 per cent in Syria" (2019, p. 16; Institute for Economics and Peace, 2019, p. 16). Iraq and Syria are both Muslim majority countries.

In November 2015, Trump reiterated the idea of closing mosques (Krieg, 2015) and floated the idea of creating a database of Muslims in the United States (Diamond, 2015). That month, Rania and Reem invited me to the Islamic Society of Western Massachusetts for the first time. In describing that first visit (Chapter 13), I shared my cultural awkwardness. On that evening, and in my many visits that followed, for Iftar, community meetings, and Interfaith gatherings, I was never fearful of Muslims. But I heard and felt the fear of those at the mosque and in Arabic Community Club, who knew that simply walking into a mosque, playing on the mosque playground, or wearing a hijab could make you a target of violence from right-wing extremists in the United States.

ALL ARE WELCOME HERE

Later that month, Jo Comerford approached the Arabic Community Club (ACC) and Families with Power about the idea of organizing a community event, which we decided to call "All Are Welcome Here Dinner." I had known Jo for many years as a local activist, Jackson Street School parent, Morning Math Club volunteer, and MoveOn organizer. FWP and ACC helped organize the event, which occurred in February 2016. It hosted hundreds of immigrants and refugees, including many who had recently arrived from Syria, for a dinner at Jackson Street School. FWP and ACC members reached out to houses of worship, schools, adult education programs, and community contacts to invite immigrants and refugees, and to arrange transportation and interpretation in Arabic, French, Chinese, Spanish, and Somali.

Rania designated quiet carpeted rooms where people could pray; she put up signs and helped organize the program around the time for prayers. Devout Muslims pray five times each day: Fajir (sunrise), Dhuhr (noon), Asr (afternoon), Maghrib (sunset), and Isha (night). The prayers take 5 to 10 minutes. The appropriate time for each prayer is about 20 minutes from the call to prayer. The time for each prayer shifts daily. And yes, there's an app that gives the time for each prayer each day.

Abdul helped organize local agencies and organizations to staff information tables in the gymnasium. He compiled handouts with information for newcomers, everything from How Schools Work, where to find English classes and houses of worship to where to buy Halal meat. Our U.S. Congressperson, Representative Jim McGovern, came to visit with and welcome immigrants and refugees; he spoke, calling the anti-immigrant sentiment of the political right "out of touch" and "detestable." Many religious leaders of all faiths attended, including many active in the sanctuary movement.

In December 2015, after advocating that the families of suspected terrorists be "taken out," in violation of international law (LoBianco, 2015),

Trump criticized Obama for not using the phrase "radical Islamic terrorism" (Herb, 2015). That same month, he referred to Muslims as "sick people" (Friedman, 2015). He called for a "total and complete shutdown of Muslims entering the U.S." (Shabad, 2015). In March of 2016, he said, "I think Islam hates us. . . . There's a tremendous hatred there" (Schleifer, 2016). In July 2016, while accepting the Republican presidential nomination, Trump spoke about "brutal Islamic terrorism" (Plumer, 2016). I cannot possibly list every hateful thing Trump said about immigrants and Muslims, but I want you to understand this was the "theme music" blaring on the national stage during this period, when the Arabic Community Club was meeting regularly, quietly growing and building community.

"If They Come for Us, You Will Protest, Right?"

Wednesday, November 9, 2016, was one of my hardest days as a teacher. In my Massachusetts bubble, I believed the strong polling that predicted Hillary Clinton would win. With other union members, I had been focused on Massachusetts Teachers Association's "NO on 2" campaign, urging people to vote down a ballot question that sought to expand charter schools in Massachusetts. Like many of my colleagues, I was stunned and devastated by Trump's Electoral College victory.

Many of my immigrant students were in tears, asking, "Is Trump going to kick us out? Is he going to take my mother?" How can you learn math if you are afraid that your mother won't come to pick you up after school because ICE snatched her? Or that you will be kicked out of the United States because of your religion? We talked about the election, how Hillary Clinton won the popular vote and how Donald Trump won the Electoral College vote (authentic math practice in reading, writing, and comparing large numbers) and how Trump would be sworn in on January 20, 2017.

Our school is also a polling place, so before and after school on election day I had been holding a "NO on 2" campaign sign on the street. One of my 1st-grade students said, "I saw you outside school with a sign yesterday, Ms. Cowhey. If they come for us, you will protest, right?"

I choked back tears. What could I, one measly little elementary math teacher, do to protect my students and their families from ICE and the 400 anti-immigrant policies that would rain down from the Trump Administration? I wasn't sure how, but I said, "Yes, I will always fight for you and your families."

PRIORITIES FOR A BEAUTIFUL BUT BROKEN WORLD

That afternoon, our principal, Gwen, invited all staff to gather after dismissal to check in, to share thoughts and feelings. She had invited her friend and social justice activist, Rev. Dr. Andrea Ayvazian, to join us. I took notes,

made a sign, and hung it up in my classroom to give myself the strength to
keep going. Here is what Andrea shared:

> When we face obstacles, struggles, and setbacks in our efforts to help
> mend, repair and heal this beautiful but broken world, remember this
> triad of priorities:
> 1. Strengthen your commitment to care for yourself; if we lose you to
>   exhaustion, we all suffer;
> 2. Show compassion, generosity and caring to others; it will help their
>   hearts and yours as well;
> 3. Organize, connect, and collaborate; take hands and strengthen each
>   other as we continue this work.

That morning, Gwen made a routine announcement that Arabic Community
Club would be meeting at 5 p.m. that afternoon. Even before 5:00, as Rania,
Rasha, and I were setting up, Gwen and other staff members started to
come in the classroom. There were paraprofessionals, other teachers, and
our counselor. They asked Rania if it was okay for them to participate, saying that they wanted to be there in solidarity. Rania welcomed them.

More of the regular members of Arabic Community Club arrived, as
well as some other Muslim caregivers. One was an Iranian woman, whom
I knew as a Morning Math Club parent. (Persian, or Farsi, not Arabic, is
the primary language of Iran.) She was not a devout Muslim, but she explained how three aspects of her identity—being a woman, a Muslim, and
an Iranian—made it almost impossible for her to find professional employment as an industrial engineer in the United States. The reason? American
factories contracting with the federal government required high-level security clearance. A Moroccan family also came for the first time. My husband,
Bill, who had never come to Arabic Community Club before, came too.

In that frightening moment, when anti-immigrant, Islamophobic, and
misogynist sentiment rose like a wave to elect Trump, the Arabic Community
Club was there like a magnet, drawing all kinds of community members together, as a site of refuge, solidarity, and strength. We were not all Arabic
speakers, or all Muslim. We were not all immigrants or women. But we
were a community. We did some of what we usually did (introducing ourselves around the circle in Arabic, sharing coffee and food) but mostly, we
listened and bore witness to how this day had felt for Muslim members of
our community.

One member told us how she experienced two Islamophobic, anti-
immigrant aggressions that very morning at work. These were not the first
harassment incidents on her job; she'd been harassed before for wearing the
hijab and praying on her lunch break. When she entered the workplace that
morning, an emboldened coworker confronted her, saying, "Trump won!
You should leave! Go back to your own country!" She simply said that she

was an American citizen, that she was in her own country. Later, she was called to the factory floor, where a machine had stopped working. She asked what was happening just before the machine stopped working. A coworker started yelling at her, saying if she was an engineer, she ought to know, and insulted her as a woman, a Muslim, and an immigrant. When she reported these incidents to her boss, he did nothing to protect her; he told her that she should stop making trouble. She quit.

SOLIDARITY IN THE STREETS

After Trump's election, some FWP members, fellow educators, and I began to attend more meetings at the Pioneer Valley Workers Center (PVWC) in Northampton. We became part of Solidarity in the Streets (SiS), a network building the infrastructure to stop state violence against working people, including immigrants and people of color, as well as to organize a powerful working-class movement. SiS launched a round-the-clock bilingual emergency hotline to respond to workplace abuse, raids, deportations, and hate crimes.

Sanctuary cities, also known as "safe cities," limit their cooperation with federal immigration enforcement agents in order to protect low-priority immigrants from deportation, while still turning over those who have committed serious crimes. While cities may try to protect undocumented immigrants, their ability to defy state law is minimal, and in Massachusetts (and 37 other states) undocumented persons may not obtain a driver's license. Driving suddenly became a lot more dangerous. In surrounding towns and on the interstate, there were increasing incidents of drivers being pulled over for minor infractions, such as a broken taillight, being arrested for driving without a license, and being brought to jail, where ICE could then detain and deport them. In a nearby city, a father was pulled over after dropping off his young son at school and arrested for driving without a license. Soon ICE was processing him for deportation.

SiS mobilized a campaign to fight (and eventually stop) the father's deportation and collected diapers and food to help his family while he was detained. SiS organized a network of volunteer drivers to take immigrants safely to and from school, work, and legal, immigration and medical appointments, to reduce the risk of arrest and deportation. SiS provided training for volunteer drivers willing to go to the site of an arrest in progress, to drive the car away so that it wouldn't be towed, and to bail people out of jail, often in the middle of the night, before ICE could detain them. Volunteers also provided transportation for family members to visit a parent in sanctuary at a local church. Often people say, "I disagree with family separation and all these anti-immigration policies, but what can I do about it?" This kind of driving was a way for volunteers to take meaningful action. Neighbors and accomplices were needed, not White saviors.

Solidarity in the Streets was organized into committees. In addition to the committees that organized drivers and bilingual folks to staff the 24-hour hotline, there was a Rapid Response Team of hundreds of volunteers on a text list who had pledged to mobilize in case of an immigration raid. As interest grew, SiS needed large spaces to train the many volunteers. Gwen opened our school for these on weekends, and many educators participated in the trainings.

One day, just after dismissal, a call came into the school office from nearby Hampshire Heights that ICE (Immigration and Customs Enforcement) was in the neighborhood. I called Rose, a codirector of the workers center, to come verify their presence. Several trained colleagues and I went right to the neighborhood. ICE had left minutes before, but we were able to figure out where they had been. Rose arrived and immediately visited the apartment where ICE went, while we checked in with other families in the neighborhood who were shaken. Rose learned that ICE was looking for a man who wasn't present that day. She left the hotline number for him to contact, which he did.

As SiS organized with more people in crisis, its experience and community credibility grew. SiS produced business cards in multiple languages with the hotline information and multilingual "Know Your Rights" leaflets about what to do if ICE comes to the door. We put up a bulletin board just inside the school's front door, full of multilingual information about immigrant rights and ways to get involved. Jackson Street School, cooperating with many community organizations including the workers center, hosted large community "Know Your Rights" meetings. Immigration lawyers, some of whom were Jackson Street School parents, provided accurate information and resources. These sessions employed our already established habits of providing transportation, childcare, and interpretation.

TAKING A STAND FOR IMMIGRANT RIGHTS

I learned that some Massachusetts Teachers Association (MTA) locals had organized standouts for immigrant rights. A "standout" is when a group of people, usually led by members of the educators' union, often joined by students, families, and other community members, stand in front of a school building with signs during a high-traffic period. Often there are speakers, singing, and chanting of slogans. In 2017, in cooperation with my local union and the workers center, FWP organized standouts in front of our school in support of immigrant rights as well as the campaign for driver's licenses for all. We invited administrators, school committee members, and city councilors. Many joined us, along with a diverse group of students and their families. FWP members made beautiful posters in Spanish, Arabic, and English.

Through Solidarity in the Streets, we learned that in a family with undocumented caregivers at risk for deportation and American-born children, it

**Figure 14.1. FWP member Sue Brow and Jackson Street School teacher Tom Chang
join students, families, and educators at the standout for immigrant rights
before school (2017).**

was important to have valid passports for all the children. If one parent was
deported and the other parent wanted to return to the home country with the
children in order to reunite the family, they could not get passports for the
children at that point without the permission of the detained or deported parent. This created a Catch-22 that could strand the children in the United States.

When the Trump administration canceled Temporary Protective Status
(TPS) for people from Haiti and El Salvador, endangering a family at our
school, an immigration lawyer told them that one parent had to go to the
home country and legally reenter the United States, and then the other. This
was risky, given the chance that either parent might not be given permission to return. Educators chipped in to raise funds for the family to obtain
passports (including help to cover expenses while the breadwinner was out
of the country). Their plan succeeded.

Valentine's Day Standout

Not so much roses and chocolates. This morning, after a few texts back and
forth, and struggling to open the frozen-shut doors of my car, I pick up a box of
munchkins, one of my former students, Blanca Diaz, and her mother. During our
drive to school, Blanca tells me about the book she and all the 5th-graders are
reading, titled *This Book Is Anti-Racist* (Jewell, 2019). She tells me they are learning
the history of how Black and Latinx people have been treated, and how they have
organized.

Figure 14.2. Rania Al-Qudsi and Blanca Diaz hold homemade signs in Arabic, Spanish, and English at a standout for immigrant rights at Jackson Street School (2017).

Blanca Diaz wrote this poem in 2nd-grade and read it aloud at our first Immigrant Rights Standout at Jackson Street School in 2017.

Not Aliens!

Our skin isn't green.
We don't have antennas.
We don't have lots of eyes.
We don't live in outer space.
We don't eat gross stuff.
We are not aliens.
We are people
just like
you!

We're planning to stand out in front of our school to demand passage of the Work and Family Mobility Act, so that everyone, including undocumented people, can get a license to drive legally, obtain car insurance, and safely drive to work and school without fear of detention and deportation. Blanca understands this fear is why many families she knows have to waste so much money on taxis.

It's sunny and 20 degrees, but it feels much colder when the wind blows. We can feel the love on the street as we hold signs in Spanish, English, and Arabic. The crossing guard waves and calls hello. A man names José arrives; he says that when his kids attended our school in 1980, he and other Latinx parents took over the school and demanded Hispanic Heritage Week. Blanca tells José about *This Book Is Anti-Racist*. José says that he would be willing to come speak with her class about this local history.

People introduce themselves to each other. Rebecca is walking her kindergartner to school. She joins us and says hello to Michael from Grow Food, who is standing out with us. Lourdes calls a greeting when she sees Rania coming, wearing a thick shawl over her hijab and coat. Lourdes is there with her two kids, Isabela and Yhazir, who came yesterday to help us make posters. Rose from the workers center arrives, with her 3-year-old daughter, Bay, who is warmly dressed. She is whining.

Bay reminds me of my daughter, who was brought to many picket lines and protests when she was that age. Oy, to be the child of an activist! Rose is setting up the battery-operated sound system and microphone. I ask Bay if she would like to help me with passing out the munchkins. She stops crying a moment to consider this offer, then nods and follows me. Bay doesn't actually ask, "Would you like a munchkin?" But she has incredibly large, expressive eyes, so she just looks up at each person; if they nod, she puts her mittens in the box, working her hands like tongs to catch a munchkin and present it to them.

The crowd chants, "What do we want? Driver's Licenses! When do we want them? Now!" Rose, State Senator Jo Comerford, and others speak to the crowd. Passing families wave and honk their support. At 8:40, we pack up so that kids can get to class.

We gather up the posters and bid our goodbyes. Ms. Diaz, who is shivering, comes inside to help me drop off the posters for next time. We see Rania in the lobby, and I introduce her to Ms. Diaz. Rania, whose daughter is now in middle school, says that she wants to volunteer at Jackson Street School, for an education class she is taking at the community college. I invite Rania to volunteer at Math Club on Tuesday mornings, and she is excited to hear that math club is still going, even though I've retired.

Rania invites Ms. Diaz to the Friday night potlucks in her neighborhood, where they've been discussing concerns about bullying. Rania, Ms. Diaz, and I walk out together, as they continue their conversation. When we reach the sidewalk, Rania and Ms. Diaz hug each other. The wind blows bitter cold, but they keep hugging each other an extra moment. (February 14, 2020)

Having My Neighbor's Back

On Martin Luther King Day in 2017, at a workshop at Jackson St. School, I heard Attorney Tahirah Amatul-Wadud say, "If I have my neighbor's back and she has mine, I don't have to fear a man in Washington" (Cowhey, 2017). Her words stayed with me that January as Trump was inaugurated and in the months and years that followed.

How Schools Work developed trusting relationships and collaborative spirit through immigrant caregiver leadership and partnerships with community organizations and educators. When immigrant families came under attack, these groups mobilized quickly to defend and support each other. It taught all our students by example how a community organizes itself to protect its members, striving to make "We will defend each other" not just a slogan but a reality.

As I write this in 2021, we are still fighting for the passage of the Work and Family Mobility Act in Massachusetts. In 2019, two caregivers from Jackson Street School were elected to state office, becoming the first women to hold each of their positions. Jo Comerford represents us in the Massachusetts Senate, and Lindsay Sabadosa represents us in the House. While it is great to have state lawmakers fighting for progressive education, labor and immigration legislation, like the Work and Family Mobility Act, it doesn't mean we automatically win every battle. We continue to work with statewide coalition partners on these campaigns.

MARCH 2020

When the COVID-19 lockdown began, many undocumented workers immediately lost their employment or were forced to continue essential work in unsafe conditions without personal protective equipment, health insurance, or accurate public health information in their language. Most undocumented workers faced an immediate loss of income, but were not eligible for unemployment insurance. They didn't receive stimulus checks, even though they'd been paying taxes for years and the children in their households were often U.S. citizens.

The workers center immediately launched an "undocu-worker fund." Many community members who were able to work remotely and didn't suffer loss of income donated their stimulus checks to the fund. This helped hundreds of undocumented workers pay rent and utility bills during the pandemic. Our bilingual school counselor quickly notified families about the fund.

The workers center offered training in unemployment advocacy with Representative Lindsay Sabadosa. The state system was idiosyncratic and hard to navigate, especially without a computer or internet connection. That advocacy helped numerous families from our school receive the unemployment benefits they'd earned. In at least one situation, the payment of the overdue unemployment benefits allowed the family to pay rent and avoid eviction. If they had been evicted, that parent would have lost custody of her children.

Networks like How Schools Work and Solidarity in the Streets and organizations such as Families with Power, Arabic Community Club, and

Pioneer Valley Workers Center all cultivate leadership and build strong relationships within and among different portions of our community. They connect people and help them recognize their shared interests. A Muslim woman who is documented and has a driver's license is willing to stand up for the right of undocumented community members to obtain a driver's license. And undocumented immigrants are willing to take a stand against a Muslim travel ban. People who connect through these grassroots organizations increase their power to mobilize and support each other. These organizations, even the smaller ones, are those that defend us and mobilize our resistance.

On January 27, 2017, my colleagues and I attended the emergency rally for immigrant rights organized by the Pioneer Valley Workers Center and a coalition of local organizations in Springfield, MA. In my speech that night, I said, "Start small, but start now. This is the very nature of grassroots organizing. We need to dig in so deep we can't be weeded out" (Cowhey, 2017).

CHAPTER 15

Working With Other Organizations

Families with Power cooperated with other organizations for many reasons. Cooperation builds solidarity and community. It can be mutually beneficial. The differences between organizations can be complementary. Geographically, one organization might have a broader reach and the other may have a more local but deeper reach to a specific constituency. Goals of one organization may overlap with goals of another organization, so it makes sense to work together toward those goals. As an organization, FWP lacked material resources that organizations we worked with were willing to share. We learned to think critically about developing respectful and cooperative relationships with other organizations.

In the chapter about healthy eating, I described a meeting to recruit more immigrant gardeners to a new community garden. The story illustrates what collaboration between organizations looks like. New FWP gardeners needed to meet the garden organizers; English language learners needed to receive information. The returning FWP gardeners served as an important bridge for new gardeners to trust the garden organizers. The immigrant families who got new garden plots were members of FWP or their friends. We were crowded in Santa's living room, with people filling every couch, kitchen chair and step, but Santa's warm *"mi casa es tu casa"* hospitality made everyone comfortable.

What Worked Well in This Collaboration?

- The Grow Food organizers genuinely wanted to develop long-term relationships with diverse gardeners, as collaborative partners. They agreed to hold the meeting at Santa's home instead of the beautiful but unfamiliar library where people might not feel comfortable.
- Grow Food welcomed the idea of having the host open the meeting.
- We made the meeting linguistically accessible, in English and Spanish, with much of the English being spoken by participants for whom English was a second language.

> • We made the "family field trip" to the vocational school where
> registration would take place and to the community garden so that
> people would feel confident when they went back the next week to
> register.

For FWP, a good collaborative partner asks, listens, and respects our ways of doing things. They recognize the leadership of our members and appreciate that our members have expertise and influence.

WHAT ASSUMPTIONS DO POTENTIAL ORGANIZATIONAL PARTNERS BRING?

Collaboration with other organizations always takes work. There are often good intentions and lots of assumptions. For example, some mainstream organizational and school assumptions are that everyone:

- has an email account
- checks it regularly
- has reliable internet service
- has a device, with storage space to download apps
- knows how to open attachments and read spreadsheets
- reads and writes comfortably, in English.

Other assumptions are that every organization:

- wants to do everything quickly and efficiently
- wants to get bigger
- wants grants and publicity.

FWP often deliberately did certain things in "less efficient" ways because efficiency was rarely the point. We enjoyed spending time together, so members expected our meetings to include a social aspect that made everyone feel seen, heard, and respected. For this reason, we geared most of our activities to small numbers. We preferred to be crowded in a small space rather than be overwhelmed by too large a space.

We always appreciated it when a community organization seeking to collaborate with us was willing to examine its assumptions and usual ways of doing things. As we worked with other organizations, we noticed and appreciated when they really listened and when they were open to change.

APOYO AT THE PTO

When FWP started in 2007, members said that they did not feel welcome in our school's PTO. Josefina described attending a PTO meeting as feeling like "a black bean in the middle of a bowl of white beans." Others said, "I went to a meeting once, and there was nobody there like me." From the beginning, FWP was its own unique organization, not an alternative PTO. We developed our own programs in response to community need and interest. We had a strong constituency and our own ways of doing things. PTO leaders noticed and grew to respect FWP. PTO members came to FWP family dances, dinners, and Math Club and began to offer support.

In 2013, the Jackson Street School PTO invited Elba to become copresident, with Gwen. Many FWP members didn't understand the PTO, but our sense of *apoyo* was strong. No one wanted Elba to have to go to a PTO meeting all alone, so a lot of FWP members went with her, *por apoyo* (for support). Since Elba was running the meeting, they felt comfortable asking questions and making suggestions about the proposed activities. Since Elba was the copresident I also started attending PTO meetings regularly, *por apoyo*. I was surprised how rarely teachers attended.

Under Elba's leadership, the PTO changed. Our PTO prided itself on its successful fundraising. Elba proposed a "fun-raiser" instead: The PTO could rent a roller-skating rink and invite students, families and educators to skate together. Why? To have fun together and to get to know each other. This was a new idea. Elba also proposed to rent school buses to carry students, families, and educators to a children's museum on a Saturday to enjoy a free program. At first, another PTO member tried to clarify that the bus was for people who *didn't* have cars, right? Elba said no, the bus was for everyone to ride together, whether they had cars or not, to get to know each other. Definitely a different approach.

Elba's family moved to Florida in June, 2015, so she gave up her role in the PTO, but her leadership left its impact. I continued to attend PTO meetings semi-regularly and found the group appreciative of advice and proposals. The PTO continued to be very supportive, with many of the families I met at PTO showing up with their children for standouts about immigration rights, funding public education, and a fair contract. Kim was a member of the School Council for years.

The Jackson Street School Inclusiveness Checklist was developed by the JSS School Council, Parent-Teacher Organization, and JSS Staff in 2017. It invited event organizers to consult with Principal Gwen Agna so that she could help them think through some of these questions as they plan. The checklist stated that inclusivity is a goal to strive toward and asked people proposing school events to respond to the following considerations:

- Can you recruit a diverse planning team to help think about the event? Has anyone done this before that you can ask for advice?
- If there are fees associated with the event (including fundraising events), *please* use a suggested donation (rather than a fixed fee) with a no-questions-asked sliding fee scale.
- Please also consider giving some free tickets to the event to Ms. Agna for the JSS staff to discretely pass out to students they think could benefit from free tickets.
- Will there be childcare provided at the event?
- Please consider how families with limited transportation can access the event. Can you help arrange transportation or carpools?
- Please consider whether translation services will be helpful and appropriate, and if you are able to make these services available.
- Please consider doing direct outreach and active recruitment with families who might otherwise be left out, including event info in a robo-call, and printing outreach materials in Spanish and/or other languages. (Note: the district policy is to provide materials for ALL families in English/Spanish.)
- Please consider whether this event might be inadvertently excluding or off-putting to some families. Please consider how it would feel to be at this event if you had limited English, limited funds, or a nontraditional family structure. Is there anything you can do to make the event welcoming and inclusive?

OFFERS, ASKS, AND INVITATIONS

In 2008, Roberta Wilmore contacted FWP. Roberta was an African American professional who had worked in the equestrian world for decades before buying a small farm in Ashfield, 45 minutes from Northampton. She started the Children's Equitation Center (CEC), a nonprofit dedicated to supporting racial and economic diversity in equestrian sports. CEC programs focused on mentoring young people's leadership skills and supporting their strengths. That was as important to CEC as good riding skills. Through fundraising, Roberta had been able to offer scholarships to kids in Boston, Washington, D.C., and elsewhere to participate in CEC programs. When she heard about FWP, she wanted local children to be able to participate as well.

Some FWP caregivers, like Eneida and Maria, who had grown up riding horses in Puerto Rico and Ecuador, wanted their children to have that opportunity too. Eneida hosted a meeting and invited Roberta to tell us more. Roberta asked the children how they felt about horses. Several said they were scared. When Roberta encouraged them to say more, Raymond said, "I guess because they have really big noses—like, they breathe on you a lot." Roberta acknowledged that these were large and powerful animals—with big noses—and that part of working with horses was learning to respect and develop trust with them.

It became clear that Roberta wasn't trying to turn our kids into ribbon-winning jumpers in jodhpurs. She believed working with horses could teach confidence, respect, honesty, and humility. She saw it as an opportunity for children to learn self-control, compassion, and teamwork. She taught children the significance of people of color owning land and farming in the United States. She taught them the history of land theft and obstacles to land ownership created by systemic racism. She taught the economics of different careers in the equestrian industry and the real cost of owning a horse. Children could also learn to ride, but that wasn't the main thing. In fact, Roberta said that if you only wanted to ride, this wasn't the program for you.

Roberta also spoke directly to the caregivers. As a parent herself, she asked them to make a long-term commitment to their children's participation. The program charged on a sliding scale, but she asked caregivers to make some financial commitment. After an invitation to visit her farm before making any decision, we made a family field trip there together. As we ate lunch and explored the farm, Roberta answered questions and listened to the children and caregivers.

Figure 15.1. Roberta Wilmore and her dog, Sherpa, welcome Families with Power children and caregivers to Lee Ella Farm in Ashfield, where they learned more about the Children's Equitation Center before deciding whether to register for CEC's program (2014).

Figure 15.2. Maria meets one of Children's Equitation Center's ponies, Tea Biscuit, held by the author's daughter and CEC volunteer, Mairead Blatner, during a Families with Power field trip to Lee Ella Farm (2014).

After Roberta had met with all their caregivers, ten children signed up. Roberta came to school with a van to drive the kids to her farm for Thursday afternoon and weekend activities. The children had riding lessons, took care of horses, visited other farms, met outside professionals, and went to horse shows. At the end of the first season, Roberta invited the families back to the farm, to see what the children had learned. Some children had learned to ride. They all learned about different jobs in the equestrian world.

Each child, including those who had been afraid, shone in a unique way. Eneida's son Juan was a quiet boy who had a special connection with animals. On our class field trips to the marsh, he always spotted the snake or frog that everyone else missed. At the farm, Juan loved grooming the horses in a beautiful meditative style. My daughter, Mairead, had been very shy, but CEC pushed her beyond her comfort zone with assignments to interview strangers at horse shows and make phone calls to solve authentic problems on the farm. Raymond, who had been afraid of the horses' big noses, had developed an interesting skill that he called "horse dancing." He stood directly in front of the horse's face and swayed, then danced. Raymond persuaded the horse to move its head in response; he taught the horse to dance with him.

Other after-school and summer programs with CEC followed. CEC closed around 2015, but 14 years after that first house meeting with FWP, Roberta is still a mentor to some of those young adults, whose lives changed for the better because of their time with CEC.

I share this story about FWP's experience with CEC as an example of an offer to collaborate. Roberta heard about FWP and learned that one of our goals was leadership development. That aligned with one of CEC's goals. Roberta wanted to connect with the community FWP was embedded in. FWP never imagined having an equestrian program, but when Roberta reached out to us, it resonated with Eneida and Maria. They told other caregivers about how strong, free, and powerful they felt riding horses as girls. When Eneida organized the house meeting to introduce Roberta to FWP, we started a slow and gradual process of building relationships and trust. There was no rushing on either side. Roberta was African American, and the majority of our members were Latinx. Both organizations shared the cultural value of prioritizing relationship building and the goal of helping our children succeed in authentic ways.

Roberta didn't ask us to "send people" to CEC. She offered to collaborate, to develop a program that would be a good fit for our children. CEC offered scholarships with a sliding scale. Roberta stated her expectation that families would pay something and saw this expectation as a sign of her respect toward our families. It wasn't charity. This relationship between FWP and CEC started with an offer, not an ask.

An Ask

I think of "an ask" as another organization asking us to do something that will benefit them without understanding FWP's goals or demonstrating interest in building a mutually beneficial relationship.

At times the audacity of some organizations that approached FWP amazed us. Here's an example of an ugly pattern: An organization would contact FWP and say something like, "We want more diversity in our organization, so could you send people to our next meeting?" Tacky variations on this theme included, "We got a grant for diversity and inclusion and need more people of color in our organization. Could you recommend one of your members to join our board?" This was a major red flag. We read this as a sign that the organization was too disconnected to take the time to build authentic relationships themselves; instead, it felt as if they were looking for a temp agency to rent people of color (for free).

Once we partnered with an organization that didn't respect FWP members' leadership. We learned from our experience, sometimes painfully. It was frustrating, but we stuck it out in order to complete the program successfully for the community members who engaged with it. We learned to be more explicit about our goals, criteria, and ways of doing things as we partnered with other organizations.

Families with Power remained clear on who we were as an organization, even as others tried to squeeze us into their own boxes, such as "immigrant organization," "Latina mothers," or "school group." We never changed our definition of FWP to suit anyone else.

Invitation to Collaborate

Sometimes FWP invited collaboration. How Schools Work is a good example of that. We came up with the idea of an educational project that would foster reciprocal learning between immigrant families and educators. FWP and Casa Latina had the resources to create a version of this ourselves, but we invited potential partners, the district early childhood program, and Center for New Americans, who we knew shared this goal. Through this collaboration, our members learned about them and their members learned about us. By working together, we had greater impact.

When FWP set a goal of healthier eating, we reached out to farmers, public health workers, and food justice organizations who shared that goal. They wanted to work with our members long-term. We developed equitable and respectful partnerships that grew and deepened in authentic ways.

WHAT ABOUT FUNDING?

Families with Power never sought or accepted funding from the school district or government. From the beginning, we saw that government funding can be used to co-opt and control grassroots organizations. If organizing

Figure 15.3. Families with Power members tour Prospect Meadow Farm with director, Shawn Robinson, and the author's son and farm staff, Robeson Cowhey. Left to right: Elba Heredia, Angela Robles, Robeson Cowhey, Roque Sanchez, Eliaz Robles, Shawn Robinson (2011).

depends on government funds and that organizing challenges the status quo, the government can tell the organization to stop organizing. If the organization doesn't stop, the government can cut its funding. Furthermore, during the time an organization receives government funding, it may find itself redirecting its energy from recruiting volunteers and donations from the community to writing and managing grants, further increasing the organization's dependency on government funding.

We received a one-time grant from Southern Poverty Law Center, which supported our very first weekend retreat in 2007. Northampton Education Foundation (NEF) gave us a grant to support our Family Writing Project. Within a year, a Northampton Education Foundation board member offered to let us use her family's large farmhouse for our annual retreat. Members decided that instead of using grant money to give each family a stipend for childcare, we'd rather bring all our kids with us for the retreat, to see if they found it as fun and empowering as the adults did. We were able to sustain the retreats for years without grant funding.

FWP didn't actively seek grants. Instead, we developed a long-term relationship with NEF and trusted that we could ask them for small grants to support specific projects, such as our Financial Literacy Project or Kime Project. We learned that it was easier for a family to make a 6-week commitment to a project if they received dinner, transportation, materials, and a small stipend. The NEF grant cycles, application, reporting, and disbursement processes were familiar and worked for us. NEF community members could see the results of their investment in FWP, trusting us to develop thoughtful proposals to meet real needs.

For many years, Elba Heredia Cartagena and a large crew of FWP volunteers organized an annual "Love Your Family Dinner" with a delicious

Figure 15.4. Elba Heredia and Anabel Romero serve food at the FWP Love Your Family Dinner (2014).

Puerto Rican menu in the school cafeteria. This joyful event always drew a crowd. We decorated with flowers and balloons. Members proudly wore their FWP tee shirts. FWP adults and youth were visible as the leaders of the event. Many local businesses donated food. The dinner happened to raise money, as many who attended made donations, and those helped us pay future expenses like snacks at our reading parties, cafés, and family dances and food at our annual retreats. Many of our projects didn't require much funding at all.

We realized that we didn't need to own all the resources necessary for a project if we could find people and organizations who supported our mission and were willing to share resources. We didn't need or want to own a large building with our own large kitchen, childcare room, dormitory, meeting rooms, a garden or farm, dining hall and multipurpose rooms in order to run our programs. We just needed partners in our school and community who would listen to our vision and trust that we would take care of these resources responsibly.

THE PRESS AND SOCIAL MEDIA

FWP rarely pursued publicity. In part, this was because some members preferred privacy (living "under the radar") for reasons like legal status or not wanting to be located by a former abuser. Also, most of our members (and potential members we wanted to reach) didn't regularly read the local newspaper.

Many people have the habit of taking photos and videos on their cell phones. Some of them don't think to ask permission before posting the photo on social media. It happens all the time, but that doesn't make it okay. Once I noticed someone narrating a video she was making at an immigration standout, where some of the participants were undocumented, and some had other reasons they didn't want to be photographed. I asked her to stop. FWP had conversations within our group to learn how members felt about being photographed. Photographers should ask permission first, after stating clearly how and where the photo could be used and for what purpose. It should be up to the subjects to say what they are comfortable with, such as a close-up photo of someone's sign, or a distant shot from the back of the crowd.

If we received an unsolicited request from the media, we didn't drop everything and twist ourselves up in knots to please them. First, we found out where they were coming from, what the larger story was, and how they were referred to us. FWP discussed requests before accepting or declining. It's fine to say no, thank you. Sometimes we wrote our own articles and worked with a publication's photographers (Cowhey, 2009).

SOCIAL CHANGE MOVEMENTS

When we organize, some historical context helps. No single book teaches you everything you need to know. After organizing and learning for more than 40 years, I have so much more to learn. We can learn lessons, positive and negative, from every movement, no matter how large or small, famous or obscure, long- or short-lived. From the Combahee River Colony to the Northampton Association for Education and Industry, from the Highlander Folk School to the Movement for Black Lives, we need to learn from the struggles of those who came before us as well as from those organizing alongside us today.

Schools should teach Black, Indigenous, Latinx, and Asian-American history year-round because it *is* United States history. Since most don't, many of us have a limited and distorted view. Many schools time their biography unit with Black History Month, "killing two birds with one stone." They designate February as the time to learn about Rosa Parks, Rev. Dr. Martin Luther King, Jr., and Malcolm X. This biographical approach focuses on individual, often charismatic, leaders. This draws attention away from their more powerful contributions in movement building. While their stories are inspiring, most of us will not become charismatic leaders. Nevertheless, many of us can learn to be effective organizers and movement builders.

I remember in June 2020 seeing Patrisse Khan-Cullors, one of the founders of Black Lives Matter, interviewed by Trevor Noah on The Daily Show shortly after the murder of George Floyd. At one point, Noah brought up a criticism that he'd heard, that the Movement for Black Lives was a "leaderless movement." Patrisse Khan-Cullors pointed to the history of Black movement leaders being targeted for assassination and said that no, this was a "leader-*full* movement." I thought of her words at every protest I attended after that.

In my community there was a young Black trans activist who was brave and energetic. She led many protests with a strong and supportive group of other activists who were mostly young, queer people of color. As an older White person, I showed up with my sign, water bottle and mask, listened to instructions, amplified with the "mic check" command, and followed the lead of these young activists. The folks I went with stuck together and took care of each other. It was *not* my job to have a witty sign to draw attention to myself, to take selfies or photos of others in the crowd to post on social media, to initiate or change chants or take rogue action to provoke the police or agitate others. The tension was palpable; discipline was critical.

Many protests and the city council testimony of hundreds of residents yielded a 10% cut in the Northampton police department budget, which resulted in the removal of school resource officers. It created a policing review commission which held hearings and collected testimony. The commission made recommendations to reallocate resources to create alternative (non-police) ways to respond to mental health, drug addiction, and domestic violence emergencies. It created a Department of Community Care to implement this new vision. As the summer of 2020 so clearly demonstrated, there are thousands of great young leaders: disciplined, ready, willing and able, training themselves up in this "leader-full" movement.

Language Justice

There is nothing cheap or convenient about language justice. And yet it is just and therefore necessary. When I started teaching decades ago, interpretation for IEP meetings was arranged on the fly, pulling in a bilingual clerical worker, aide, or teacher. There was usually no interpretation provided for district or municipal meetings. Sometimes, at school meetings in our district, an administrator might say, very loudly, in English, "Raise your hand if you don't speak English!" or "*Si tu habla español*, go over there!" These awkward commands were usually met with stony silence and stillness. In response, some schools stopped offering interpretation, on the basis that the service went unused.

For many years in FWP organizing, I thought of interpretation (which is oral) and translation (which is written) as practical necessities, in order to communicate: to understand and be understood. Fluent bilingual FWP members usually volunteered to interpret. I am ashamed to say I took that for granted. In our meetings, someone would speak in English or Spanish, and then it was interpreted into the other language. Since everything was said twice, it effectively doubled the length of our meetings, which led my husband to affectionately call us Families Without Watches. When FWP went to Highlander's Homecoming in 2007, we learned about land acknowledgments and taking the time to recognize all the languages spoken by participants in the room; we incorporated those elements into our practice.

I don't remember hearing the term "language justice" or seeing it in practice until I attended Pioneer Valley Workers Center (PVWC) meetings in 2016. Upon arrival, organizers offer everyone a headset for simultaneous interpretation. Fluent bilinguals decline the headsets. Organizers introduce the interpreters for the event and thank them in advance. One of the interpreters walks the group through how to select the appropriate channel for their language, how to control the volume and test their equipment. For a monolingual Spanish speaker, it goes like this: When someone speaks in Spanish, their earphones are silent and they hear the speaker directly. When someone speaks in English, they hear the voice of the interpreter in their earphones simultaneously interpreting the speaker into Spanish. If they address the group in Spanish, everyone will hear and understand them in their chosen language. It works the other way around for a monolingual English speaker. Neither language is privileged over the other.

In March 2020, I attended the first PVWC Workers' Assembly of the COVID-19 era on Zoom. It offered an interpretation option that worked like the simultaneous interpretation described above. This kind of simultaneous interpretation does not lengthen or interrupt the flow of the meeting. It requires that all speakers stick to a single language, speak more slowly and pause occasionally to allow the interpreter to catch up. Simultaneous interpretation can be exhausting. For this reason, it is best practice to alternate between interpreters or give them scheduled breaks. PVWC hires professional interpreters from Just Words Cooperative, which is dedicated to language justice and pays its interpreters a fair wage.

Budgets reflect priorities and can include a line item for interpretation. If a school or organization lacks interpretation resources, they can write grants to hire interpreters, purchase headsets, get a Zoom account with an interpretation line or arrange to share with another organization. If we value language justice, we have to invest in it. In this manner, we will begin to normalize language justice in our communities and schools.

"WE MAKE THE ROAD BY WALKING"

When Paulo Freire said, "We make the road by walking," in dialogue with Myles Horton, he was paraphrasing the Spanish poet Antonio Machado. Families with Power didn't have a road map for collaboration with other organizations. We grew and learned through that work. Sometimes collaborations enabled us to provide programs and opportunities for our families that we could never have imagined, like the horse program with Children's Equitation Center. Sometimes we "made the road by walking" in dialogue with partner organizations and professionals as we explored the route to healthier eating and thought critically about all the obstacles that challenged us. We learned about important issues like language justice and effective approaches to organizing. We joined partner organizations in campaigns—for immigrants' rights, increasing state funding for public schools, and raising the minimum wage—that we wouldn't have had the time, energy, skills, or resources to launch on our own. We learned from our experiences how to be better collaborative partners, how to negotiate and when to hold our ground.

At our first FWP retreat, members described how they felt in our school and community: invisible, isolated, ignored, *outcast*. Our work with other organizations helped members realize that they were not only leaders within Families with Power and our school. They were leaders in our community.

CHAPTER 16

Sticking With the Union

No book about educators engaging families and community would be complete without a chapter about educator unions. Unions' collective bargaining power increases significantly with community support. In return, unions earn that support by using their collective bargaining power to advance the interests of the community. Unions and communities have overlapping membership and are natural allies.

GO DOWN AND JOIN THE UNION

I joined the teacher union when I was hired in 1997. Excited to attend my first union meeting, I quickly became disillusioned. I heard complaints about the contract negotiations. I asked, if it was that bad, why weren't we talking about a strike? Everyone looked at me as if I were an idiot. The union president said, "Because in Massachusetts, it's *illegal* to strike. If we strike, *I* could get hauled off to jail!"

As a child growing up in New York in the 60s, I learned about the Taylor Law, passed in 1967. My father was an active member of the teacher union; dinner conversation topics often included the union and the Taylor Law. It created a state labor board to resolve public employee contract disputes through mediation and arbitration but punished strikers with fines and jail time. Nevertheless, teacher unions struck. For example, in 1978, the Levittown United Teachers struck for 53 days. Each day teachers were on strike they were fined two days' pay. The union was fined $170,000; their president was sentenced to 20 days in jail. Teacher' unions knew the law and struck anyway. Every time my father's union struck, we teetered on the brink of foreclosure. But despite the Taylor Law, New York teacher unions struck and won, again and again.

Massachusetts outlawed strikes by public employees in 1919. Over the years, teachers in Lexington, Hanover, Franklin, Quincy, and other locales, mostly in the eastern part of the state, struck, sometimes facing arrest and substantial fines. In 1980, 1,800 teachers struck in nearby Springfield for 18 days. Twenty-seven strikers were jailed and the union faced substantial fines. The risks and costs of a strike are high; the decision to strike is never made lightly. After two years of negotiations, in 2019 the Dedham Education Association voted 255 to 2 and struck, defying injunctions. The union organized for a year before the strike, among its members and out in the community, knocking on doors, attending parent-sponsored coffee conversations in homes between parents and educators. The union rallied, organized standouts, and had hundreds of members showing up at school committee meetings. They struck on a Friday, negotiated through the weekend, voted on a new contract, and returned to work on Monday. Even where public employee strikes are illegal, they are not impossible.

I was unimpressed with my union in Massachusetts. I paid dues and voted in local elections. Our contract negotiations dragged on. Some of the most racist and classist teachers in my school were the loudest members. I believed in labor organizing, but I also knew that many unions, like other institutions in the United States, had been racist. I focused my energy elsewhere.

EDUCATORS FOR A DEMOCRATIC UNION (EDU)

Kim and I became union activists in 2014, late in our careers, when we recognized the real possibility of transforming our union. Unions are, or can become, powerful vehicles, not just for economic justice for educators, but for economic, social, and racial justice for students and their families across our state. We learned how educator unions and communities can fight for each other. That motivated us to get more union training and to get more involved.

We first became active at the invitation of Educators for a Democratic Union (EDU), a progressive caucus in the Massachusetts Teachers Association (MTA). They recruited us to become delegates to the MTA statewide annual meeting.

EDU was running Barbara Madeloni, a rank-and-file member, for MTA president, challenging the union's old guard. Madeloni envisioned a more deeply democratic union that would strategize our defense of public education and education workers, by holding forums developed in alliance with parents and students across the state to discuss and develop a richer, more humane and democratic vision of public education than that promoted by corporate education reform. She proposed to make the fight for economic and racial justice a centerpiece of our organizing within and beyond the union, including fighting for a progressive tax and fully funded education from preschool through college. Kim and I attended the MTA Annual Meeting where we voted for Madeloni and began to learn about the democratic processes within our union at the state level.

Dan Clawson wrote in *Jacobin*, "In 2014, when Barbara Madeloni was elected president of the 116,000-member MTA, she was both an improbable winner and an unapologetic leftist" (Clawson, 2018). Madeloni shook up the past practice of union leadership accepting bad policies and dehumanizing mandates handed down to us by the state; they had not asked members' opinions about whether the policies and mandates were right, but only how best to implement them. Madeloni charted a new path, with the slogan, "When we fight, we win!"

In 2016, the MTA led the Save Our Public Schools Campaign to defeat Question 2, which proposed to greatly expand charter schools. Charters drain large amounts of money from local public-school budgets. The "Yes" Campaign, largely funded by corporate donations, vastly outspent us. Our grassroots campaign harnessed the credibility of educators talking to neighbors, friends, and families about the real impact of charter school expansion in our communities. Defeating Question 2 was a bright spot in the 2016 election.

In early 2017, I signed up for the MTA's "Next Generation" training for rank-and-file members. We used *Secrets of a Successful Organizer* (Bradbury et al., 2016), published by Labor Notes, as facilitators asked questions to probe the dynamics of power in our locals.

In 2017, I ran as a rank-and-file candidate to represent 13 locals in my region on the statewide MTA Board of Directors. I met with local presidents in surrounding communities, including small rural districts that had felt disconnected from the MTA. At the last minute, an old-guard candidate ran against me, confident she'd win. I hadn't run for office before and felt sick to my stomach at the prospect. Dan Clawson, EDU organizer and strategist, calmly said, "You're not going to quit. You're going to win. You've been counting votes, right?"

Dan had helped me figure out the maximum number of delegates in my region that could possibly show up to the MTA Annual Meeting and then I had to make sure I knew more than half that number would show up and vote for me. Getting them to show up was the hard part. The meeting was a day and half long, two hours away in Boston, where hotels and meals were expensive. Small locals were entitled to two delegates but often didn't have the money in their budgets to pay for gas, tolls, and hotel for even one person. I talked with locals about supporting a democratic union with more rank-and-file leadership. We discussed carpooling between locals, splitting hotel rooms or staying with relatives or friends in the Boston area. I reached out to all 13 locals. I attended their meetings and met local presidents for coffee all over western Massachusetts. I organized and counted votes. And I won.

As I listened to those locals, I became aware of fights that I hadn't heard of before. At the first meeting I led as a board member with a handful of other presidents, we brainstormed the idea of wanting to create something

Figure 16.1. Audrey Murph-Brown, Mary Cowhey, Kim Gerould and Barbara Madeloni at an MTA rally for public education in Boston, following the MTA annual meeting (2017).

like a "bat signal" that we could send out to other locals for support. For example, if there was a critical action at a school committee meeting in South Hadley, we wanted a way to activate union members from other locals in the region who lived in South Hadley to call their school committee members and show up with signs.

All In

I became a building representative for Northampton Association of School Employees (NASE, a wall-to-wall union covering all education employees, including custodians, bus drivers, paraprofessionals, clerical workers, teachers, and counselors). Other building representatives and I helped organize a communication system during the "All In" campaign in 2017. This was in anticipation of the Supreme Court's anti-union Janus Decision in June 2018. Similar to the old "phone tree," each building had a team of members willing to communicate regularly with a list of fellow union members. Unlike a phone tree passing a message in one direction, these members gave updates and engaged in 1:1 conversation to really learn where members were coming from, what they were willing to do with the union and anything that was presenting an obstacle to their greater participation. The "All In" campaign's goal was to organize more forcefully in the face of the Janus attack on public sector unions, which could have otherwise decimated union membership.

In the Fall of 2017, the MTA worked with Raise Up Massachusetts on campaigns that gathered enough signatures to get two questions on the ballot: one to raise the minimum wage to $15/hour and another to create paid family and medical leave. This campaign intersected with the interests of Families with Power members. Shirley, FWP member and a single mother who worked three minimum wage jobs, thought I was kidding about a $15 an hour minimum wage. She laughed and said, "$15 an hour! If I had $15 an hour, I'd be RICH!" Both initiatives became law.

Bargaining for the Common Good

In February 2018, West Virginia teachers stunned the nation with a two-week strike that shut schools in all 55 counties, winning higher wages and improved health benefits. Those militant West Virginia teachers inspired educators in Oklahoma, Colorado, Arizona, Kentucky, and North Carolina to take action and win impressive gains. At the MTA summer conference that year, we met union activists from United Teachers of Los Angeles (UTLA), "bargaining for the common good" in their contract fight as they built the groundwork for a strike.

UTLA was inspired by the work of the Caucus of Rank-and-File Educators (CORE) in Chicago and the 2012 teacher strike "for the schools Chicago students deserve." UTLA formed its own progressive caucus, which pushed UTLA to work with parents and community organizations to identify issues of common concern in their contract campaign. The caucus demanded the union invest in both rank-and-file and community organizing. After a slate of progressive unionists took power in 2014, they spent 4 years developing rank-and-file leadership at every worksite.

In January 2019, 30,000 UTLA members struck for 6 days. In addition to bargaining for wages, they demanded smaller class sizes, nurses, librarians, and counselors in every school, legal support for undocumented students, and an end to "random" search practices, which disproportionately targeted students of color. UTLA teamed up with a student-led group including parents and teachers. Previously, the district said issues like the random search policy were not subjects for bargaining, but once teachers, students, and families were on the picket lines, the district had to bargain for the common good. Random searches ended by June 2020.

WeMEAN: Building the Bat Signal

In August 2018, MTA activists from across Western Mass met to make the "bat signal" idea a reality. We formed Western Mass Educator Action Network (WeMEAN), with a mission to work in solidarity and take action across the region to improve student learning conditions and members' working conditions. The WeMEAN "bat signal" would summon activists across the region to show up in solidarity.

That summer, the MTA kicked off a campaign called Fund Our Future, to address the historic issue of underfunding our state's public schools. In Western Mass, WeMEAN urged school committees to back our demands. We organized community forums. We marched and rallied, and organized letter writing campaigns and phone banks. We wore Red for Ed(ucation) on Fridays; we wore red tee shirts, pants, and dresses. At my school, we also held weekly standouts of educators, parents, and students to press for more equitable state funding.

In the winter of 2019, the state house in Boston, two hours away, was not paying much attention to 50 or so people standing in the cold every Friday morning with signs and banners in front of schools in Northampton while passing cars honked their support. Our state senator, Jo Comerford, and state representative, Lindsay Sabadosa, both sponsored critical legislation. They spoke at our community forums and rallies and joined our weekly standouts when their schedules permitted. Those weekly standouts in front of school as well as the weekly "Red for Ed" Fridays were part of a larger fight. That fight resulted in the passage of the Student Opportunity Act in November of 2019. The Act updated the state's foundation budget for public schools for the first time in 25 years, to bring more than a billion dollars in additional funds to public schools each year.

TURNING POINT

When Families with Power teamed up with Pioneer Valley Workers Center and our local educator union to standout for immigrant rights, students and caregivers turned out one afternoon to make dozens of beautiful hand-drawn posters in Spanish, Arabic, and English. They turned out the morning of the immigrant standout too, even though some were directly targeted by Trump's anti-immigrant and anti-Muslim policies; some came from countries where standing on the street with a sign could get you killed.

The participation of union members, workers center members, and other Jackson Street School families provided a feeling of strength in numbers. Immigrant parents weren't out there alone. That standout for immigrant rights didn't make headlines. It didn't need to. It was the first time in my career that I saw families and community members participate in any union activities. And it was the first time I saw the union show up for immigrant and low-income parents in a public and political way. They weren't just staff members showing up for a delicious meal at the FWP Love Your Family Dinner. They were standing together on the street with signs in front of our school.

Figure 16.2. Principal Gwen Agna and educator union members Deirdre Johnson and Kim Gerould joined students, families, and fellow educators to stand out for immigrant rights at Jackson Street School (2017).

After that first standout for immigrant rights, it became the new normal for families and union members to stand out shoulder to shoulder. I learned that when an educator union fights for students and families, students and families will show up to fight for the union.

I didn't know that when I started teaching in 1997, and I didn't know anywhere it was happening. I went to my first Labor Notes conference in 2018 and connected with United Caucuses of Rank-and-File Educators (UCORE, a growing national network of locals and caucuses within the teachers' unions). It blew my mind. I hadn't realized there were educators across the country thinking this way about transforming their unions.

CHANGING OUR LOCAL UNION

In 2018, I helped a fellow EDU activist, Sadie Cora, run for and win election as president of my local, challenging our old-guard leadership. Sadie and the bargaining team demanded open bargaining for the first time in our local's history, lifting the black box of secrecy that had always hidden past negotiations. Through the All In campaign we had activated our rank and file members and strengthened our communication and mobilization capacity in every building. We used that to turn out crowds of rank-and-file union members to observe every negotiation session so that district negotiators couldn't pit one unit against another. Rank-and-file members stopped calling it "the union" and started calling it "our union," not saying, "What is the union going to do about it?" but "What can we do about it?"

Figure 16.3. FWP member Sue Brow and her son, Jordan Lopez Brow, joined the rally with MTA members in Springfield to demand full funding for public schools (2019).

Just as we'd developed the habit of wearing red on Fridays, we printed and distributed red union tee shirts to all members to wear on negotiation days, to show our solidarity. When the negotiations stalled, the union negotiating team and the whole crowd of members would caucus to discuss the issues. We had heated debates and decided our next steps through discussions and votes. The union organized a community forum focused on our community values, with over 100 attendees.

With the help of WeMEAN, Northampton Association of School Employees activists turned out hundreds of educators, parents, students, retirees, and community members with signs to rally outside before school committee meetings. Public comment periods went on for hours in support of the union's demand for a fair contract. Labor allies from the Pioneer Valley Workers Center and the Western Mass Area Labor Federation (WMALF) joined us.

Our union is 80% female, with many women being the primary breadwinners in their families. Northampton prides itself on feminism. Yet for years, the administration told our union that we were "too big" for the city to afford to give us a raise. At the time, average teacher pay in Northampton ranked 270 out of the 289 districts in Massachusetts. Some workers in support units were making less than the state minimum wage, so our union demanded $15/hour as a minimum pay rate as part of our initial set of unified demands.

Eventually, negotiations broke down and our union members voted to "work to rule," a labor action in which union members pledge to follow their contracts to the letter and not do any additional unpaid work. High school students staged a walkout in support of the union. Every morning, union members stood out in front of our buildings, joined by hundreds of students, caregivers, and community members. Shortly before the official start of the school day, we packed up our signs and banners and entered the building en masse. Every afternoon, we poured out of our classrooms, met up in the lobby and walked out together, to stand out again. Teams of union activists from locals throughout our region, activated by the WeMEAN "bat signal," showed up at our school standouts and at our city hall and school committee rallies. Just as we had shown up at their school committee meetings, rallies, and standouts, they were showing up at ours.

Those students, caregivers, and community members didn't come out of thin air. We'd been building that solidarity like a muscle for years. We'd practiced and developed the routines of wearing red, standing out, showing up with signs with and for each other. Our school community stood with our union when we fought for social justice issues like immigration rights, raising the minimum wage, paid family and medical leave, and more equitable state funding for public schools. When our union stood up and finally fought for the fair contract we deserved, our students and families stood with us and spoke out for us at school committee and in letters to the editor, demanding a fair contract. We were ready.

The contract fight was exhausting. And "work to rule" is difficult for teachers like me who routinely arrive for work early and leave late. The labor action stopped all the voluntary extra things we do at school. It wasn't easy, but the solidarity inspired and strengthened us. We ended the school year still engaged in the "work to rule" action. Large weekly rallies of union members, supported by students, families, and community members, continued on the steps of City Hall throughout the summer, before we finally signed an historic contract in August 2019. The 3-year contract included 3% annual raises for teachers and cafeteria workers, 4% raises for educational support professionals for the first year and 3% for the next two years. Clerical and custodial workers' pay scales were made consistent with the higher pay scales of other city workers in similar positions.

WHEN SIZE MATTERS

The largest labor organization in the state, the Massachusetts Teachers Association (MTA), can leverage its power in statewide campaigns that impact our local districts and schools. It doesn't matter if, when we start, we don't have organizing skills or experience. State and national unions use part of our dues to provide free training in organizing skills, such as how to be a union rep, negotiate contracts, and build membership.

MTA took a stand to fight for immigrant rights and against White supremacy. MTA made its commitment to racial, economic, and social justice material by supporting coalition work with labor unions and community organizations. These include MA Jobs with Justice, a coalition of more than 150 member organizations.

MTA's professional trainings regularly include book groups to read and discuss books such as *How To Be An Antiracist* by Ibram X. Kendi and *White Fragility: Why It's so Hard for White People to Talk About Race* (2018) by Robin DiAngelo. MTA also offers movie nights with discussions of films such as *Pushout: The Criminalization of Black Girls in Schools* (Morris & Atlas, 2019; based on Morris, 2016) and a slate of workshops on racial, economic, and social justice topics.

When I started teaching in 1997, I was unimpressed with my local union, which seemed dominated by racist and classist bullies who were afraid to take action against injustice. I had no idea how to fight racism and classism in the union. I had no idea how to build a militant union that would fight for its members and our students. What I learned, albeit late in my career, was that rank-and-file union members can transform their union, at the state or local level. We can change it. We can say how we want our union to be. We can campaign and vote for leaders and create a budget that puts our values into practice.

If rank-and-file members want better contracts, we can run and elect local leaders who will use open bargaining and bring all our coworkers to the negotiating sessions. To address injustice in our schools, we can bargain for the common good. If we have a record of fighting for what our community values, we can organize our community to stand with us during contract fights and statewide legislative campaigns.

Daring to be Powerful

When I dare to be powerful, to use my strength in the service of my vision, then it becomes less and less important whether I am afraid.

—Audre Lorde

When I have the courage to stand up with my union to demand the public-school funding, dignity, rights, wages, and working/learning conditions educators and student deserve, I am not just standing up for my interests. Union activists are role models, not just for coworkers, but for students and families. This is what activism looks like. This is what it sounds like when you dare to use your voice. This is how it feels to be part of a group demanding justice.

"Families" and "community" are never a monolith. Not everyone will agree with you on everything, but families and community members who trust and respect you will listen to what you have to say. That trust and respect will carry a lot of weight. And our unions, at the local, state, and national levels, need to connect with and listen to low-income and immigrant caregivers and families of color. When union activists are engaging families and communities in their schools, we open up two-way communication and build authentic relationships.

Finding Allies

When we struggle alone, we can easily feel overwhelmed and discouraged. With others, we find strength. Therefore, we need to know where we can find allies, at a local, state, or national level. Connecting with others helps us see our local struggles in a broader context. In our case, we learned from other activists what worked and what could have worked better. We met educators from West Virginia to Los Angeles who took huge risks, demonstrating that when they fought, they won. We learned that labor organizing comes down to the hard work of mapping our workplaces and communities; of having one-to-one conversations in which we listen and find common ground; of tirelessly inviting participation as we rally people together.

Educator unions are yet another avenue for educators to collaborate with families and community. Don't be discouraged if you don't yet have a union, or if your current union is ineffective or out of touch with the larger struggle for economic, social, and racial justice, or if your coworkers seem apathetic. Remember that nothing stays the same. Change doesn't happen without struggle. Educators are learning to get good at this.

Students watch educators all the time. Remember that 1st-grader who asked me, "If they come for us, you will protest, right?" the day after Trump was elected? When he had seen me the day before with a sign outside school, he was too young to be able to read what my sign said (to vote against charter school expansion). But he could "read" that standing in front of school with a sign was "protest." He believed someone with the courage to protest, even if she was a skinny old math teacher, would fight for his family. That year he learned he was right.

The Roots Are Down There

And don't think the garden loses its ecstasy in winter. It's quiet, but the roots are down there, riotous.

—From the poem "Form is Ecstatic" by Rumi

The process of writing and rewriting this book has pushed me to reread *The Long Haul* (Horton et al., 1998), *Pedagogy of the Oppressed* (Freire, 2018), and *We Make the Road by Walking* (Horton & Freire, 1990), and for that I am appreciative; I did not engage in this much "scholarship" in 15 years of organizing Families With Power. In some ways it feels like a luxury that I did not have in all those years of teaching school, engaging in all the FWP educational projects and residential workshops, and participating in union organizing, all while raising my children and taking care of my mother. Reflecting on this recent rereading helped me see that what we were doing in FWP incorporated the ideas of Paulo Freire and Myles Horton even more than I had previously realized.

Additionally, my thoughts return to the question, *Who am I to write this book?* I try to ignore the voice that says I am "just" a teacher. There's a part of me that always feels a little "less than" in a setting like an academic conference, where people asked me what university I was with (Jackson Street School) and what courses I taught (1st and 2nd grade). I am proud to be a teacher of young children, a popular educator, and a writer, and I encourage more teachers to write about their practice and reflections.

GROWING GRASSROOTS LEADERS

In writing these stories down and talking with these members of FWP, Eneida made me realize the importance of what we did. Recently we had tried and failed to reconnect with a member of FWP who struggled with addiction, to talk with her about the book and ask permission to use her name. Eneida understood the reasons why publishers require permission, but said, "I still wish we could include her name. I know she would say that her years as a leader in Families with Power were the proudest of her life, the best thing she ever did."

That made me think about Myles Horton talking about the idea that really took form at Highlander, the idea of "people learning from each other." Horton wrote: "You don't need to know the answer. You can help people get the answers. . . . You have to respect their knowledge, which they don't respect, and help them to respect their knowledge" (Horton & Freire, 1990, p. 55). When the FWP member mentioned above attended her first workshop, she talked about feeling "stupid" at school. By the end of that weekend, she was transformed by the ways that being part of FWP helped her to recognize her own knowledge and see herself as a leader.

In our first weekend workshop, I remember how people responded to Horton's description of grassroots leaders who "are not official leaders but people who are recognized as having leadership qualities by the people they live and work with. . . . Whatever strength and influence they have will be based on their serving the people who have accepted some of their leadership. . . . You can build your strength from the bottom up instead of the top down" (p. 146). For our members, some of whom had described themselves as "outcasts" because they had not graduated from high school, or had been labeled as learning disabled, or because they did not yet speak English fluently or because they were not a citizen, or because they worked in service sector jobs where they felt invisible, this was a radical and inviting idea. At the conclusion of that workshop, Irma Lucena looked at the other members and said, "I feel proud to be part of this group. Thanks for having the confidence in me that I could be a leader. I have a reason now to fight for more than my family."

In many ways, I think that it was an advantage that so many of our members felt like outsiders within the school when we started. Horton's description of Highlander working "outside the system" was appealing because, as he said, "we would . . . be completely free to do what we thought was the right thing to do in terms of the goals that we set for ourselves." He described experimenting with ways to do social education outside the system "with more validity than we could inside the system, because we didn't have to conform with anything. Nobody could tell us what to do. We could make our own mistakes and invent our own process" (Horton & Freire, 1990, p. 200). FWP followed Highlander's path of popular education; we weren't forced to conform with expectations or regulations, or to report "results" to any authority. For example, Rania said that when she proposed the Arabic Community Club, no one pushed back to say that was weird or something that we couldn't do. Members were free to think outside the box and not conform with what schools usually do.

In *Pedagogy of the Oppressed*, Freire wrote: "Many political and educational plans have failed because their authors designed them according to their own personal views of reality, never once taking into account (except as mere objects of their actions) the *men-in-a-situation* to whom their program was ostensibly directed. . . . They approach the peasant or urban masses with a project that may correspond to their own view of the world, but not to that of the people" (Freire, 2019, p. 94). I think of FWP's "bottom-up" educational projects, like Eneida's idea of Family Reading Parties, Elba and Edwin's Morning Math Club idea, Josefina's Financial Literacy Project idea, and Rania's Arabic Community Club idea. Often, an FWP member had an idea and then collaborated with an educator, like Elba asking Ms. Totty to help develop what became the Kime Project for teaching families self-defense and more. Sometimes FWP members collaborated with community partners like a farmer and public health director to create a pilot like the Jackson Street Farmers Market. No outside academics or administrators cooked up these ideas from an outside perch *for* or *about* these students and families. Even as innovative educators, Kim and I couldn't have designed these projects ourselves. In *Pedagogy of the Oppressed*, Freire warned that no truly liberating pedagogy "can remain distant from the oppressed by treating them as unfortunates and by presenting for their emulation models from among the oppressors. The oppressed must be their own example in the struggle for their redemption" (2018, p. 54). These programs succeeded because of their grassroots leadership and bottom-up design, by creating and being their own examples.

Characteristic of popular education, these programs responded to authentic need and grew organically as a result of ongoing dialogue, reflection and action. Freire (2018) wrote about critical experiments in education that would seek out "ties which link one point to another and one problem to another" (2018, p. 74), and we saw this time and again with FWP's educational projects. In trying to solve the problem of how to teach math games to parents to play with their children, Elba connected it to the problem of how parents who were not raised with the culture of reading aloud could help their children with reading and proposed "family math parties" like the Family Reading Parties. Edwin connected that idea to the problem of caregivers who work an evening schedule not being able to participate in school activities and proposed Morning Math Club. A discussion at Café about weight, body image in the media, and health connected to the problem of exercise, sparking Elba's idea of Family Dances for fun and exercise. The problem of access to healthy food sparked the pilot of our own farmers market. That led to the food demonstration tables, which then led to healthy cooking classes. These connections that link one problem to another remind me of mycelium in the forest, a web of tiny, subterranean fungal threads from which mushrooms grow when conditions are just right (Del Conte & Læssøe, 2008, p. 19). These networks can stretch underground for miles.

When we started FWP in 2007, we didn't know where it would lead, or how it would look or work. And we did not worry about that or let it stop us. In FWP, Kim and I were popular education facilitators. We were not organizers, but educators—what Freire calls "teacher-students," engaging in critical experiments in education with other FWP members. Freire describes the result of dialogue in problem-posing education: "The teacher is no longer merely the one-who-teaches but one who is himself taught in dialogue with the students, who in turn while being taught also teach" (2018, p. 80). These teacher-student and student-teacher roles remained fluid in FWP projects over the years, from Family Reading Parties to How Schools Work and Arabic Community Club.

POPULAR EDUCATION IN PRACTICE

We learned about the practice of popular education from *The Long Haul* (Horton et al., 1998), so that we didn't repeat the Highlander staff's early mistake of trying to move from theory to practice, which they corrected when they saw they weren't reaching people. Horton wrote:

> We reversed the usual process: instead of coming from the top down and going from the theoretical to the practical, trying to force the theory onto the practical, we learned you had to take what people perceive their problems to be, not what we perceive their problems to be. We had to learn how to find out about the people, and then take that and put it into a program. . . . We were now in an out-of-schooling situation where the ways of learning were different. . . . We had to unlearn and relearn from them. It was only then that we could begin to build a base . . . that gave us roots among the people and in their problems. (pp. 140–141)

In *The Long Haul*, Horton wrote about the idea of having two eyes that he doesn't use the same way. One eye would be trained upon how people perceive themselves, using observations of body language, speech, personal preferences, ideas, how they live. The other eye would envision ways that they could move forward: "It's not a clear blueprint for the future but movement toward goals they don't conceive of at the time." He didn't separate these two ways of looking: "If you have to make a choice between moving in the direction you want to move people, and working with them where they are, you always choose to work with them where they are . . . otherwise you separate yourself from them" (1998, pp. 131–132).

While I felt pretty confident about seeing with that first eye, I tried to remain cautious about my "other eye," lest it get too bossy. I often felt this tension between my "two eyes," but I am grateful that I had Horton's advice to follow. The results of our practice demonstrated his wisdom.

SUPPORTING EACH OTHER AND HELPING OUR CHILDREN SUCCEED

These principles of popular education from Highlander Folk School informed what we did through Families with Power because our purpose was articulated by the families themselves. Our goal was never to spread nationwide or to become famous or even very efficient. The Common Core language of "college and career ready," standardized tests, and "adequate yearly progress" don't define FWP's goals. Our members had stated our goal simply: to support one another and help our children succeed. Our members defined success as their children reaching adulthood, being happy and connected strongly to their families and community, and able to support themselves and their families.

As I look back over the last 15 years of FWP history and attempt to share some of these stories with you, I am reminded of microbial communities—invisible to the naked eye—making fertile and healthy soil that can grow food to nourish our community. Some FWP members have passed away or lost touch, but they still inspire and nourish us. We continue to learn, grow, and support each other and our children. Those who were toddlers at those first Family Reading Parties and Family Writing Projects are now in high school, applying to college. The older children are now in their 20s and early 30s. Some have become parents themselves. I think of our community, and the fertile soil we have nurtured here: the webs of relationships that bind us together and help us grow, like the billions of microorganisms and thin threads of mycelium stretching, branching, and communicating for miles and miles underfoot.

*   *   *

Sometimes people ask me if FWP is "still active." I say that we aren't running any programs at the moment, but that our relationships are still alive. Throughout the pandemic, we have stayed connected, sharing necessities like food and toilet paper among families who didn't have the cash on hand to stock up when the lockdown started. We still check in with and support one another, navigating unemployment benefits and health issues, caring for loved ones and grieving their deaths. We've been celebrating new accomplishments, such as closing on a first home, graduating from community college, or applying to 4-year colleges. We help one another write resumes and prepare for Zoom job interviews. We share leads for jobs and vaccination appointments. Families with young children are hoping to have Family Reading Parties outside when the weather warms. This is how Families with Power works: There is mutual giving and receiving, without keeping score.

At our first FWP retreat in 2007, Maribel, one of our cofounders, said, "I learned you don't need twenty or fifty people to move a mountain. You start with who you have." That insight has guided us all these years. You have read stories from one community, a small city in western Massachusetts. These were stories about what we tried, the mistakes we made, what worked and what didn't work so well. I share them in the hope that our feelings and problems, our ideas and enthusiasm, will inspire you and your community. I hope you will be encouraged to take the time to deepen relationships beyond your cultural comfort zone and look at what is familiar from someone else's perspective. I like to imagine you and I will find ourselves in the not-so-distant future sitting together, drinking coffee and talking about your teaching, organizing, and about what matters to the families in your communities.

References

Abu-Lughod, L. (2013). *Do Muslim women need saving?* Harvard University Press.

Anderson, S. J. (Director) (2007). *Meet the Robinsons*. Walt Disney Animation Studios.

Basu, T. (2015, October 21). Donald Trump says he would consider shutting down radical mosques. Time. https://time.com/4082627/trump-mosques-minimum-wage/

Beatty, A. (2007). *Iggy Peck, architect*. Abrams Books for Young Readers.

Beatty, A. (2013). *Rosie Revere, engineer*. Abrams Books for Young Readers.

Boaler. J. (2008). *What's math got to do with it?* Viking Penguin.

Bradbury, A., Brenner, M., & Slaughter, J. (2016). *Secrets of a successful labor organizer*. Labor Notes.

Cenoz, J. (2009). *Towards multilingual education: Basque educational research from an international perspective*. Multilingual Matters.

Centers for Disease Control and Prevention. (2021a). *Preventing adverse childhood experiences*. https://www.cdc.gov/violenceprevention/aces/about.html

Centers for Disease Control and Prevention. (2021b). *Preventing adverse childhood experiences*. https://www.cdc.gov/violenceprevention/aces/fastfact.html

Chittenden, K., & Messenheimer, M. (2019). *Susie King Taylor, an African American nurse and teacher in the Civil War*. https://www.loc.gov/ghe/cascade/index.html?appid=5be2377c246c4b5483e32ddd51d32dc0

Clawson, D. (2018, June 28). The legacy of Barbara Madeloni. *Jacobin*. https://jacobinmag.com/2018/06/barbara-madeloni-massachusetts-teachers-association-edu

Cowhey, M. (2006). *Black ants and Buddhists: Thinking critically and teaching differently in the primary grades*. Stenhouse Publishers.

Cowhey, M. (2009). Learning to roar. Learning for Justice. https://www.learningforjustice.org/magazine/fall-2009/learning-to-roar

Cowhey, M. (2017, February 6). Dig in so deep that we can't be weeded out. *Daily Hampshire Gazette*. https://www.gazettenet.com/Columnist-Mary-Cowhey-on-wake-up-call-to-organize-so-every-American-can-safely-exercise-First-Amendment-rights-8145661

Deak, J. (2010). *Your fantastic elastic brain: Stretch it, shape it*. Sourcebooks.

Del Conte, A., & Læssøe, T. (2008). *The edible mushroom book*. DK Publishing.

Denton, P., & Kriete, R. (2000) *The first six weeks of school*. Northeast Foundation for Children.

Diamond, J. (2015, November 20). *Trump would 'certainly implement' national database for U.S. Muslims*. CNN. https://www.cnn.com/2015/11/19/politics/donald-trump-barack-obama-threat-to-country/index.html

DiAngelo, R. (2018). *White fragility: Why it's so hard for White people to talk about racism*. Beacon Press.

Dweck, C. S. (2006). *Mindset: The new psychology of success*. Random House.

Dweck, C. S. (2013). "Teaching a Growth Mindset" at Young Minds. https://www .youtube.com/watch?v=kXhbtCcmsyQ

Felitti, V. J., Anda, R. F., Nordenberg, D., Williamson, D. F., Spitz, A. M., Edwards, V., Koss, M. P., & Marks, J. S. (1998). Relationship of childhood abuse and household dysfunction to many of the leading causes of death in adults: The Adverse Childhood Experiences (ACE) Study. *American Journal of Preventative Medicine, 14*(4), 245–258.

Freire, P. (1998). *Teachers as cultural workers: Letters to those who dare teach*. Westview Press.

Freire, P. (2018). *Pedagogy of the oppressed* (50th Anniversary Edition; M. B. Ramos, Trans.). Bloomsbury.

Friedman, D. (2015, December 13). *Trump cites 'sickness' in defense of Muslim immigration ban proposal*. Fox News. https://www.foxnews.com/politics/trump-cites -sickness-in-defense-of-muslim-immigration-ban-proposal

Galvin, W. F. (2002). *Question 2: Law proposed by initiative petition: English language education in public schools*, in *The official Massachusetts information for voters* [Brochure]. Massachusetts Secretary of the Commonwealth.

González, N., Moll, L., & Amanti, C. (2005). *Funds of knowledge: Theorizing practices in households, communities, and classrooms*. L. Erlbaum Associates.

Harry, B., & Klingner, J. (2005). *Why are so many minority students in special education? Understanding race and disability in schools*. Teachers College Press.

Herb, J. (2015, December 6). Trump: Islamic terrorism will get solved when Obama 'gets the hell out.' *Politico*. https://www.politico.com/story/2015/12/trump-islamic-terrorism -obama-216462

Horton, M. & Freire, P. (1990). *We make the road by walking: Conversations on education and social change*. Temple Univesrsity Press.

Horton, M., Kohl, J., & Kohl, R. (1998). *The long haul: An autobiography*. Teachers College Press.

Institute for Economics & Peace. (2019). Global terrorism index 2019: Measuring the impact of terrorism, Sydney. http://visionofhumanity.org/reports

Irving, D. (2014). *Waking up white: Finding myself in the story of race*. Elephant Room Press.

Jewell, T. (2019). *This book is anti-racist*. Frances Lincoln Children's Books.

Johnson, J. (2015, September 30). Donald Trump: Syrian refugees might be a terrorist army in disguise. *The Washington Post*. https://www.washingtonpost.com/news/post -politics/wp/2015/09/30/donald-trump-syrian-refugees-might-be-a-terrorist-army-in -disguise/

Joseph, M., & Ramani, E. (2006). English in the World does not mean English everywhere: The case for multilingualism in the ELT/ESL profession. In R. Rubdy & M. Saraceni (Eds.), *English in the world: Global rules, global roles* (pp. 186–199). Bloomsbury.

Kendi, I. X. (2016). *Stamped from the beginning: The definitive history of racist ideas in America*. Public Affairs Books.

Kendi, I. X. (2019). *How to be an antiracist*. Random House.

Kingsolver, B. (2007) *Animal, vegetable, miracle*. Harper Collins.

Krieg, G. (2015, November 16). *Donald Trump: 'Strongly consider' shutting mosques*. CNN. https://www.cnn.com/2015/11/16/politics/donald-trump-paris-attacks-close -mosques/index.html

Ladson-Billings, G. (1994). *The Dreamkeepers: Successful teaching for African-American students*. Jossey-Bass.

Lawson, S. (2020). *This is major: Notes on Diana Ross, dark girls, and being dope.* Harper Perennial.

LoBianco, T. (2015, December 3). *Donald Trump on terrorists: 'Take out their families.'* CNN. https://www.cnn.com/2015/12/02/politics/donald-trump-terrorists-families /index.html

Macedo, D., & Freire, A. M. A. (1998). Foreword. In P. Freire, *Teachers as cultural workers: Letters to those who dare teach.* Westview Press.

Minoui, D. (2021). *The book collectors of Daraya: A band of Syrian rebels, their underground library, and the stories that carried them through a war.* Picador.

Morris, M. W. (2016). *Pushout: The criminalization of Black girls in schools.* The New Press.

Morris, M. W., & Atlas, J. (Producers). (2019). *Pushout: A documentary.* Women in the Room Productions.

Nieto, S. (2008). *Dear Paulo: Letters from those who dare teach.* Paradigm.

Paris, D. (2012). Culturally sustaining pedagogy: A needed change in stance, terminology, and practice. *Educational Researcher, 41*(3), 93–97.

Plumer, B. (2016, July 22). *Full transcript of Donald Trump's acceptance speech at the RNC.* Vox. https://www.vox.com/2016/7/21/12253426/donald-trump-acceptance -speech-transcript-republican-nomination-transcript

Pollan, M. (2007). *The omnivore's dilemma: A natural history of four meals.* Penguin.

Reynolds, J., & Kendi, I. X. (2020). *Stamped: Racism, antiracism, and you.* Little, Brown Books for Young Readers.

Richardson, K. M. (2019). *The book woman of Troublesome Creek.* Sourcebooks.

Schleifer, T. (2016, March 10). *Donald Trump: 'I think Islam hates us.'* CNN. https://www .cnn.com/2016/03/09/politics/donald-trump-islam-hates-us/index.html

Scott Foresman (Publisher; 2017). *Investigations 3.* Scott Foresman.

Sesame Street. (2014, September 10). *Sesame Street: Janelle Monáe: Power of yet.* https:// www.youtube.com/watch?v=XLeUvZvuvAs

Shabad, R. (2015, December 7). *Donald Trump calls for a "total and complete shutdown" of Muslims entering U.S.* CBS News. https://www.cbsnews.com/news/donald -trump-calls-for-total-and-complete-shutdown-of-muslims-entering-u-s/

Souto-Manning, M. (2010). *Freire, teaching, and learning: Culture circles across contexts.* Peter Lang.

Stenmark, J. K., Thompson, V., & Cossey, R. (1986). *Family math.* Lawrence Hall of Science.

Tatum, B. D. (2017). *"Why are all the Black kids sitting together in the cafeteria?" And other conversations about race.* Basic Books. (Original work published 1997)

Taylor, S. K. (2006). Reminiscences of my life in camp. University of Georgia Press. (Original work published 1902)

Trelease, J. (2019). *Jim Trelease's Read Aloud handbook* (8th ed). Penguin. (Original work published 1982)

Vargas, C. (2015). *Incorporating social justice ideology into English language teaching* [Unpublished undergraduate thesis]. Marlboro College.

Weil, S. (2000). *Waiting for God.* Harper Perennial. (Originally published 1950)

Winter, J. (2005). *The librarian of Basra: A true story from Iraq.* Clarion Books.

Winter, J. (2010). *Biblioburro, a true story from Colombia.* Beach Lane Books.

Wright, R. J., Stanger, G., Stafford, A. K., & Martland, J. (2006). *Teaching number: Advancing children's skills and strategies* (2nd ed.). Sage.

Index

Note: Names marked with asterisks (*) are pseudonyms to protect participants' privacy.

About the Author

Mary Cowhey is a cofounder of Families with Power/Familias con Poder. She was an elementary public school teacher for 22 years. She is a grassroots community organizer, parent, union activist, writer, community gardener, and winner of numerous awards for teaching, including a Milken National Educator Award, the Massachusetts Public Health Association's Frontline Award, and MA Agriculture in the Classroom's Excellence in Agricultural Science Teaching Award. She lives in Northampton, MA.

Left to right: Eneida Garcia, Bill Blatner, Mary Cowhey, Elba Heredia Cartagena, Angela Robles, Janet Namono, Kim Gerould, and Josefina Rodriguez gather for a Families with Power reunion in July 2021. All of these members, as well as Pallavi Bandalli, and Rania Al-Qudsi, shared their stories and reviewed large portions of the manuscript for accuracy. This book would not have been possible without their vital help in sharing our stories. (Photo: Roberto Irizarry)